PROFESSIONS
of DESIRE

PROFESSIONS

Lesbian and Gay Studies

Edited by *George E. Haggerty*

of DESIRE

in Literature

and *Bonnie Zimmerman*

THE MODERN LANGUAGE ASSOCIATION OF AMERICA
NEW YORK   1995

Pages 213, 214, 216: Constantin Brancusi, *The Kiss*, 1907–08, 1909, 1912. © 1994 Artists Rights Society (ARS), New York/ADAGP, Paris

Page 226: Earvin "Magic" Johnson and Isiah Thomas. Photo: Andrew Bernstein/*Sports Illustrated*

Page 227: Darryl Strawberry and Keith Hernandez. Photo: AP/World Wide Photos

Page 228: *Tank McNamara*. © 1990 Millar/Hinds. Dist. Universal Press Syndicate. Rpt. with permission. All rights reserved

LIBRARY OF CONGRESS CATALOGING-IN-PUBLICATION DATA

Professions of desire : lesbian and gay studies in literature / edited
  by George E. Haggerty and Bonnie Zimmerman.
    p.   cm.
    Includes bibliographical references and index.
    ISBN 0-87352-562-0 (cloth) — ISBN 0-87352-563-9 (paper)
    1. Gays' writings, American—Study and teaching.   2. Gays'
  writings—History and criticism—Theory, etc.   3. Gays' writings,
  English—Study and teaching.   4. American literature—Study and
  teaching.   5. English literature—Study and teaching.
  6. Homosexuality and literature.   7. Lesbians in literature.
  8. Gay men in literature.   9. Canon (Literature)
  I. Haggerty, George E.   II. Zimmerman, Bonnie.
  PS153.G38P76   1995
  810.9'92064'07—dc20   94-28342

Cover art by Anne Yanagi

Published by The Modern Language Association of America
10 Astor Place, New York, New York 10003-6981

Set in Trump Medieval
Printed on recycled paper

DEDICATED TO
Louis Crompton AND *Dolores Noll*

AND

IN MEMORY OF
Michael Lynch

Contents

Acknowledgments

This project has had wide-ranging and enthusiastic support. We would like to thank both the Gay Studies Division of the Modern Language Association and the Gay and Lesbian Caucus for the Modern Languages, which have been behind us from the beginning. At the Modern Language Association's Book Publications office, Adrienne Ward got this book off to a promising start, Joseph Gibaldi and Martha Evans have been enormously helpful editors, and Elizabeth Holland has been a fine editorial coordinator.

Claude Summers suggested a volume such as this some years ago, and Michael Lynch began negotiations with the MLA just before he died, in a sense passing the project on to us. We are grateful for their inspiration.

This book would not have been possible without the powerful essays we received, and we would like to thank everyone who contributed. We admire their courage and that of all those who work in the field of lesbian, gay, and queer studies.

For their support of editorial meetings and research travel, we thank the Regents of the University of California; the Committee on Research and the English Department of the University of California, Riverside; and the Women's Studies Department at San Diego State University. For their bibliographic and editorial energy, we are grateful to Kate Burns, Erik Kruger, and Cynthia Morrill.

Finally, for all sorts of support, we thank our partners, Philip Brett and Berlene Rice.

GEH
BZ

Preface

The setting of a recent murder mystery is the 1990 Modern Language Association convention in Chicago. A killer is running amok. Among the victims is an aggressively gay professor from Johns Hopkins, amorally infatuated with Michel Foucault and Jacques Derrida. Before the convention winds down, the unlikely team of Boaz Dixon, a Chicago detective, and Nancy Cook, an assistant professor, turns up with the murderer. Before Professor Cook mutates into the Nancy Drew of the modern languages, she is an acerbic observer of her colleagues. Reading the MLA program, she and a friend, Jennifer, come across a paper title that dismays them: "Lesbians at the Racetrack: Toward a Queer Theory of Gambling." " 'Queer Theory'!" Nancy groans. "What's next? 'Spic Theory'? 'Kike Theory'? I don't understand this. How can you force a word of hatred into another person's mouth and expect it to turn into a word of acceptance?" Jennifer responds, "It's pretty queer, all right. . . . Weirdosity-laden" (73–74).

If Nancy and Jennifer were not characters in a minor novel, I would make *Professions of Desire* required reading for them. Then they might begin to understand why confronting negative stereotypes is essential to gay and lesbian studies in literature. Such studies would be, not "weirdosity-laden," but intelligent and often brilliant, suggestive and sometimes shocking, and a gift to contemporary culture.

More precisely, *Professions of Desire* offers three gifts to us all. First, it asks the most serious and valuable of questions about literature and culture. What are the connections, it inquires, among the literature of many periods and human sexualities? What difference does it make that Oscar Wilde was a gay man? that Gertrude Stein was a lesbian woman? And whatever do we mean by sexuality? by sexual identity? by gender identity? by desire? Where did we acquire, and how do we deploy, this vocabulary? Or where did this vocabulary acquire us? Moreover, how should we think simultaneously about sex, gender, and race? How can gay and lesbian studies guarantee the inclusion and influence of people of color?

Second, *Professions of Desire* cares about pedagogy, about teachers and their students. Our sexualities and their representations are the raw material of volatile syllabi and classrooms. Some teachers and students wish to stigmatize homosexuality ferociously. Others wish to smother it with silence. Still others, like Nancy and Jennifer, bustle among attitudes of tolerance, anxiety, and mockery. Still others, like the editors and writers of this book, wish to encourage lesbians and gay men. If classrooms are to be of use, we must learn to speak together in them, but, as *Professions of Desire* rightly tells us, we cannot speak together decently unless we break the interlocking gags of the stigma against homosexuality and the mockery of it.

Third, although the rhetoric of *Professions of Desire* is most often that of the contemporary scholar-critic, the tone of this book is special. It is at once playful, ironic, fearless, resolute, and angry. This tone is also grieving, because of the pain that gay men and lesbian women have suffered in the past and because of the monstrous waste that AIDS produces in the present. Today, elegies compose our realism.

The *Oxford English Dictionary*, that great prop of literary and cultural studies, reminds us that the word *weird* once meant having the power to control fate or destiny. In this sense, *Professions of Desire* is a wonderfully weird book. It shows gay and lesbian scholars claiming both the power to count the ways in which their culture has denied them and the power to control their own fate—yes, even to redefine the meaning of *queer*. "Weirdosity-laden?" Let us, finally, take it as a term of praise.

Catharine R. Stimpson
Rutgers University, New Brunswick

Work Cited

Jones, D. J. H. *Murder at the MLA.* Athens: U of Georgia P, 1993.

Introduction

For more than two decades, lesbians and gay men in the profession of language and literature have been engaged in researching, interpreting, theorizing about, and popularizing lesbian and gay writers, gay and lesbian textuality, the sexuality of literature, and the literature of sexuality. One important site where this work has gone forward has been the annual meeting of the Modern Language Association of America. The story of the founding of gay and lesbian studies at the MLA has been recounted clearly and concisely by Adrian Tinsley in the *Gay Studies Newsletter*.

As Tinsley notes, the first formal gay studies seminar at an MLA convention took place in 1973; it was called "Gay Literature: Teaching and Research." The following year's convention included five additional sessions as well as the forum "Homosexuality in Literature," presided over by Catharine Stimpson and featuring Christopher Isherwood as a speaker. The Gay Caucus for the Modern Languages (later renamed the Gay and Lesbian Caucus for the Modern Languages) began functioning as an allied organization of the MLA at the same convention. That year, the caucus began sponsorship of the newsletter *Studies in Gay Literature*, which evolved into the current *Lesbian and Gay Studies Newsletter*. As a result of efforts by the caucus, the MLA established, in 1981, the Division on Gay Studies in Language and Literature. The division currently numbers about nine hundred members and continues to sponsor several panels at each annual MLA convention.

The idea for this book emerged at the 1989 convention. *Professions of Desire* reflects the range of, and trends in, current research, scholarship, and pedagogy devoted to lesbian and gay literary studies; and it includes significant examples of lesbian and gay critical analysis, careful theorizations of possible areas of investigation, and thoughtful meditations on what it means to be lesbian, gay, or queer in the classroom. It represents an attempt by scholars who have been involved in lesbian and gay studies in literature to discuss their concept of the field and to demonstrate, to both specialists and nonspecialists, teachers and students, how they carry their concepts into the classroom and into their own critical and theoretical work.

The collection begins to suggest the scope and diversity of the field and the people working in it. It emerges at a moment of unprecedented openness in the academy (although the sting of backlash is already being felt) and of unprecedented hope outside it (although public violence forces us to face the cost of our openness). Those of us willing to "profess" desire, inside the classroom and beyond it, have learned how much we risk in doing so; but we have also realized that the risks are worth taking. Those of us who have staked our careers on the viability of gay and lesbian studies and who have viewed the closet as an impossibility—we have helped to clear a space within literary studies for rethinkings and reassessments, for deconstructions and reconstructions, for queering and outing, to be sure. But we have also made room for students who want to see literature from this perspective, who want to understand the workings of desire in and around literary texts, and who want to understand how sexuality has functioned in modern Western culture. This collection demonstrates a range of what is possible and offers direction to anyone who wishes to figure sexual difference into his or her classroom or research or writing. In addition, it provides materials to those who are attempting to open their own closet doors or to create the right conditions in which students might choose to open theirs, professing desire and making it their profession as we have done here.

The title *Professions of Desire* is meant to convey just that idea: this is a field that one does not enter so much as come out in. One's own sexuality is always at issue, and there are no easy answers to questions about identity and its (mis)representations in and around literary texts. As many of the essays in this volume suggest, moreover, desire asserts itself in constantly challenging and revealing ways in the gay or lesbian studies classroom. In the texts to be studied and the students to be taught, desire emerges as the trope that is figured most often, argued most persuasively, and experienced most deeply. What we profess, then, what we are professors of, is not desire itself but the figuration of desire in ourselves, our students, the texts we discuss, and the culture we analyze.

Not so much a field in the classic sense as a theoretical approach to literature and culture, lesbian and gay studies have taken their place in the academy and challenged everyone involved in the study of literature with new materials, new approaches, and new ideas. No longer content to "identify" writers or works as gay or lesbian, people working in this area have been central to the movement called cultural studies, reexamining the relation between literature and culture, problematizing the notion of identity, and rethinking the function of literature in relation to sexuality on the one hand and cultural production on the other. Happily, there is still room for readings of canonical figures such as Oscar Wilde and Gertrude Stein, as this collection demonstrates. But what constitutes a "reading" has shifted so profoundly that essays such as those by Eve Kosofsky Sedgwick, Jeffrey Nunokawa, and Karla Jay in this volume are among the most interesting cultural analyses to be found. Moreover, it is within the gay or lesbian studies classroom that identity has been most rigorously challenged and most carefully theorized. Even when studies are focused on the question of identity politics, as they often must be these days, the availability of sexual identity for political action is by no means taken for granted. Finally, and most important, scholars working in gay and lesbian studies have been increasingly conscious of hegemonic practices in the academy and have worked to figure difference of various kinds not just in their own work but in the field as a whole. Lesbians and gay men of color have made such important contributions in this area—in critical and theoretical analysis, to be sure, but also in writing and filmmaking and performing—that monoculturalism no longer has a place among us. In our classrooms and outside them, in our research and beyond it, lesbian and gay literary studies matter now, in a way they have never mattered before.

Unlike some previous collections, this book is committed to giving voice to the broadest possible range of individuals working within a loosely defined area of scholarly activity. The contributors to the volume themselves identify as lesbian, gay, or queer, and they work on writers, texts, or situations that are similarly definable, either directly, because of their overt interest in same-sex desire, or implicitly, because the issue of sexuality can be interrogated in them. The different histories of lesbian studies and gay studies are nowhere more apparent than in their different attitudes toward questions of ontology. While the question of what makes a "gay" text has been largely ignored, lesbian criticism has focused on the issue of what lesbian literature is, as the essays by Lillian Faderman, Paula Bennett, and Marilyn Farwell suggest. The context of feminism surely helps to explain some of the concern with definition among lesbian writers, as does the historical phenomenon of "romantic friendship" among married women. If definition has not been as compelling an issue among gay men, perhaps it is because the (white male) literary tradition offers so many astonishing inroads that definition seems almost beside the point. Another anomaly is the theorization of pedagogy. Until recently, pedagogical essays were by definition "anecdotal." Although the writers in this volume have not sacrificed the potential of anecdote, they have carried the discussion of pedagogy to a new level of theoretical sophistication. Again, there is no common approach to the issue of lesbian and gay pedagogy, and essays as diverse as those by Gregory Bredbeck, Sue-Ellen Case, Joseph Litvak, David Román, and Yvonne Yarbro-Bejarano offer an astonishing range of approaches rather than a prearranged set of conclusions.

Of course, as editors of a collection such as this, we cannot claim to be innocent of motives and agendas of our own. Some may see such an agenda in the subtitle of this collection. But we are not intending to publish a book on "lesbian and gay studies" without recognizing the complications inherent in the arrival of a controversial new old term of identification: *queer*. *Queer* has become a site of contestation since it has been hailed, on the one hand, as a term of coalition between and among lesbians and gay men but derided, on the other, as an effacement of the specific subject positions delineated by these two groups. While we, the editors, do not identify primarily as queer, we recognize that some who cannot (or choose not to) identify as lesbians and gay men and who may have come to be dissatisfied with the perceived classism, racism, and Eurocentrism of these terms may need the queer position from which to speak. Queer in this context has become the chosen position for many individuals who have come to be dissatisfied, in other words, with the politics that mark the terms *gay* and *lesbian*.

Identity politics has mattered historically in gay and lesbian studies, and it continues to matter, at least strategically, as an answer to the forces that oppose us. *Lesbian* and *gay* have not outrun their usefulness in the struggle for equal rights, nor does *queer* replace them in any but the most provisional way. All these terms and the concepts behind them are necessary in the classroom as well as in the streets. We hope that this volume, instead of systematically addressing questions of identity, identity politics, and terms of identification, opens all these issues for discussion from various points of view. If there are recurring attempts at definition here, they come from a feeling that we lack power until we know who we are. Those attempts are by their nature frustrated, however, because no identity, not even the identities we have fought for, can be fixed. Nor can the texts we study be determined by our readings any more definitely than they have been determined by others to which we object. These are vexed and vexing problems not just for those of us in this field but for others in fields more or less circumscribed than our own.

Various readers of this book in manuscript have insisted that we outline the terms of contradiction among the essays here and that we articulate what we see as the "fault lines" in lesbian and gay studies.

Neither of us feels that these fault lines are of major interest to us or to a majority of the readers of this book. Aside from its broadly divergent areas of interest, this book does not represent a field in conflict. Many issues that occupy current academic attention are present here, to be sure, but it would be wrong to suggest that the book is about them or that those of us involved in teaching in these fields are trapped within such controversies. For whatever difficulties we have faced, we are now more able to move toward more open classrooms, more exciting programs, greater political awareness, and greater independence than we have been at any time in the past. In other words, we have much to feel good about, and this volume represents that good in a variety of ways.

"Teaching Positions," the first section in *Professions of Desire*, includes four essays by writers who theorize pedagogy at the same time that they analyze their own positions in and around the classroom. These writers make various demands of lesbian and gay literary studies, questioning the field and what it is capable of achieving, problematizing the role of the professor in a gay or lesbian classroom, and arguing the cultural importance of pedagogical activity. George Haggerty argues that it is best to attack head-on the accusation of "promoting homosexuality"; he also asks what it means to teach gay studies and discusses how sexuality can be taught. Joseph Litvak describes what is at stake when a professor comes out of the closet; he tells the story of his own undergraduate homophobia as a way of explaining the levels of difficulty represented by sexuality in the classroom. Joseph Chadwick considers what it takes for humanities teachers to combat homophobia and tries to open up the concept of multiculturalism to include gay culture. In discussing the phenomenon of the "new dyke," Sue-Ellen Case attempts to redefine pedagogy from a lesbian subject position; she talks about subcultural fashions and the threat of self-appropriation implicit in "the look." All these essays seek to redefine what we ask of our students as well as of ourselves.

"Canons and Closets," the volume's second section, carries this discussion of pedagogy a step further. Focusing on curricular and organizational shifts that lesbian and gay studies programs warrant, these essays challenge canons and reclaim literary traditions. Lillian Faderman defines and chronicles lesbian literature, examining the influence of "sexology" on lesbian self-identification and the difficulties of categorizing lesbian texts. Stephen Orgel suggests how the literature of the English Renaissance can benefit from an approach that emphasizes sexuality; he urges those involved in the study of the field to reexamine their assumptions and to recognize that not even the greatness of great books is to be thoughtlessly assumed. Karla Jay argues that teachers of lesbian and gay studies need to explode the long-standardized canon of modernism, not just by outing already canonized figures but also by opening the canon to the vast range of writers that misogynist, racist, and anti-Semitic critics have ignored in establishing the field. Cheryl Clarke considers the problem of identity in a closeted African American classic, and she explains the intricacies of homosocial desire in the practice of passing. Paula Bennett's overview of lesbian poetry in the United States describes how sexual preference can be a site for poetic invention and redefines an entire poetic tradition.

The next section, "Sameness and Differences," begins to articulate the problems of identity in lesbian and gay studies. David Román talks about the organization of a specific lesbian and gay studies class and the function of difference in that context; he investigates the various subject positions we bring into our classrooms, the implications of teaching difference, and the uses of our work outside our classrooms and professional organizations. Yvonne Yarbro-Bejarano argues that the categories of race are neither static nor self-explanatory in lesbian and gay studies; she demands, moreover, that the field and its organizers emphasize multiculturalism, not just in topics discussed but also in priorities. Focusing on the uses of pornography in the gay and lesbian studies classroom, Earl Jackson, Jr., asks what the ground rules should be for discussing sexually explicit subject matter. Marilyn Farwell considers the degree to which lesbian identity has been closeted in the study of narrative; according to Farwell, lesbian narrative affirms a place for lesbian subjectivity and rewrites desire from the position of both lesbian and other female characters in a story. Gregory Bredbeck suggests the difficulty of distinguishing queer pedagogy from the manipulative pedagogies of the classical and more recent pasts, and he argues that "heterosexual pederasty" is "the condition of meaning in pedagogy," a condition on which the theorization of learning depends.

Finally, the section "Transgressing Subjects" gathers a group of essays that pose a direct challenge to the status quo, at the same time demonstrating most powerfully what queer studies can achieve. Jeffrey Nunokawa refutes the assumption that gay identity is formulated in Wilde's *Dorian Gray*; instead, he says, the pedagogical model universalizes homosexual desire and therefore deprives it of its potential for personal identification. Opening *The Importance of Being Earnest* to a queer reading that redefines avuncular relations, Eve Kosofsky Sedgwick urges us to "forget the name of the father," if only long enough to contemplate who might take his place. Phillip Brian Harper discusses how fear of miscegenation works to minoritize subjectivity; he explores the assumptions of heterosexual love in various representations of "The Kiss" and connects his findings to the confusion of public and private in *Iola Leroy*. In the closing essay, Michael Moon theorizes mourning in a rereading of Emerson and Whitman; he challenges the Freudian notion that mourning is a "completable" task and asks us instead to consider Whitman's call for a more intimate relation with our dead.

It is our sad task to announce that one of the contributors to this volume, Joseph Chadwick, has died from complications resulting from AIDS. Those of us who knew Joe will miss him deeply. Everyone who reads his essay here will begin to understand why.

George E. Haggerty, *University of California, Riverside*
Bonnie Zimmerman, *San Diego State University*

Work Cited

Tinsley, Adrian. "Louis Crompton, Dolores Noll, and Gay Studies in the MLA." *Gay Studies Newsletter* Mar. 1981: 1–4.

PART 1

Teaching Positions

"Promoting Homosexuality" in the Classroom

George E. Haggerty

IN MEMORY OF JOHN A. SEAMSTER

An infamous law in England (section 28 of the Local Government Act of 1988) forbids the use of materials that "promote homosexuality" in any government-sponsored activity, and similar language crops up in various documents in the United States, usually when reactionary leaders are listing the horrors of what they call the "gay agenda." The first response of lesbian and gay faculty members to the accusation that they are promoting homosexuality would probably be to laugh. *Homosexuality*, after all, is not a term with which many of us identify, nor is simple promotion an activity that we consciously pursue. Most of us, as professors of literature, understand that no discussion of a literary text is complete until sexuality—homo or hetero—in and around that text has been addressed. But that is not promotion, we might tell ourselves; that is teaching.

In the essay "A Talk to Teachers," James Baldwin writes:

> The purpose of education is, finally, to create in a person the ability to look at the world for himself, to make his own decisions, to say to himself this is black or this is white, to decide for himself whether there is a God in heaven or not. To ask questions of the universe, and then learn to live with those questions, is the way he achieves his own identity. But no society is really anxious to have that kind of person around. (4)

11

Our society seems especially anxious that certain questions not be asked: a school board in Vista, California, for instance, has recently insisted that creationism be taught alongside evolution as an alternative theory of biological development. An arts council in Georgia, in almost the same week, canceled all arts funding rather than sponsor Terence McNally's *Lips Together, Teeth Apart*. And in Oregon, local authorities are legally permitted to reject any civil rights bills that include sexuality as a right. As gay and lesbian faculty members, we have a duty to give our gay and lesbian students—all our students, really—the tools they need to achieve a sexual identity in a society that is determined to make that identity an impossibility. That duty includes being open about our own sexuality, of course; it also means being open to the sexualities of texts and the sexualities of students.

When we open our classrooms to an awareness of sexuality, sexual desire, gender difference, and other oppressive "otherings," we not only acknowledge that we *do* but also claim that we *must* "promote homosexuality": the phrase we have heard used against us in so many contexts should become our rallying cry. Until we accept the challenge that society continually taunts us with, we will be unable to create an agenda that is really gay or a world that is really our own. As a community, we seem in a certain sense to have accepted the terms that the hegemonic culture, which labels as "promotion" any discussion of homosexuality that is not homophobic, has set for this discussion. We argue, that is, that we do not, would not promote homosexuality and that our teaching is unaffected by our sexual orientation. I think we must argue precisely the opposite. We do promote homosexuality and indeed offer one of the few contexts in which the thoughtless and demeaning label can be reinvested with personal and cultural meaning. But we must also try to find ways to teach our students to be gay and lesbian, to show them that it is possible to flourish as lesbians and gay men in a culture that does everything it can to silence and oppress us. If we do not promote homosexuality in the classroom, we are surely promoting heterosexuality. And in our culture that is merely redundant.

The editors of a recent volume of pedagogical theory argue:

> By assuming a position in the classroom, . . . the teacher makes it possible for the student to become aware of his position, of his own relations to power/knowledge formations. . . . [T]he subject of . . . (post) modern pedagogy is a partisan subject: one who— far from being "well-rounded"—self-reflexively acknowledges his own partiality, in the sense of both incompleteness and commit-tedness. . . . The space of culture is therefore opened up for differ-ent organizations of the real.   (Zavarzadeh and Morton 11–12)

This project sounds impossibly idealistic, but considering what is at stake, we need to take it seriously. After all, the forces of the academy and the world at large are doing all they can to see that we do not accomplish it. They are always already in collusion to keep us on the defensive. As Simon Watney remarks:

> [T]he narrative of "homosexual promotion" should be regarded as a powerful fantasy which permits some heterosexuals to legitimately dwell on the image of children's bodies as objects of (homo)-sexual desire, and, moreover, as its active *subjects*. . . . [T]he discourse of "promotion" of homosexuality should be recognized as an essentially pre-modern construction, that is only able to conceptualize homosexual desire in the likeness of sinister, predatory perverts, luring innocent victims to their doom, having corrupted them from within.   (399)

I think that it is time for us to appropriate this "pre-modern construction" for our own liberatory ends. As teachers of lesbian and gay studies, we must encourage gay and lesbian students to see the traces of homophobia in the academy and to challenge those limits to personal freedom with a powerful political agenda that questions all the assumptions on which the "state apparatus" of education is founded. Gay and lesbian professors have to teach their students to be gay and lesbian, that is, because few people in authority inside or outside the academy can or will.

We can teach our students to be gay only if we teach them how much it matters in this society to challenge the cultural determinism of our age—the elitist, racist, heterosexist values that are everywhere celebrated as if they were values per se—and to demand the space for our various differences and the alternative organization of power that our "promotion" would promote. We might begin by telling them that much of gay and lesbian culture has been suppressed and hidden and marginalized in the academy, even in recent years, and that heterosexuality is "promoted" in every corner of the academy almost, as it were, by default. Our project is not just to open up Marlowe, Whitman, Dickinson, and Woolf to discussions of different sexualities; it is also to uncover the ways in which the entire canon has been founded on an attempt to silence the voices that could give a differently constituted "us" a sense of our newly re-created selves.

In the introduction to *Epistemology of the Closet*, Eve Kosofsky Sedgwick writes:

> Has there ever been a gay Socrates?
> Has there ever been a gay Shakespeare?

> Has there ever been a gay Proust?
> Does the Pope wear a dress? . . . A short answer, though a very
> incomplete one, might be that not only have there been a gay
> Socrates, Shakespeare, and Proust but that their names are Socra-
> tes, Shakespeare, and Proust; and beyond that, legion—dozens
> or hundreds of the most centrally canonic figures in what the
> monoculturists are pleased to consider "our" culture, as indeed,
> always in different forms and senses, in every other.   (52)

What this startling assertion affirms is that our traditions are already
available for a rediscovery of the place of (homo)sexuality in our culture.
Critics in every field are rereading texts and opening canons in just such
a spirit of rediscovery, as this volume affirms. As professors of literature,
moreover, we need to approach all texts from the point of view of
sexuality to learn from them the various ways in which gay and lesbian
"identities" have been brutalized and silenced. We can promote homosexuality only if we teach our students that much effort has gone into
suppressing it here in the academy and everywhere else. Once our students understand the dynamics of this silencing, and the threat to monoculturalism that it presupposes, they will discover in their own
experience a liberatory tactic that opens canons in life as well as in
literature—canons of race and class as well as those of sexuality and
gender. Chris Weedon suggests that the classroom is a "site of struggle
for power to fix meanings, to define ways of understanding the world
and to justify and guarantee the social relations that discourses support"
(53). In approaching texts in the literature classroom, we have to be
willing to make ourselves aware of the conflict of identities surrounding
the creation and reception of those texts. Whatever "meanings" we
produce must emerge from the shared experience of the classroom.

But how, as antiessentialists, can we base a pedagogical technique
on a concept as problematic as that of identity? Diana Fuss says that
"[n]o where are the related issues of essence, identity, and experience
so highly charged and so deeply politicized as they are in the classroom.
Personal consciousness, individual oppressions, lived experience—in
short, identity politics—operate in the classroom both to authorize and
to de-authorize speech." We can all imagine the uncomfortable situation
in a gay studies classroom when "identity politics" foreclose discussion
with the ruthless claims of experiential knowledge. As Fuss argues,
"The appeal to experience, as the ultimate test of knowledge, merely
subtends the subject in its fantasy of autonomy and control. Belief in
the truth of Experience is as much an ideological production as belief
in the experience of Truth" (113–14). For gay and lesbian students,
however, experience has taught a valuable lesson of homophobia and

its various manifestations in modern and postmodern culture. It seems to me that the "truth" of this "experience" is too valuable to sacrifice to the ideal of theoretical unassailability. All students are victimized by the status quo in our culture, but lesbian and gay students have been victimized on so many levels and in so many ways that they cannot defer to others—by which I mean *any* others—who only imagine, however theoretically profoundly, how (homo)sexuality figures in their lives. Lesbian and gay students' needs are more urgent than is the constant deferral that postmodern theory presupposes. Experience *must* count in the gay studies classroom, just as it counts among activist theorists themselves. Fuss talks about "the complicated process of identity formation" (100), which is at least in part transacted in experience that, however culturally determined, is significant in personally painful but also theoretically complicated ways. Not to recognize the value of that experience to the field of gay studies is to risk its loss—another silencing that we cannot easily afford.

Still, experience, no matter how telling, can function in the classroom as the privileged signifier that brutalizes and oppresses with all the violence of the law it is trying to subvert. Rather than use experience as a ground on which to silence other oppressions, oppressions of race and class in particular, or to oppress with other forms of silence, gay and lesbian students need to learn about the politics of oppression in their own lives as well as in the cultural context that, after all, determines what they mean when they call themselves lesbian or gay. In the gay studies classroom, we need to resist both the temptation to fetishize identity and the claim that personal experience provides ultimate truth. Our students can find an alternative to experience through literature by acknowledging difference and theorizing their own cultural construction, as they learn about representations of subjectivity throughout a rich and varied (multi)cultural history. What a gay or lesbian studies classroom can accomplish is an open confrontation with the various essentialisms that threaten to silence difference in any classroom: we must liberate students from the various oppressions that have shaped their social "identities." Fuss says, following Louis Althusser, that "if experience itself is a product of ideological practices . . . then perhaps it might function as a window onto the complicated workings of ideology" (118). A pedagogy of gay and lesbian studies needs to theorize just such an understanding of experience: can we look at how we have been constructed as gay and lesbian subjects without sacrificing the identity politics that some of us still see as crucial to our advancement? Maybe we can do so by looking into our own oppressions and by understanding how, even in our minority position, we exert a majority power on others outside our particular differences. By doing so, we can begin to confront homophobia on its own ground and transform the classroom into a laboratory for real social and ideological change.

As some readers may well object, a middle-class gay white male can argue for ideological change, and all it usually means is a larger office or a bigger salary for himself. "Homosexuals" have, after all, been the agents of oppression in many contexts—but in none more virulently than in the academy. In an article entitled "Resistance to Sexual Theory," Juliet Flower MacCannell develops Jane Gallop's argument about the relation between pedagogy and pederasty, which have gone hand in hand, as it were, since the time of Plato. From *this* feminist perspective, the connection between pedagogy and pederasty represents "the old order": "coercive, ideological heterosexuality which is actually rooted in homosexuality" (MacCannell 75). MacCannell's point is of course meaningless if we try to apply her "homosexuality" to any behavior that transpired longer than a hundred or so years ago. David Halperin has shown that, whatever the Greeks offer as a model for male relations in Western culture, it is not what we have learned to call homosexuality. Be that as it may, the place of an antiliberationist model of homosexuality in the academy is all too familiar. Gay faculty members, white gay male faculty members, have a lot to answer for. More than one closeted homosexual has wielded his straight-seeming rod of authority to set standards and to shut out those who do not measure up to his own usually sexist, usually racist, and always monocultural ideal. But the key to this exercise of power is the key to the closet door itself. As Sedgwick has shown, the closet has closed the American mind in countless ways. But the coercive old order is precisely what we eschew in coming out; coming out as gay professors liberates us from the compulsion to victimize our students with what we know or to tease them Socratically with its desirability. It offers instead a mutuality and a recognition of difference that builds relations, both "between the sexes" (MacCannell 71) and among "different" (because politically aware) subjects and subjective differences. Sedgwick says that "no one *can* know in *advance* where the limits of a gay-centered inquiry are to be drawn, or where a gay theorizing of and through even the hegemonic high culture of the Euro-American tradition may need or be able to lead" (53). While the first move in this liberatory tactic is the opening of the closet, the coming out of the faculty also entails a new responsibility. For the gay white male, unlike his "homosexual" counterpart, it means questioning the privilege of his position and putting his easily passable "identity" on the line. If the gay white male professor is still racist, sexist, or elitist in the old ways, in the ways that the academy always has been, he only hurts himself. Because as deeply as he might have desired to be one of the boys, his very act of coming out of the closet had made him the boys' enemy. His future lies with difference: his potential allies are similarly marginalized members of the academy whose agenda for rereading and redesigning the canon is a project to be celebrated and shared.

"Different organizations of the real," then, are precisely what we as lesbian and gay faculty members owe our students. For if we leave them as we found them, if by our silence or our shame we teach our students that the dominant culture was right about us all along, then we are merely replicating the traditional function of education. By acknowledging our own complicity, by challenging our whiteness, gayness, empoweredness, we help to point the way toward change.

I close with an anecdote, which I call the anecdote of the sympathetic colleague. When I told this colleague the title of this essay, he responded with a look of concern. "You know," he said, "the climate is just so bad right now, so rife with censorship, that you really should think twice before using a title like that." I responded that I thought it was important to challenge the climate he described. The next day, I saw him again. "I've been thinking about your paper," he told me. "I think you should use the word *gay* instead of *homosexual*—that way it doesn't sound as if what you are talking about is sex." But I *am* talking about sex—the function of sex both in our culture and in our lives. Our concern has to be the personal, sexual self-determination of our students, which can only happen when they are encouraged to recognize the oppressions in which they participate as well as those of which they are victims. For gay and lesbian pedagogy to succeed, we must be willing to take the risks: of constructionism, essentialism, institutionalization, and appropriation and of whatever our openness entails for us personally. None of these risks is as great as the threat of the status quo: our culture has for too long taken our silence for granted.

Works Cited

Baldwin, James. "A Talk to Teachers." *Multi-cultural Literacy: Opening the American Mind.* Ed. Rick Simonson and Scott Walker. The Graywolf Annual. Vol. 5. St. Paul: Graywolf, 1988. 3–12.

Fuss, Diana. *Essentially Speaking: Feminism, Nature, and Difference.* New York: Routledge, 1989.

Gallop, Jane. "The Immoral Teachers." *Yale French Studies* 63 (1982): 117–28.

Halperin, David M. *One Hundred Years of Homosexuality and Other Essays on Greek Love.* New York: Routledge, 1990.

MacCannell, Juliet Flower. "Resistance to Sexual Theory." Morton and Zavarzadeh 64–89.

Morton, Donald, and Mas'ud Zavarzadeh, eds. *Texts for Change: Theory/Pedagogy/Politics.* Urbana: U of Illinois P, 1991.

Sedgwick, Eve Kosofsky. *Epistemology of the Closet.* Berkeley: U of California P, 1990.

Watney, Simon. "School's Out." *Inside/Out: Lesbian Theories, Gay Theories.* Ed. Diana Fuss. New York: Routledge, 1991. 387–401.

Weedon, Chris. "Post-structuralist Feminist Practice." Morton and Zavarzadeh 47–63.

Zavarzadeh, Mas'ud, and Donald Morton. "Theory Pedagogy Politics: The Crisis of 'The Subject' in the Humanities." Morton and Zavarzadeh 1–32.

Pedagogy and Sexuality

Joseph Litvak

THE FRENCH LESSON

Near the end of my career in junior high school, I heard a mildly titillating story about a certain teacher—a French teacher—at the high school I was to attend in the fall. (Why, as in Eve Sedgwick's "A Poem Is Being Written"—an important model for this essay, by the way—is it always a French teacher? If French teachers didn't exist, American culture would no doubt have to invent them. Come to think of it, it sort of *did* invent them.) It seemed that if you took French, as I planned to do, you might well end up in the classroom of a certain Mr. Boyer. And it seemed—here's the titillating part—that Mr. Boyer, whose name was almost too good to be true, was famous at the high school for "liking boys." Though it's been a long time, I'm pretty sure my gleeful informant managed to embellish his tale with suitably lurid images of lechery and molestation.

I think the reason this memory has stayed with me for so long is not that the conversation in question revealed to me something scandalously new but, rather, that it confirmed an intuition that I had been forming ever since who knows when. In other words, while the story about Mr. Boyer had as its salient theme the *abuse* of pedagogical power, it actually illuminated something about the *normal* functioning of teachers in relation to students. In its sensationalistic way, the story emphasized that the classroom—any classroom—is a highly eroticized space: eroticized in different ways and with different effects, depending on the gender and sexuality of the teacher and the gender and sexuality of the students, but eroticized nonetheless—even or especially when the teacher goes strictly by the book and when nothing recognizably erotic takes place in that classroom.

I won't deny that a large part of my interest in this story

amounted to sheer prurient curiosity about Mr. Boyer and his alleged advances: If Mr. Boyer likes boys, I undoubtedly asked myself, will he like me? And if he likes me, will he do to me what he does to the others? Yet what was ultimately more compelling about the story was its dramatization of the insight that "liking boys" and, for that matter, "liking girls"—where those euphemisms designate homosexuality and heterosexuality in general—were not merely extracurricular activities. Rather, they were ways of being that our teachers carried into their classrooms and communicated to us, whether or not they wanted to, as much as if not more than they did the authorized subject matter of algebra, American history, English, and, of course, French. Ostensibly, sexuality was the most "personal" thing about a person, not just a private matter but in some sense the very essence of privacy, that which is by definition "nobody else's business." It was becoming clear to me, however, that acquiring *cultural* literacy—as one is supposed to do in school—meant, to no small degree, acquiring *sexual* literacy, not learning how to exclude the private from the public but learning how to read the private as it is everywhere obliged to manifest itself *in* public.

My point is that, if you grow up in this culture, you become remarkably sophisticated, well before college age, about the sexuality of your teachers—more sophisticated, perhaps, than about your own sexuality, which, as they say, is another story. This sophistication doesn't consist primarily in an explicit trading of information about sexual organs and practices, though it usually includes plenty of that kind of exchange. What defines it best is an acute, often merciless receptivity to the ways in which the sexual "truth" about a person spreads out to suffuse everything he or she says and does, especially at the level of apparently nonsexual words and deeds and especially when he or she is unconscious of their "true" significance.

I am drawing, of course, on Michel Foucault's distinction between sexuality and sex. For Foucault, sexuality is not reducible to what you do in bed; unlike sex, which is a biological category, sexuality is a cultural, a discursive, category—perhaps *the* category whereby we learn, in this culture, to make sense of the world. Sexuality, as Foucault formulates it, is the "putting into discourse of sex" (12). Being sophisticated about sexuality thus means being able to pick up on the innumerable ways in which our culture makes sex speak. It is this sophistication, I take it, that was at work not only in my friend's story about Mr. Boyer but also, for example, in all the endless little jokes that—like lots of students—my classmates and I would make about our teachers, not always behind their suggestively vulnerable and vulnerably suggestive backs.

I suppose I should come out at this point as, among other things, a compulsive mimic. By the ninth grade I'd built up a repertoire of (more or less cruel) imitations of almost all the teachers in the school. (Becoming a certain kind of class clown—everybody loves a clown—is of course one of the strategies a lot of gay or protogay kids adopt to survive in the intensely homophobic worlds of junior high and high school.) I think I realized even then that my imitations—of both female and male teachers—got a lot of their bite from an insistent playing up of whatever was most uncomfortably indicative of a given teacher's erotic specificity. Whatever little verbal or gestural tic seemed most decisively to betray the secret of his or her desire, that was what I would zero in on to the delight of my peers. Not surprisingly, however, the imitations that were most in demand were those of teachers thought to be gay. (And by *gay* here, I mean "gay men." Significantly, it almost never seemed to occur to me or my "friends" that any of our teachers might be lesbians; in this respect, we were no doubt obeying the cultural imperative to misrecognize—or simply *not* to recognize—lesbian lives and meanings, even when they're staring us in the face.) If apparently straight teachers had to be worked up into figures of fun, then apparently gay male teachers (needless to say, none of our teachers ever came out to us) seemed "naturally" hilarious. That is, if our sophistication about the sexuality of straight teachers was largely subliminal, what we "knew" about our gay teachers, we "knew" consciously, ostentatiously, aggressively.

In "Tearooms and Sympathy," Lee Edelman examines heterosexist culture's "insistence on the presentation of the gay male body as public spectacle" (154). As Edelman argues, this spectacle primarily serves not to satisfy some voyeuristic urge of the straight spectator but, rather, to "shore up 'masculinity' by policing the borders at which sexual difference is definitionally produced" (159). As a junior impressionist, I was more than happy, I'm afraid, to serve as a rookie cop—to assist, that is, in this enforcement of sexual boundaries, whereby the increasing visibility and problematicality of the gay man promotes the increasing invisibility and unproblematicality of straight society as a whole, but especially of the straight man. It wasn't long, then, before I was regaling my classmates with my wickedly acute rendition of Mr. Boyer—but of a Mr. Boyer who, despite my junior high school friend's ominous assurances, spent most of his time trying to pass rather than making passes. So what my routine consisted of, essentially, was a florid amplification of all the little ways in which the notorious French teacher revealed not so much his homosexuality as his closetedness; it was a question, in short, of ruthlessly bringing out his techniques for not coming out, techniques that were thereby seen repeatedly and delectably to backfire. If I was thus performing the cultural work of presenting the gay male body as public spectacle, I was presenting it the way straight society likes most to see it—as hiding ashamedly from a supervisory agency that it can never really elude, so knowing, so expert is that agency in detecting that body's every ruse, in exposing all the ironic accidents whereby it predictably puts itself into discourse.

In doing Mr. Boyer, as I remember all too well, one of my favorite shticks was to ape his recitation of what seemed to be one of *his* favorite shticks, about how "just because two men love each other, society assumes they're homosexuals." The joke, you see, was that he wasn't fooling anyone; eventually, with some egging on from my friends, the line was expanded into "just because two men live in the same house, just because they sleep in the same bed, just because they like to fondle each other's genitals. . . ." But while I thought that the joke was on Mr. Boyer, it turned out, of course, that the joke was on me. I congratulated myself at the time for what I took to be the sophisticated truth-telling implicit in my unmasking of this necessarily cautious gay teacher, who seemed every inch the less than gay, pre-Stonewall stereotype of "the homosexual," of the queer in the old, untransvalued sense of the term, with all its abjective violence. But in my wittiness I was unwittingly locking myself into the very double bind that he was enacting—into the tight paradoxical space of closeted homosexuality, whose emblem, as D. A. Miller has suggested in *The Novel and the Police*, is the open secret.

As a version of the open secret, Mr. Boyer's line about what society erroneously assumes wasn't just part of a cover-up, although that was certainly one of its functions: it was also, as now seems painfully obvious, the only means he had, in that homophobic time and at that homophobic place, for claiming a modicum of pedagogical control over the interpretation of his own sexuality—for letting us know that he *had* a secret and for cluing us in on what that secret might be. If, on the one hand, we recognized something depressingly dishonest and banal in the "just because x, it doesn't mean y" logic of his formulation, on the other hand, we chose not to recognize that he was also, through the same formulation, holding open the possibility that two men might love each other and that it *might* mean that they *were* gay. Or, rather, *I* chose not to recognize that. I chose, that is, to close the closet door on myself if not on Mr. Boyer. And for the next eight years, I, too, would be inhabiting the constrictive, attenuated realm of compulsory ambiguity typified by "just because two men love each other, society assumes they're homosexuals."

Did anything ever "happen" between Mr. Boyer and me? Well, yes, sort of. Somehow it came about that I needed to stay after class one day and go over some explication de texte. Sitting next to Mr. Boyer at his desk, I suddenly felt his hand on my thigh, which is where it stayed, decorously and discreetly, for the next half hour, until it was time for me to leave. Along with a sense of relief that nothing more had happened, there was probably something in my response equivalent to the line in the old Peggy Lee song: "Is that all there is?" But I can't have been all that disappointed, since, long before this hands-on instruction, I had already learned the sad lesson that Mr. Boyer had to teach me: that decorousness and discretion, rigorously maintained as a system of furtive, halting, or merely half-hearted words and gestures, of thighs and whispers, were indeed all there was to a certain socially constructed model of male homosexuality, the only model, I might add, available to a gay—or, rather, extremely unavowedly protogay—high school student in Richard Nixon's middle America of 1971.

THE LESSON OF PAUL DE MAN

Let me elide my college years, which, like many gay undergraduates, I spent in a painful sort of sexual fugue, and fast-forward to New Haven, Connecticut, and the year 1978, when I found myself enrolled in the comparative literature department at Yale—more specifically, in Paul de Man's graduate seminar. (Since you could still do French in comp. lit., the French connection—along with everything it stood for—wasn't exactly severed; moreover, though de Man himself was from Belgium, that status could seem at the time a sufficient metonymy for Frenchness *tout court*.)

Admittedly, to talk about this particular pedagogue under the rubric of pedagogy and sexuality may seem not so much novel as simply beside the point. Since the discovery of de Man's wartime writings, the relevant terms of discussion would appear to be, shall we say, pedagogy and politics or pedagogy and anti-Semitism. My aim is hardly to dismiss those issues: they're very much on the scene of what I want to say; but I want to focus for a minute on a somewhat different (though inextricably related) kind of politics and ideology—the politics and ideology of gender and sexuality. A memory of de Man that keeps coming back to me, along with the more obviously resonant ones, is of a class on Yeats, in which de Man, slipping into the apparently digressive mode that was one of his pedagogical hallmarks, began to relate a rather funny—if probably apocryphal—anecdote about Yeats's private life. I can't reconstruct it very well anymore, nor would it seem particularly funny even if I were to do so, since the point is that I'm no longer willing to sell it as a piece of humor. It took off from some casual remarks about the symbolism of the tower in Yeats, which led to a story about how Yeats insisted on living in a tower on the outskirts of town. In case we were interested in buying a tower, de Man continued, we should know that there wasn't any shopping nearby, which meant that poor Mrs. Yeats had to ride her bicycle into town three times a week to get groceries for her husband, for which he finally rewarded her—here's the punch line—by referring to her in "The Circus Animals' Desertion" as "that raving slut / Who keeps the till" (336).

A lot of people in that intensely cultish class clearly got a kick out of this disarmingly loose-jointed story, which seemed to epitomize the cool irony for which de Man was famous. (You have to realize that this was still prefeminist Yale.) I, for one, thought both the story and de Man were pretty cool, which is why, as soon as I got a chance to teach Yeats myself, I recycled the bicycle story as though it were my own. And for several years, that routine played as well in my classroom as it had in de Man's, though it probably would have gone over even better if I had done it in a Belgian accent. But although I wasn't doing the accent, I was still, of course, engaged in a process of imitation—this time, imitation of a heterosexually identified male mentor, whose pedagogical style virtually defined, for me, what might be referred to as "teaching as a straight man." By 1982, when I arrived at Bowdoin as an assistant professor and started playing de Man (whose name, especially in contrast with Mr. Boyer's, has an obvious allegorical resonance), I had already acknowledged to myself that I was gay and had been living for some time with my lover, the aforementioned Lee Edelman. Yet while the mask was therefore off in my "private" life, I was still trying to keep it on in the classroom, not so much through a conscious policy of deception as through the largely unconscious ideological programming that constitutes what it means to become a teacher in this culture.

If becoming a teacher means, for many people, becoming a straight male teacher, a role for which de Man was my model, what does his Yeats anecdote tell us about that role? For one thing, insofar as it is an anecdote, it tells us that teaching as a straight man is no more nonnarrative than teaching as a gay man is nontheoretical. But it does say something about a certain straight male strategy of using narrative to overcome narrative. In relating his story, and in relating it as he did, de Man, I would argue, was giving us a lesson in how to ascend from narrative into theory.

Nothing could have been more seductive, at the time, than the way in which he appeared to be telling us something about himself even as he kept us at a calculated distance or in which he appeared to be giving himself up to the pleasures of free association even as he subjected his discourse to the strictest possible discipline. Nothing could have been more seductive, as I say, unless it was his enactment of a certain bored, urbane knowingness vis-à-vis the dreary realities of marital politics.

Now, it might have seemed that de Man was thus offering a feminist or even a potentially lesbian and gay critique of patriarchal, heterosexist domesticity, but it didn't seem that way at all, not just because of his identification as heterosexual but also because of the grimly totalizing force of his irony itself. If, that is, the humor of the story seemed to consist in its equal opportunity cynicism, if the joke was as much at Yeats's expense as it was at his wife's, its ultimate effect was to install *de Man* in the tower, catapulting *de Man* to the supreme position of the normative, disembodied consciousness that, not controlled by the discourse of sexuality but controlling it, sees everything, knows everything, and remains blankly indifferent to everything. Staging his own evacuation as a desiring subject, de Man stunningly transformed himself into something like a transcendental ego.

As Miller has argued, it may not finally be that much fun to perform this kind of "theoretical" self-abstraction: it can recall "the professional deformation that positively requires such alienation for efficient job performance—and not just, of course, from those who aren't white, male, or heterosexual-identified, but also (even more, of course) from those who . . . are so entitled" ("Black Veil" 52). Whatever its costs to the performer, however, the performance, as I've said, had an extremely seductive effect on at least one member of the audience, and I'd wager that similar performances in similar classrooms seduce a lot of people into becoming professors themselves. But if there's something undeniably sexy about appearing to empty yourself of all sexual desire, this paradoxical trick is more available to those whose social entitlement most requires it: it is more available to straight men than to anyone else. What allows straight men to bring it off convincingly is that it already constitutes a large part of their social construction *as* straight men. From Ernest Hemingway to Kevin Costner, from Dick Tracy to Dick Cheney, the strong, silent type has been the dream of masculinist American culture, where acting like a man means acting like you're not acting at all, since the ones who make sexual spectacles of themselves are women and gay men. As performed by gay men and by both lesbians and straight women, the straight male disappearing act may not, therefore, be a surefire hit.

However much the paradoxicality of the act seems to resemble that of, say, the open secret, the two techniques have different consequences for classroom politics: where the straight male power play registers as a tour de force, the closeted gay or lesbian teacher's compulsory ambiguity seems, like all compulsions, forced on him or her; the difference, if you will, is as great as that between Mr. Boyer and de Man. As for my own reception, I have no idea how many of my students took my teaching as a straight man for the real thing and how many of them read my act as I had read my high school French teacher's; when you're in the closet, as Sedgwick reminds us, you never really know what people think. After several years at Bowdoin, at any rate, it started to become harder for me to tell the difference between being in the tower with de Man and being in the closet with Mr. Boyer; the mask of male heterosexual privilege began to seem oppressively indistinguishable from the mask of homosexual constraint. And that's what takes us to our third and final story.

GOODBYE, MR. CHIPS

Even if I hadn't stopped teaching Yeats a few years ago, I would still have stopped telling de Man's story in class. As my teaching, along with my scholarship, became increasingly feminist, the idea of getting comic mileage out of Mrs. Yeats's exploitation came to seem increasingly grotesque. But if feminism itself was becoming my new pedagogical vehicle, it, too, served partially to dissimulate: although I was perfectly sincere in my critique of patriarchy, my male feminism tended to serve as a way of teaching against heterosexism and homophobia without actually having to come out. In other words, I believed in what I was telling my students, but I wasn't telling them the whole story. And while this reticence seemed pragmatically defensible at the time, it had some rather disturbing practical consequences.

For example, the semester before the one in which I wrote the first version of this essay, I was teaching a seminar called Literary Theory. One of the texts for the course was Terry Eagleton's book of the same name. Somewhere around Columbus Day, we were discussing his chapter on poststructuralism, whose alleged political impotence Eagleton asserts through a parodic rehearsal of the writings of the gay French critic Roland Barthes—there's that French connection again. Things were going relatively well until I decided to point out the strains of francophobia, erotophobia, and homophobia in Eagleton's prose. Incorrigible ham that I am, I chose to mock Eagleton's mockery of Barthes by enacting my own parody of the virile, salt-of-the-earth political activism that Eagleton privileges over Barthes's ostensibly effete, apolitical, all too Parisian autoeroticism. After miming with fist and palm the pounding phallic thrust of Eagleton's macho Marxism as it goes to inseminate an implicitly feminized social reality, I proceeded to figure, by contrast and with even greater brio, the various masturbatory pleasures of the nonreferential textual play that Barthes celebrates.

Though this bit seemed at first to be going over fairly well, I began to suspect that something was wrong when one of the women in the class, looking rather unamused, turned to another woman and started a conversation I couldn't hear. And sure enough, about a week later the first student came to my office to tell me that something had indeed been wrong: that while the five men in the class had obviously been enjoying my routine, she and both the other women in the class had been feeling acutely alienated, as though the classroom had suddenly been transformed into the men's locker room. Now, when this student confirmed my suspicions, my response was one of considerable chagrin: I felt, to be perhaps dangerously candid, as though I had been caught with my pants down, in the full criminal sense of that cliché.

I tried to cover, or recover, myself by explaining to the student, and subsequently to the class as a whole, that I had intended my little performance as a feminist debunking of Eagleton's phallocentrism. I talked about how, in attempting to deconstruct the locker room, only to reconstruct it on some level, I had inadvertently illustrated one of the acknowledged predicaments of deconstruction in general. And this explanation was all true, as far as it went. Yet the problem was that it didn't go far enough. For the students who thought I was straight, my profession of good faith may have seemed a little abstract, not to say downright unconvincing. But for the students who thought I was gay, the open secret of my sexuality may have seemed even more discrediting. For as long as I let that sexuality remain an open secret, as I'm pretty sure it was for some if not all of the students, my professions of solidarity with the women in the class could always be called into question; that is, it could always be inferred that, while pretending to support the female students, I was far more interested in trying to charm the male students—that my apparent subversion of the phallus constituted an excuse for trying to get a rise out of it.

In another text that we read in the Literary Theory seminar, a critic named Gerald M. MacLean, who comes out unmistakably as a married heterosexual man, writes: "I don't think anyone has begun to examine fully the range of erotic interactions between students and teachers. In class I flirt, consciously and consistently. But I play for laughs and flirt with the men too" (149). A straight male teacher can say that and get away with it: if it's understood that when he's "flirting with the men" he's just "playing for laughs," it goes without saying that when he's playing it straight—flirting normally and normatively—the "students" interpellated as the objects of that flirtation are all female students. I don't know too many straight female teachers who would say the equivalent of what MacLean says, but if they did, chances are they'd seem to be asking for trouble. Were a lesbian teacher publicly to acknowledge sexual interest in her students, she'd most likely open herself up to the charge of using her classroom as a recruitment center. And in a culture perpetually haunted (and thrilled) by the possibility that pedagogy might turn into pederasty, such a statement by a gay male teacher still has to be made with a certain circumspection. So in trying (as I was indeed doing) to win my male students over to feminism, was I also flirting with them? At Bowdoin, I answered, "Maybe I was." Here I can say, more bluntly and with a certain air of insouciance, "Of course I was." But the flirtation depended crucially on my closetedness: if I wanted the male students to "like me," I wanted them to like me not as a teacher who "liked boys" but as one of the boys, as what our culture, in all its strong, silent eloquence, calls a regular guy.

I've mentioned, of course, my suspicion that this masquerade was being perceived as such. But I still wanted to have it both ways: not so differently from Mr. Boyer (who had even better reasons for playing it safe), I was trying to speak out of both sides of my mouth at once, obliquely making certain gay-affirmative points while counting on a vague presumption of my heterosexuality to legitimate them—and not only to legitimate them but also, frankly, to make *me*, well, more desirable as their purveyor. At the same time, however, I was beginning to find the contradictions of this double bind intellectually and politically untenable, emotionally enervating, and just generally not worth it. Under such circumstances, how could the masquerade not begin to wear thin to the point of transparency? The masturbation episode, as I came to call it, seemed to exemplify everything that was inauthentic and off-target and uncomfortable-making about the seminar in which it occurred, and it forced me to do some rethinking about the kind of teacher I wanted to be.

CODA

As a result of that rethinking, I came out to one of my classes the following semester. The coming-out story is supposed to have a happy ending, but my experience with that class was less than happy. Too many of the comments on the end of the semester course evaluation forms boiled down to some version of "the teacher emphasizes sex too much" or of the less guarded "the teacher emphasizes homosexuality too much." If the actual discourse of the class hadn't quite prepared me for the formulaic dismissiveness of these parting shots, it may simply have been because a lot of the students had made the cynical decision that the best way to get through the course was by treating my gay pedagogy as the particular orthodoxy to which they would have to pay lip service until a more palatable alternative came along. In effect, they ended up trying to reconstruct the gay male teacher as the straight male teacher they wished he had been in the first place.

Of course, they couldn't quite succeed, less because of any conscious resistance I may have offered than because of the irrepressible interference of an older model of the homosexual teacher, a model that, for all its apparent obsolescence, our culture just won't give up: the model of—who else?—Mr. Boyer. Hoping to transcend the opposition between teaching as a straight man and teaching as a pathetic closet case, I wound up reinscribing that opposition in my own person, back in the familiar territory of the pedagogical double bind. For if I took on some of the straight man's power—without any of the seductiveness that goes with it—I found myself stereotyped at the same time as the bearer of a sexuality popularly conceived either as a surrender of power or as an abuse of it.

In no way do I claim to speak as the representative gay pedagogue. But from my own nonuniversal vantage point, it seems that, no matter how knowing and sophisticated a gay male teacher is in his management of his own pedagogical-sexual performance, he remains susceptible to the following interpretations: For many straight male students, he's both contemptible (he wants to be treated "like a woman") and threatening (he wants to treat you like one). For many straight female students, his homosexuality means either that he's misogynistic (he doesn't like women) or that he's merely indifferent (he won't play his prescribed role in the academic version of *Father Knows Best*). For many closeted lesbian, gay, and bisexual students, he's someone who might blow your cover. And even for many out lesbian, gay, and bisexual students, he's less a role model than, given the pervasive ageism of the culture, well, both contemptible and threatening again.

This isn't to say that there haven't been some good moments in classes where I've come out. But I've come to realize that when you teach gay, just as when you try to teach straight, certain discomforts may be irreducible as well as inevitable for all concerned. If you like to think of yourself as an oppositional critic, and as someone who carries his or her critical activity into the classroom, then maybe you have to accept the fact that you can't simultaneously *épater les bourgeois* and charm their pants off.

As the lesson of Paul de Man might go to show, of course, the opposition between teaching as opposition and teaching as seduction is no less deconstructible than any other. But as that lesson also shows, not all oppositional pedagogies are equally seductive. Professing a relatively unseductive oppositionality can seem like another form of self-censorship, a de Manian ascesis without any of the mystique such a pose so successfully confers. Moreover, if you're gay, the position of pain in the institutional ass is never entirely voluntary. Yet if it chooses you as much as you choose it, you *can* figure out your own way of occupying it, of playing with and against it, and in the process you can both have some fun and teach people some lessons for which they may not thank you but that may not feel merely like discipline and punishment either.

Bowdoin College

Note

This essay is the abbreviated text of a lecture I first presented at my home institution, Bowdoin College, in the spring of 1990. Readers will quickly recognize that, in addition to being about pedagogy, it is a pedagogical exercise; it was originally written for a specific undergraduate audience, and it retains the traces of that specificity. I presented a revised version of the essay at the Homotextualities conference at the State University of New York, Buffalo, in October 1991. In recasting the essay for that occasion, I framed and modified the original structure with remarks designed for a more professional audience; some of those changes have also been preserved here, especially in the coda. Thus, though my title might suggest a certain global reach, the essay is the condensed record of two quite local performances, for two quite different audiences. It of course addresses a third audience as well—the audience of its current readers, who, I assume, might appreciate this brief account of its history.

Works Cited

Eagleton, Terry. *Literary Theory: An Introduction.* Minneapolis: U of Minnesota P, 1983.

Edelman, Lee. "Tearooms and Sympathy; or, The Epistemology of the Water Closet." *Nationalisms and Sexualities.* Ed. Andrew Parker et al. New York: Routledge, 1992. 263–84. Rev. and rpt. in *Homographesis: Essays in Gay Literary and Cultural Theory.* New York: Routledge, 1994. 148–70.

Foucault, Michel. *An Introduction.* Trans. Robert Hurley. New York: Vintage, 1980. Vol. 1 of *A History of Sexuality.*

MacLean, Gerald M. "Citing the Subject." *Gender and Theory: Dialogues on Feminist Criticism.* Ed. Linda Kauffman. Oxford: Blackwell, 1989. 140–57.

Miller, D. A. "The Administrator's Black Veil: A Response to J. Hillis Miller." *ADE Bulletin* 88 (1987): 49–53.

———. *The Novel and the Police.* Berkeley: U of California P, 1988.

Sedgwick, Eve Kosofsky. *Epistemology of the Closet.* Berkeley: U of California P, 1990.

———. "A Poem Is Being Written." *Representations* 17 (1987): 110–43.

Yeats, W. B. *The Collected Poems of W.B. Yeats.* New York: Macmillan, 1974.

Toward an Antihomophobic Pedagogy

Joseph Chadwick

Since the late sixties, gay culture has blossomed in the United States. This is not to say that gay culture didn't exist in the United States before then, only that in recent years this culture has gained public visibility, acquired some political power, and produced a wide array of gay-identified businesses, institutions, organizations, and artistic work.

During the same time, various ethnic, women's, and (to a lesser degree) class cultures in the United States have gone through similar processes. The public emergence and political struggles of these cultures have created an overall crisis in the way we think about relations both among these ethnic, gender, class, and sexual groups and between those groups and the "dominant" culture—a crisis complicated by the fact that one may participate in more than one of these cultures (including the dominant) at the same time. The notion of multiculturalism is one of many diverse responses to this crisis. It represents a productive attempt to find a coherent and nonoppressive way to think about and act on matters of cultural difference. Too often, however, we assume that the term *multiculturalism* refers fundamentally to issues of ethnic difference. I don't want to deny the importance of those issues, but I do want to insist that they be raised in conjunction with questions of sexual difference as well as of gender and class difference (though I won't take up those issues here), especially since, in the United States, ethnic and sexual attitudes and stereotypes often blend and blur. Gay culture exists in this country, even if what it consists of remains a healthily unsettled question and even if it is fragmented by fault lines of ethnicity, class, and gender. We must take into account gay culture—or better, gay cultures—when we think of the questions summed up by the term *multicultural*.

Further, since the answers we get to a question are often dictated by the terms in which the question is posed, if we are to take the line of thinking sketched above into the field of pedagogy, we will need to alter the questions posed by multiculturalism—and many other questions that we ask when we teach.

What would such a changing of pedagogical questions look like? To answer this, I propose a name for the practice, offer a couple of questions as grounding assumptions for it, and then look at some situations—specifically, students' essays—where it is called into play. For some of the same reasons that we speak of feminist (rather than, say, antisexist) teaching or theory, it is tempting to call the practice I'm describing gay or gay-identified pedagogy: to do so would be to insist that, to engage in this practice, one must take up the struggles that attend gay existence in this society (as men must take up women's struggles to engage in various feminist practices). It is also tempting to call this practice anti-heterosexualist pedagogy, since that name locates the source of the problems to which this practice responds not in the *homo* of *homophobia* but rather in the *hetero* of *heterosexualism*—that body of beliefs and attitudes centered on the assumption that heterosexual relations constitute true, normal, or natural sexual relations. For the purposes of this essay, however, I stick to the term *antihomophobic* pedagogy, since it emphasizes that such a pedagogy is a crucial task not only for gay teachers but also for any teacher in this society.

My first thesis, one implicit in the stands that various activist groups have taken in the struggles over AIDS research, is that any research question or pedagogical strategy that does not pursue an actively antihomophobic course when issues of sexual difference arise (or that simply tries to evade those issues) must be in some degree homophobic. There's no room for neutrality here, since neutrality means letting the normal, institutionally and socially sanctioned current of homophobias flow on undisturbed. Floating for a moment into the more rarefied reaches of literary criticism, specifically to critical treatments of Proust's *A la recherche du temps perdu*, one finds Eve Kosofsky Sedgwick articulating this thesis. She challenges the current critical tendency to insist on "a notional 'undecidability' or 'infinite plurality' of 'difference' " in a text like Proust's, a text that "has its terms and structure so intimately marked by the specificity of turn-of-the-century sexual crisis that to imagine a floating-free of those terms, or an infinity of non-homosexual marked alternatives to them, is already a homophobic form of understanding" (246).

My second thesis, a crucial one for any practice of antihomophobic pedagogy, reading, or even conversation, is announced by D. A. Miller in a recent essay on Hitchcock titled "Anal *Rope*":

Where homosexuality is concerned, the sophistication that has learned how to drop the subject in passing must be just as suspect as the balder mode of panic that would simply drop the subject, period. In a culture where variously sharp excitements . . . greet the mere nomination of the subject, a truly offhand reference to male homosexuality must hardly be credible, least of all from a heterosexual-identified man whom this category has likely served half his life to bully into good behavior.   (116–17)

As Miller suggests, there is virtually no such thing as an "offhand" or "passing" reference to homosexuality in this society. Any reference, even the most oblique and apparently marginal, demands some kind of antihomophobic reading and response, be it direct or equally oblique.

Miller's claim finds powerful confirmation in my first example of student writing, essay A. The assignment for this essay called for a profile of someone that included physical detail, mannerisms, and action. In the first version of essay A, the writer, a freshman living in a dorm, told how his roommate, a senior whom he names Mr. X, tried to get into bed with him one night while he was sleeping. The writer thought of reaching for the knife that he kept under his pillow but instead simply told Mr. X to get out. The rest of the essay consisted of a homophobic tirade that relied entirely on stereotypes and the standard epithets that serve as weapons in verbal gay bashing.

My strategy of response to this essay was dictated by my sense that the event had provoked a powerful panic in the writer (witness the detail of the knife). Any direct confrontation on the issue of homophobia, I thought, would only turn into one of those hostile, specular face-offs that men use to evade other forms of embrace. So I took an oblique approach and told the writer that, because his essay relied heavily on stereotypes and clichéd epithets, it did not fulfill the assignment; I suggested that he rewrite the essay, possibly even about someone else, and rely more on detail and action.

As a result, the writer produced a new version of the essay, still focusing on Mr. X, but this time recounting situations when Mr. X pretended to some expertise on subjects about which he knew little. The only remaining trace of the first version's outpouring of panic appears in the following passage: "The phone call I was waiting for finally came. I felt sort of relieved because it gave me an excuse to leave the room and get away from that queer, irritating stare that he always gave." If one reads this passage in isolation, the word *queer* might seem to qualify as an example of an offhand or casual homophobic gesture. But if one reads it against the essay's first version, one has to conclude, first, that the whole episode of Mr. X's attempt to get into the writer's bed and all the hysterical panic let loose by that episode have been condensed into the single adjective *queer* and, second, that the issue of homosexual-homophobic panic has, in a telling displacement, been turned into the issue of whether Mr. X knows what he pretends to know. The revision of essay A not only supports Miller's claim about the impossibility of offhand references to homosexuality but also suggests that certain psychoanalytic notions—condensation, displacement, disavowal, hysteria—may prove particularly useful in formulating questions about such references. Those notions, that is, can be appropriated for a strategy of antihomophobic reading that would certainly have to be part of any practice of antihomophobic teaching.

The second example, essay B, demands a somewhat different strategy of reading and response. In this case the assignment called for an essay about a situation in which some aspect of the writer's identity made her or him feel out of place, foreign, or even threatened. Essay B, titled "Discrimination and Me!" recounts a Hawaiian student's angry reaction to being taken for a Mexican during a visit to California with his high school track team (an experience common enough that the Hawaiian comedian Andy Bumatai has a routine about it). The essay includes the following passage:

> I walked into the restaurant and waited in line behind three girls on my track team. The man who took their order looked at them and said, "Good evening ladies, welcome to Carl's Jr., may I take your order?" So, thinking nothing of it, I waited in line and when he saw me, he gave me a disgruntled look. "What would you like?" he told me. "Huh," I said, as he looked at me and said, "Oh, es que servirle ese?" Right then I knew he thought I was Mexican as I looked at his cocky face and his clicking of his gums at me. Our team's head coach, Mr H., heard everything and tried to hold me back, as I began to calmly approach the little shit who had to be so hostile to me. I looked at him and said to him in Spanish, "Eh pendejo, cállate la boca tu maricón." Well in English this translates to "Asshole, shut your mouth you faggot." Then for some uncontrollable reason I found myself and my arms around his neck, and his body off the ground and on the countertop. Repeatedly, I felt my head and his bouncing off each other. All of a sudden I just stopped the pounding, went to the van and just sat there.

An antihomophobic reading of this passage might go something like this. First, the apparently offhand epithet "faggot," used here more as a gesture of contempt than as a definite claim about the restaurant employee's sexual disposition, is not so offhand as it seems. It is backed up by an act of physical violence described in terms that could refer to either strangulation or embrace: "for some uncontrollable reason I found myself and my arms around his neck. . . ." Second, the head-to-head confrontation in this passage follows precisely the ritual pattern of specular, symmetrical hostility that homophobic sociality enforces in many situations. The almost automatic, ritualized response is confirmed by the writer's use of locutions that deny the speaking *I* any role as agent of the violence: "I found myself and my arms around his neck . . ."; "I felt my head and his bouncing off each other." Finally, the use of homophobic insult as a weapon of revenge against perceived ethnic insult not only supports my earlier argument about the blurring of ethnic and sexual identities and thus about what the term *multicultural* should include but also suggests that for men in this society, a term like *faggot* may pack an even harder punch than any comparable ethnic slur. It suggests as well that homophobically structured rituals of specular confrontation may be at work in a good many situations in the manifest content of which issues of sexual difference never even appear.

I responded to this passage from essay B with the following comment:

> You need to make clearer what the fundamental issue at stake in this essay is—the fact that several people in California mistook you for a Chicano or the fact that many people in California discriminate against Chicanos. Or is it something else altogether? I read it as an essay about how one kind of discrimination often breeds another. The Carl's Jr. worker apparently doesn't like Chicanos and, by speaking to you in Spanish, suggests that you are one. You respond by calling him a "maricon," suggesting that you don't like gay men and that he is one. You later say that "a person should not pass judgment on another person that they don't really know," but your narrative shows how hard it is to stick to that principle in the heat of the moment.

This response seeks to take up the issue of homophobia directly but without setting up a repeat of the kind of confrontation that the essay narrates. My rhetorical stratagem was to discuss the issue in relation to its effect on the essay's argument. Since the sheer volatility of homophobic energies often sends them careening in directions that their subject apparently doesn't intend, they can easily disrupt argumentative consistency or coherence, so this strategy may be an effective one in a variety of situations.

The last example, essay C, argues that racism is a serious problem on college campuses in the United States but that it would be wrong to try to solve this problem by restricting the right of free expression.

The writer himself never mentions the issue of sexual difference, but he does include a quotation from a *Newsweek* article about the putative emergence on college campuses of demands for politically correct attitudes on race. For the student conforming to PC principles, the article claims,

> it would not be enough . . . to refrain from insulting homosexuals or other minorities. He or she would be expected to "affirm" their presence on campus and to study their literature and culture alongside that of Plato, Shakespeare, and Locke.   (Adler et al. 48)

This passage takes a tricky rhetorical stance. Both the student writer and the *Newsweek* article take the pose of simply defining PC principles in a relatively neutral way. The *Newsweek* article, however, places this ostensibly neutral exposition of those principles immediately after an introductory anecdote about a University of Connecticut student who was expelled from her dorm for having a sign on her door listing "homos" as one category of "people who are shot on sight"—an expulsion that the *Newsweek* article later calls "appalling" (48–49). This clear attack on PC principles also appears, though less obviously, in the word *enough* in the ostensibly neutral passage I've quoted; the word suggests that to "affirm" the presence of "homosexuals or other minorities" is indeed too much to expect. In addition, the word *enough* introduces into the *Newsweek* article's argument a racism powerful enough to reduce that argument to absurdity. To claim that refraining from insult *is* enough, that it might be legitimate simply to ignore the existence of those belonging to sexual or ethnic minorities, would, given the ethnic breakdown of the state of Hawaii, for example, mean ignoring the existence of everyone on the University of Hawaii campus (I use the term *minority* here in a purely demographic sense rather than as denoting differences of power or privilege). The homophobic content of the *Newsweek* article's argument resides in the implicit but nonetheless clear suggestion that students not be required to study the "literature and culture" of "homosexuals" "alongside that of Plato, Shakespeare, and Locke." This suggestion reduces the argument to absurdity yet again if one recalls the incontrovertible facts that homoerotic relations are central to both Plato's dialogues and Shakespeare's sonnets and that those texts have played crucial roles in the formation of certain strata of gay male culture from the Victorian era onward. Within essay C as a whole, the implicit racism and homophobia of this passage have the effect of undermining somewhat the writer's claim that, although PC principles are not the right solution, something needs to be done about racism on campus.

The points about racism and homophobia raised by the *Newsweek* passage and the points I've made about essays A and B suggest a few principles of antihomophobic reading and response—that is, of antihomophobic pedagogy. First, the panicky energies of homophobia may produce self-deconstructive inconsistencies in an essay's argument, as they do in both essay B and the essay C quotation. Second, the conflation of homophobia with racism clearly depends on the similar strategies of objectification at work in each of those impulses; but that conflation— again, as in essay B and to some extent in the essay C quotation—may also allow one of those impulses to operate under cover of the other or to legitimize the other. Third, the rhetorical strategy deployed in responding to homophobia must take into account both the student's situation and the teacher's relation to that student. This principle might seem self-evident, but it needs to be applied with special care—or tact, or force—given the volatility of homophobic emotions. Fourth, even the most oblique and apparently offhand manifestations of homophobia demand a response. Homophobia comprises a set of attitudes, emotions, and somatic responses so pervasive and so deeply embedded in the sexual, familial, and social arrangements through which we are constituted as subjects that no one, not even those most directly victimized by it, is exempt. One implication of this final principle is that we would do well to respond to homophobia—and especially homophobic assertions about canons and cultures—by recalling that homosexual desire does not exempt anyone either, not even canonical philosophers and poets. Another is that changing the questions we ask when we read and respond to student essays also means changing the questions we ask of ourselves.

University of Hawaii, Manoa

Works Cited

Adler, Jerry, et al. "Taking Offense." *Newsweek* 24 Dec. 1990: 48–54.
Miller, D. A. "Anal *Rope*." *Representations* 32 (1990): 114–33.
Sedgwick, Eve Kosofsky. *Epistemology of the Closet*. Berkeley: U of California P, 1990.

The Student and the Strap: Authority and Seduction in the Class(room)

Sue-Ellen Case

FOREPLAY

Strapping on the dildo has become the premier image of the new wave of lesbian sexual imagery and hermeneutics. Photos and ads of dildos for and with lesbians fill the pages of the underground chic 'zines as well as the slide screens of MLA panels on the lesbian. In theory circles, the psychoanalytic portrait of the lesbian with phallus as fetish is thusly fleshed out, and the fashionable new focus on masquerade and performance makes the dildoed dyke appear alluring, plenitudinous, and postmodernly perverse and dispersed. What more or less could a girl want?

The earlier dowdy dyke, who had no market muscle, who inhabited the downwardly mobile community of lesbian feminists, and who eschewed the market for the "natural," lacked the allure of commodification. Attitudes toward her appearance were reminiscent of the oft-heard comments from Americans who traveled into East Berlin on a sight-seeing day: boring, gray, and depressing without the visual excitement of billboards, display windows, brilliant commodities on the streets or on the people. The dowdy took too seriously, among other things, a utopian notion of equality in sex, and when she asked her date up to see her sketchings (up to her mommy's *jouissance* joint), they turned out to be old French feminist images of two lips and unseeable, ascopophilic holes. A dutiful daughter, with no sex toys or scenarios of power to play, and almost puritanical in her refusal of sexual images, the dowdy's appearance has been obscured by graffiti such as "essentialist" or "feminist."

In contrast, the new dyke of the visible is born out of the rib of gay male subcultural images. She peaks in photo displays of her sex toys and sexual identities, such as the photo essay in *Quim* entitled "Daddy Boy Dykes" in which the dykes are dressed as gay leather men, replete with mustaches. There, they pose as cocksuckers and ass fuckers with dildos peeking out of leather chaps. This new visibility, called "lifestyle lesbianism," is configured as a reaction against that earlier dowdy's feminism as "a justifiable response to an over politicization of the personal" in which "this new attention to lifestyle [is] a freedom, a testament to the fact that their identity is now a personal choice rather than political compulsion" (Stein 40, 41).

This display of lesbian sexual identity as proximate to phallic display has deep roots within the tradition of lesbian appearance. Once and once again it is performed as butch-femme role playing. Likewise, it appears in lesbian S and M scenarios that often conflate penetration with phallic power and its vicissitudes of appearance. After all, as Teresa de Lauretis has already worked out in "Sexual Indifference and Lesbian Representation," there are only certain ways in which lesbians can appear on the dominant heterosexual semiotic screen. However, the critical reception of the more traditional strategies of appearance, such as butch-femme role playing, has been figured through feminist theory, set against the backdrop of oppression. This tradition of configuring "lesbian" vis à vis "the gaze" addresses role playing as the only possible form of liberation in a system of representation locked tight by the erect phallus. Even Pat Califia, who would distinguish herself from orthodox lesbian feminist critiques, works off models of oppression for S and M practitioners and pornographers, pleading an almost civil libertarian case in her introduction to *Macho Sluts*. Thus, the running argument of the 1980s concludes that masquerading lesbians, oppressed, finally, by codes of invisibility, had little choice but to appropriate the phallus in order to appear. These politics of oppression allowed dykes and, for example, women of color to form coalitions and consonances among themselves, as well as with other political critiques, such as socialism.

The newer theoretical argument that accompanies the dildoed dyke asserts that, when the dyke straps on the dildo or gay male leather fashion wear, commodity fetishism overcomes dominant gender traps. Unlike the coalition politics of oppression, these are the politics of individual success. The power of these politics is in visibility and appearance. As Cindy Patton puts it in "Unmediated Lust":

> For the last few years the lesbian sex magazines have been quite openly playing with the (gay) boys. At first, there was a tinge of envy in these images, but once dressed for the occasion, we

discovered that we had already been over this turf. . . . [W]e must now deconstruct any female desire that insists that it must be constructed against masculinity. We must create images for Monique Wittig's polemic assertion that lesbians are not women. . . .

(238)

Clothes make the man. The costumes of phallicized commodities provide the necessary deconstruction of earlier naturalized systems of genderfication and (hetero)sexualization. Some even "see" fashion wear as a form of activism: "My appearance tells people that I am a sexual outlaw and an urban gender terrorist" ("S/M Aesthetic" 42). Significantly, Patton's article appears in a book on lesbians and photography because much of this new dyke posing and theorizing presupposes a camera somewhere or some version of *I Am a Camera*. Thus, the representational muscle of commodity fetishism is not merely in the buying of the dildo, the posing, the sucking, or the watching but also in the expectation of the photo of it and, ultimately, of the ad. The new dyke is constructed by her appearance in the marketplace of images—she is an ad man. Her politics are an ad campaign. Cameras are a dyke's best friend. Now this:

> In his account of the parallel rise of the photographic portrait and the middle classes, John Tagg characterises the medium as "a sign whose purpose is both the *description* of an individual and the *inscription* of a social identity." The latter function, Tagg argues, is performed both by the photograph's replacement of the earlier portrait media by which rising classes claimed their social place— the painted miniature, the silhouette and the engraving—and by its role as a commodity in itself, an object whose very purchase conferred a certain status on the purchaser. . . . Somewhere along this faultline, Krafft-Ebing's patient posed "in man's attire" with her woman lover, an image which . . . represented the social mobility traditionally afforded the "passing" woman.   (Merck 24)

The representational strategy of the new dyke, then, is a kind of photogynesis in which the dildo is a catalyst into the class of the visible. The status of commodity that the photo affords the new visible dyke is the motor for her upward mobility. The photo-ad of dyke apparel, in assimilating the subculture, makes it literally class-y. Somehow, the link between apparel and political action for women has come full circle. While the women's movement began with burning bras, the lesbian one conquers by strapping on the dildo.

While these dykes are just stepping into their liberatory leathers, John Preston, a well-known gay-leather scene pornhistoriographer is already leaving his leather behind (so to speak). For Preston, the assimilation of gay subculture into the marketplace has ruined its revolutionary potential: "Leather was gay sexuality stripped of being nice. It offended. It confronted. It took sex as its own ultimate value." But now "[i]t's been codified, measured, and packaged. . . . As we all did it, we were also popularizing it, and romanticizing it" (10, 11). Further, Preston argues, the marketing of the leather scene represses its politics, sexual identity, and sexual pleasure all at once. For him, the technomarket man fears sexual anarchy and strives for institutionalization: "Thus we have all the workshops, the endless patter of silly bottoms talking about 'the right way' to do things." Moreover, civil libertarian politics proceed from "the wimps who beg for acceptance from the larger society" (12). Preston's nostalgia signals what, for him, is the loss of an oppositional identity through leather and S and M practices that, once commodified, lose their sting.

What is at stake here is the construction of gay and lesbian appearances and sexual practices within the late-twentieth-century, high-capitalist technomarket of commodity identities. As commodities create the appearance, the appearance also creates the commodification of the subculture. Images of gays and lesbians sell straight newspapers. For example, the *Los Angeles Times* ran an article in its View section on Northhampton as a lesbian watering hole, titillating its readership with reviews of lesbian night at the local lingerie store (which found that lesbian night sold more lingerie than the former men's night did). Then, in a following week, the paper ran an insight article on how the new editor of the *Advocate* had increased its circulation by slicking up its look. In other words, the slick image of the gay and lesbian subculture brings it closer to the *Times*. Traditional marketing structures govern the production of the new dyke images. The glossy *Outlook* contrasts with the 'zines (sounds like "jeans"), which represent a similar market appearance of the rough and ready as alternative images to the glossy/dressy. In other words, what seems to be the new dyke look may only be the extension of fashion categories to the subculture.

Straight critics of technoculture have already described how sexual identity and desire are produced through media marketing. Mark Poster, in *The Mode of Information*, constructs the notion of the "floating signifier" in television ads:

> The ad takes a signifier, a word that has no traditional relation to the object being promoted and attaches it to that object. . . . These

floating signifiers derive their effects precisely from their recontextualization in the ad. Extracted from an actual relationship between lovers, romance or sexiness increases in linguistic power.
In the ad, sexy floor wax is more romantic than a man or a woman
in an actual relationship. . . . The commodity has been given a
semiotic value that is distinct from, indeed out of phase with, its
use value and its exchange value.   (58)

This surplus sexual value deployed by the floating signifier cuts both
ways in the representation of the new dyke. In strapping on the dildo
and getting off on the pose of another woman going down on it, the
dyke buys into the surplus sexual value of the recontextualized commodity. As the phallus, now a commodity, is recontextualized in lesbian
sexual scenarios, it takes on surplus sexual semiotic value. On the other
hand (once an emblem of lesbian sexual desire), the appropriation of
gay and lesbian images into straight culture semiotizes gay and lesbian
as surplus sexual values in their recontextualization. Like the referent of
the dildo in lesbian scenarios, gay and lesbian sexuality within dominant
heterosexual culture is without actual use or exchange value in the
sexual economy and is thus sexy as surplus. The effect, then, of the
appearance of the new dyke is to capitalize her—her earlier dowdiness,
just as the dowdiness of the erstwhile East Berlin (also newly capitalized)
was, in its distance from successful capitalist integration. For, as Engels
noted, the "essential character" of capitalism is in the extraction of
surplus value (700).

ENTER THE CLASS(ROOM)

In the context of sexual play, in the bars, or in 'zines ads, the dildo and
the leather chaps may introduce only another one of the new leisure
suits that mark the difference between the wage slave and the "free
individual" whose leisure identity is purchased through commodity
fetishes. Given an assumption of likeness between individuals, within
the gender system, and within economic and social liberties, playing at
power imbalances may eroticize sameness with the illusion of difference. But, if one wants to look like a dyke in the class/room, within
the workplace, and within the institution, what does this strapping on
of the dildo or dressing up in leathers mean? Playful images of power
differences between consenting adults imply something quite different
when age, authority, and economic relations are foregrounded as un-
equal. Class differences, or even prior feudalist structures, already reside
in the composition of the traditional student-teacher relationship.

In the class(room), the costume of masquerade becomes a uniform. When actual class, gender, and authority imbalances are eroticized, the social meaning of the images can become reactionary rather than liberatory. The dildoed, leather dyke, then, becomes an image that authorizes power imbalances and finds pleasure in the oppression of others. Of course, this image is disturbing only if that dyke still has any hangover from the politics of oppression. Yet most practitioners of the new look and/or of S and M scenarios emphasize the notion of consent and the power of the "safe word." In the class(room), this magic leap out of the system does not exist. The S and M scenario is at the heart of learning as it has been canonized. Does identifying as the new dyke in the class(room), then, make the visible lesbian the spectacle of the eroticization of authority and power over others?

There is a tradition of eroticizing student-teacher relations as well as actual class relations within homosexual practices that stretches back to Socrates. As David Halperin has noted, the practice of pederasty and pedagogy, of man-boy love, was elevated, eroticized, and made otherwise acceptable to academics through the enduring metaphor of the Socratic model. The privileging of the Greek classics in British universities created a "precious" model for male homosexual practices within an academic setting. Alan Sinfield extends this model further into British homosexual practices in the earlier decades of this century that were based on the eroticization of actual class differences. E. M. Forster's novel *Maurice* presents a portrait of the upper-class, university-trained (in both cultural and sexual practices) homosexual's love of a working-class man. Thus, the class- and school-sex practices of upper-class British men created a constellation of homosexual love, pedagogy, age, and class erotics. Insofar as American universities have canonized such British texts and academic traditions, the tradition continues.

Even for the lesbian, generally outside universities until a only few decades ago and definitely outside canonical images, there are still some images of teacher-student relations that create a similar tradition. The German cult film *Mädchen in Uniform* eroticizes the teacher-student seduction within an upper-class context as well as within a militaristic one. These young girls, the daughters of officers, learn to become suitable wives of military men through various disciplinary practices. The notion of the uniform in the title is a disciplinary costume that specularizes the eroticization of authority and age differences within the parameters of reward and particularly punishment—the same parameters that haunt all classroom procedures. The excitement of the unbalance of power resides in its proximity to punishment as well as to the discipline of learning. It also resides in the unavailability of the object of desire.

In contrast to the Socratic tradition of scholarly seduction, which portrays the teacher as seducer and the boy as object of seduction, the lesbian tradition eroticizes the powerful teacher as unavailable. Lesbian nun fantasies depend on such unavailability for their titillation. The power figure of the nun, whose body is mysteriously draped with something like a uniform and who practices celibacy, encourages erotic scenarios composed of self-denial and corporal punishment. Lesbian S and M scenarios also work off this tradition, both in practice and in pornography. The dominatrix-teacher, as in the film *Seduction: The Cruel Woman*, must be seduced into punishing. While the model, in this way, inverts the male Socratic one, it still shares many of the primary elements. "The Finishing School," in Califia's *Macho Sluts*, concerns a young student who resides with her wealthy patroness. Before returning to her boarding school, she enjoys another lesson in S and M scenarios, which leaves her so sore from spanking that she requires an extra cushion for her train ride back to school. Complex associations among elements of the privileged class, age difference, student-teacher associations, corporal punishment and learning, and erotics come together in such fantasies.

The very thrill, however, of the seeming contradiction between the bruised child's bottom and the velvet cushion may be only a part of the ongoing system of capitalism and class difference. Whereas Preston, Califia, and others perceive this kind of leathered, S and M image or practice as challenging to dominant structures, it may, in fact, be the playing out of those structures:

> Because selfhood is constituted out of public discourse, the state of the individual's self-comprehension will embody the state of prevailing social communication. Under capitalism, this state is contradictory. Enough truth must be told to support the illusion of self-determination. Since every significant bourgeois social need will require its contrary pretense—rivalry-friendliness, sexual domination–familial piety, compulsive accumulation–self-divesting altruism—the child must be introduced simultaneously into strategies of reality and illusion. What the child needs to know or be, but cannot be acknowledged to know or be, makes up the realm of repression. It is not that society must contain and extinguish the barbarism of the individual but that *capitalism must create the barbarism.* (Lichtman 134)

In other words, the seemingly illicit love of teacher and student, S and M scenario, or pederasty is necessary to the system of capitalism in order to create what seems to be a free sphere of self-determination. It marks the stance of self-determination by its seemingly taboo status, yet it is precisely the production of the taboo that tunes up the motor of mystification. The notion of the new lifestyle lesbian as setting personal freedom against the earlier feminist overdetermination of personal politics is, in fact, the reverse process. By acting out the seeming contradiction against any dominant ideology, such political action only sets capitalist mystification on its way.

What high technocapitalism needs is a subject trained in competition, domination, and appropriation, driven by the desire for surplus value. Once commodification means upward mobility, assimilation can pose as liberatory. Likewise, when a subculture identifies by an outside status instead of seeming to be the necessary bipolarity that drives mystification, that status can also appear as liberatory. Then, when the status is marked by commodities such as the dildo and leather wear, the saturation is complete. While the dyke believes that she is finally appearing, she is actually disappearing into the market.

Thus, when the dyke enters the class(room), she is on the stage of dominant practices. All the world's a class(room) at this point, after the so-called fall of the wall in Eastern Europe, the spread of technology and its accompanying security systems, and the ability of the market to assimilate and thus define any kind of image. Academia, once attacked as an "ivory tower" by political activists and guarded as one by the erstwhile Right, has likewise given in to the market. Intellectual fads come and go like fall fashions, the practices of commercial publishing have overcome earlier academic press procedures, and so on. In fact, gay and lesbian are this year's fad. So, while this photogynic new dyke underscores things as they are rather than an alternative, this essay on her plays into the same system.

If there is to be anything like lesbian "politics," then, they must be of another order of politics. The categories of subculture, transgression, and other like ideas have simply become part of an ad campaign. Here at the heart of my own call to pedagogy, I must admit I am newly stalemated. I tell my young queer students to read Gilles Deleuze and Félix Guattari's *A Thousand Plateaus*, macho and heterosexist as it is, or Gregory Ulmer's *Teletheory*, or some work that can address the new technoculture on terms more suited to its operations. I try to look like a dyke in the classroom in all the old ways, realizing that they read as commodities—especially since I wear a variety of costumes, ranging from T-shirts with pictures on them to ties and suit coats. The variety marks the market in the approach. I am also aware that many of the exciting new dykes in dildos have no such old-fashioned sense of politics, or even any sense of politics. If they do have it, they don't figure it laterally across economics to sexuality. This, too, is a dated model. So what do we make of the rising unemployment, the battles against abortion rights, the battles against municipal rights for gays and lesbians, the rise of neo-Nazi organizations, and the prominence of ethnic gang violence that are occurring at the same time as the extension of surplus bliss to disenfranchised groups?

University of California, Riverside

Works Cited

Boffin, Tessa, and Jean Fraser. *Stolen Glances: Lesbians Take Photographs.* London: Pandora, 1991.

Califia, Pat. "The Finishing School." *Macho Sluts.* Boston: Alyson, 1988. 63–83.

———. "Daddy Boy Dykes." *Quim* Winter 1991: 32–35.

de Lauretis, Teresa. "Sexual Indifference and Lesbian Representation." *Theatre Journal* 40 (1988): 155–77.

Engels, Friedrich. "Socialism: Utopian and Scientific." *The Marx-Engels Reader.* Ed. Robert C. Tucker. New York: Norton, 1978. 683–717.

Halperin, David M. *One Hundred Years of Homosexuality and Other Essays on Greek Love.* New York: Routledge, 1990.

Lichtman, Richard. *The Production of Desire: The Integration of Psychoanalysis into Marxist Theory.* New York: Free, 1982.

Mädchen in Uniform. Dir. Carl Froelich. 1931.

Merck, Mandy. " 'Transforming the Suit': A Century of Lesbian Self-Portraits." Boffin and Fraser 22–29.

Patton, Cindy. "Unmediated Lust? The Improbable Space of Lesbian Desires." Boffin and Fraser 233–40.

Poster, Mark. *The Mode of Information: Poststructuralism and Social Context.* Chicago: U of Chicago P, 1990.

Preston, John. "What Happened? An S/M Pioneer Reflects on the Leather World Past and Present." *Out/Look* 4.3 (1992): 8–15.

Seduction: The Cruel Woman (Verfuhrung: Die grausame Frau). Dir. Elfi Mikesch and Monika Treut. 1985.

Sinfield, Alan. "Closet Dramas: Homosexual Representation and Class in Postwar British Theater." *Genders* 9 (1990): 110–31.

"S/M Aesthetic." *Out/Look* 1.4 (1989): 42–43.

Stein, Arlene. "Style Wars and the New Lesbian." *Out/Look* 1.4 (1989): 34–42.

PART 2

Canons and Closets

What Is Lesbian Literature? Forming a Historical Canon

Lillian Faderman

Lesbian literature written by women has a short history. From the verse of Sappho, the Greek poet of Lesbos in 600 BC, to Radclyffe Hall's *The Well of Loneliness*, which was published in 1928, there is little women's writing that has been recognized as lesbian. The history is short in part because writing by women was virtually nonexistent for centuries. But it is also short because, while romantic friendship between women was an accepted social institution in Western countries from the Renaissance through the nineteenth century and while sex between women appears to have been a staple of pornography since the inception of that genre, the possibility of seeing oneself as a "lesbian" had to wait until the emergence of German and English sexologists. It was the sexologists who, in the last decades of the nineteenth century, defined that creature and called her into being as a social and sexual category.

If by *lesbian literature* we mean work in which the subject of lesbianism is clearly and explicitly the center, the history is even shorter. Many of the most interesting women writers of the postsexologist period, who might have, from personal experience, been able to reveal lesbian life in their literature, chose not to because of the social stigma attached to lesbianism. Particularly if they expected to be taken seriously as writers, they felt they could not risk their careers in dealing with a subject such as love between women, which appeared to have little universal application. The novelist Helen Hull was representative of that view. In her writer's journal of the 1950s, she lamented the untold stories of lesbian life that, she admitted, she could have told well from her personal experiences. But Hull ultimately concluded in that journal entry, "I don't want to be connected with the subject" (Papers). In fact, she has been finally "connected with the subject" as critics have come to understand her encoding of lesbian relationships in novels such as *Quest* and *Labyrinth*, but like other ambitious writers of her generation, she rationally chose to be veiled.

After the appearance of Hall's *The Well of Loneliness*, which was heavily influenced by the sexologists, a spate of books by women followed that did take the subject of lesbianism as their clear center. Like *The Well of Loneliness*, many of those works were influenced by the nineteenth-century German and English sexologists who saw lesbianism as a hereditary anomaly and the lesbian as a man trapped in a woman's body. Other women writers who published after Hall were influenced by her only in their belief that she had broken the silence on the subject, freeing them to speak as lesbians also. Their major models, however, were not Hall and the English and German sexologists who influenced her but rather the nineteenth-century French male aesthete-decadent writers, whose purpose was to "astound the bourgeoisie" (*épater les bourgeois*) through the most shocking image they could devise, namely, two women being sexual together. The lesbian in such presentations, and in those of these writers' female emulators in the early and mid twentieth century, was invariably depicted as exotically evil.

These two images—the lesbian as a medical anomaly and the lesbian as a carnivorous flower—dominated openly lesbian literature, particularly fiction, until the 1970s. At that time the American lesbian-feminist movement rebelled against images of lesbian deformity and wickedness, demanding more positive pictures of lesbians, literary role models of whom living lesbians could be proud. To that end, lesbian feminists established their own presses and publishing houses and produced a literature of brave, beautiful, and wholesome amazons, a literature that self-consciously defied the earlier German, English, and French images and defined lesbianism as the sanest, healthiest choice a woman could make.

Such works, however, are often less than satisfying. In the earliest lesbian novels, such as *The Well of Loneliness*, and their subsequent emulations, there seems to be an inverse correlation between a writer's ability to deal subtly and artistically with a subject and the specificity of her treatment of the lesbian theme. Perhaps the sexologists and moralists had made the theme of lesbianism so melodramatic that only writers who were willing to engage in melodrama would dare to undertake it. While openly lesbian poetry has more often managed to escape the problem, lesbian novels frequently suffered, and continued to suffer through the 1980s (though their messages had become entirely different from those of the earlier lesbian novels), from the limitations and distractions of their polemical concerns—the necessity, which the genre seemed to mandate, of showing the lesbian as a sinner, a victim of congenital inversion, or a happy amazon.

It is too early to generalize about the character of lesbian literature in the 1990s. But as Catharine Stimpson has observed, homosexuality has been so stringently associated with deviancy that historically it has been almost impossible for writers to ignore the connection. Writers who dealt with the subject and who were influenced by the European models supported that conjunction, "leeringly or ruefully." And those who have been influenced by the more recent American models rejected it, "fiercely or ebulliently." But whatever model writers chose, if they dealt openly with the subject of lesbianism, they generally felt constrained to create either a narrative of damnation or one that spent its energies on constructing an enabling escape (Stimpson 364). More often than not, style, subtlety, and complexity in the openly lesbian novel were sacrificed to those ends.

Openly lesbian writing (the kind that condemns, sympathizes, or glorifies—and that, with the exception of the work of occasional poets, was almost the only kind) has been very polemical up to the 1990s. It generally made a political point: lesbians are evil and should be punished; lesbians are suffering creatures and should be tolerated; or lesbians are brave, beautiful, and brilliant, and every woman should want to be one. The message dictated that the lesbian character be contrived: she must be made to turn out "right"—that is, miserable or happy, pathetic or victorious. The integrity of the work itself was often sacrificed to the message.

But must such works compose the extent of pre-1990s lesbian literature? What is lesbian literature? It has often been considered to be literature that deals with problems of coming out and coping with a homophobic society and with sexuality between women, as did *The Well of Loneliness*, the prototypical lesbian novel. But if lesbian literature is limited to that subject matter, it cannot go back much more than a hundred years, except for isolated instances, since "the lesbian" was seldom a recognized entity earlier. And if such literature must be written by a woman to be considered lesbian, its history is even shorter, since women of earlier eras seldom felt comfortable dealing with the subject of sexuality.

But perhaps literature need not confront the matter of same-sex sexuality head on to be "lesbian." Can we identify a lesbian sensibility in literature that may not be concerned specifically with lesbian sexuality and attendant matters? For example, if a work (especially one written before Hall broke the ice in 1928) criticizes heterosexual institutions, focuses on women apart from their erotic connection with men, and presents romantic friendships between women (which fall short of genital sexuality), is it lesbian? Willa Cather's *My Ántonia*, for instance, fulfills all those criteria and also presents a "male" narrator who is almost certainly a woman in masquerade. If a work evinces a fascination with androgyny and concerns itself with feminist protest, does it have a lesbian sensibility? Virginia Woolf's *Orlando* presents a character who keeps changing from male to female and back to male to illustrate the difficulties of women's plight. Is the argument for divining a lesbian sensibility in those works more persuasive when we know that both Cather and Woolf were lesbian? (On *Orlando*, see also the essays by Farwell and Jay in this volume.)

Conversely, if an author is ostensibly nonlesbian, can we nevertheless consider her work lesbian if it concerns sexual love between women? Alice Walker's *The Color Purple*, set in black rural Georgia of the 1930s, suggests (realistically) that its characters are not aware of any lesbian "lifestyle" in America or even of the concept of "the lesbian." It leaves untouched such lesbian issues as coming out or battling homophobia. But it takes as its emotional center the nurturing, loving, and specifically sexual relationship between Celie and Shug. For Celie, the relationship remains erotically charged to the end of the novel and represents the only satisfactory sexual experience of her life. Do the absence of the word *lesbian*, the oblivion to the existence of a lesbian subculture, and the author's putative heterosexuality mandate that we cannot consider such a work lesbian literature? According to Bonnie Zimmerman's working definition, contemporary lesbian fiction (1969–89) must be written by self-declared lesbians because "the nature of lesbian fiction makes it impossible to separate the text from the imagination that engenders it" (15). But it is not easy to think of a text more critical of heterosexual institutions and more positive about the regenerative effects of erotic love between women than *The Color Purple* or to conceive of how a "real lesbian imagination" could have engendered a more lesbian text.

Zimmerman also suggests that in lesbian literature of the 1970s and 1980s the central character must be "one who understands herself to be a lesbian" (15). While Zimmerman's definition is entirely appropriate to the political lesbian-feminist novels on which her study focuses, a different definition may be required for earlier novels, those written at a time when such consciousness was hard to come by and even harder to articulate in print, such as Louisa May Alcott's *Work* and Florence Converse's *Diana Victrix*. Such a definition would also cover novels that challenge the reader to struggle along with the main character to understand an inchoate lesbian development, for which the character may never have a descriptive term. In Carson McCullers's *A Member of the Wedding*, an adolescent girl crops her hair, takes a boy's name, fantasizes an androgynous existence where she can change her sex at will, assaults a young man who tries to kiss her, and by the end of the novel, enters into a satisfying relationship with another adolescent girl with whom she makes detailed plans to spend the rest of her life. Although Frankie is incapable of identifying herself as a lesbian, McCullers (herself a homosexual) presents what is almost a cliché in sexology: the adolescent history of "the lesbian." Writing in the years after World War II, under the constraint of self-censorship and possibly a not unrealistic fear of external censorship, McCullers did not dare permit even her third person narrator to state Frankie's lesbianism. But is it impossible to see the novel as lesbian because neither Frankie nor the narrator articulates what should be clear to the reader?

According to Zimmerman, the lesbian novel "places love between women, including sexual passion, at the center of its story" (15). While novels that follow that formula are clearly lesbian, must we eliminate from any "canon" (i.e., works we write about as lesbian scholars and recommend to students in our gay and lesbian literature classes, always with the distinct understanding that canons are mutable) a novel such as Jeanette Winterson's *Oranges Are Not the Only Fruit*, in which the center of the story is concerned with a girl's struggle in the context of a religious fundamentalist upbringing, and loving another woman erotically is shown to be only one of several ways in which she effects a break with her upbringing? Is it a contradiction in terms for a lesbian novel to focus on problems of, for example, frustrated ambition, on the trauma of aging, and on mortality, as they affect a character who just *happens* to be lesbian?

Can a work be seen as lesbian when it presents little or no awareness of erotic possibilities between women nor even a complaint about gender limitations? Barbara Smith, in "Toward a Black Feminist Criticism," argues that Toni Morrison's *Sula* is a lesbian novel not because Nel and Sula are lesbians but, rather, because the novel is critical of heterosexual institutions. (On Smith's discussion of *Sula*, see also Clarke's essay in this volume.) Smith's analysis expands the definition of lesbian literature, but is it excessively liberal? Could we consider Sylvia Plath's "Daddy" a lesbian text because it provides a critique of heterosexual institutions (despite the homophobia of Plath herself)? And, if we reduce the point to its potential absurdity, since *The Well of Loneliness* privileges heterosexuality (a woman gives up her beloved, Mary, to a man because she believes that Mary will have an easier, happier life as his wife), must we see it as a heterosexual novel, despite its crucial role in the development of openly lesbian literature?

For some critics, a major difficulty in trying to formulate a canon of lesbian literature has been in deciding whether a work can be considered lesbian without doing violence to the writer's intention. But we must transcend the literality of insisting that lesbian literature, even works written before the 1970s, be by a self-declared lesbian (not many writers before the 1970s were making such declarations), be about a character "who understands herself to be a lesbian" (a certain sophistication is necessary for that understanding, and interesting characters often lack such insight), and include lesbian "sexual passion at the center of its story" (censorship laws in the past and self-censorship often mandated that the depiction of same-sex erotic love not be explicit). Perhaps a work might be considered lesbian, even if it lacks any of the criteria Zimmerman stipulates for the lesbian novel of the 1970s and 1980s, if it can be shown that lesbian subject matter is somehow encoded in it. Such encoding might be blatant to the contemporary reader, as it is in Gertrude Stein's 1923 piece "Miss Furr and Miss Skeene," which Stein published in *Vanity Fair* for predominantly heterosexual readers who undoubtedly thought that her constant reiteration of the word *gay* was nothing more than an instance of her wacky repetitive style or an ironic commentary on the sad life of "spinsters." Or the encoding might be more subtle, as in Nella Larsen's *Passing,* in which race and its attendant problems are possibly used as metaphors for the social and personal problems connected with lesbianism in the 1920s.

It should not be surprising that many women who could have and would have written about lesbianism in earlier decades did not dare— or, rather, did but encoded their work so carefully that only the very knowledgeable would understand what the real subject matter was. Stein, for instance, began her literary career by writing an openly lesbian novel, *Q.E.D.*, in 1903. Then she promptly put it in a drawer and forgot about it. It was not published until 1950, four years after her death. Stein did not give up the lesbian theme in subsequent writing, but she did conceal it, sometimes through race (she retells the *Q.E.D.* story in "Melanctha," presenting the characters as African Americans rather than as lesbians), sometimes through hermetic language and structure (as in "Ada" and "Sacred Emily"). Her admonishment to Ernest Hemingway reveals her motives. Hemingway had shown her his then unpublished story "Up in Michigan," which Stein thought good but too sexually graphic because he referred to the size of his hero's penis. Stein suggested to Hemingway that such a detail rendered the story impractical, *"inaccrochable,"* like a painting with salacious subject matter, which one could never exhibit (qtd. in Hemingway 15). Yet many of Stein's works, such as "Lifting Belly," "A Third," and "As a Wife Has a Cow: A Love Story," offer detailed descriptions of lesbian lovemaking and even orgasm, if the reader is able to decode what Stein has carefully encoded.

Similarly, the poet Amy Lowell advised D. H. Lawrence to be "a little more reticent" on the subject of sex if he desired recognition as a writer:

> You need not change your attitude a particle, you can simply use an India rubber in certain places, and then you can come into your own as it ought to be. . . . When one is surrounded by prejudice and blindness, it seems to me that the only thing to do is to get over in spite of it and not constantly run afoul of these same prejudices which, after all, hurts oneself and the spreading of one's work, and does not do a thing to right the prejudice.
>
> (Damon 482–83)

Lawrence ignored her advice, but she herself followed it scrupulously. She believed that writing openly as a lesbian could do nothing to alleviate prejudice and would only ruin her literary reputation. But, like Stein, she incorporated lesbian subject matter into much of her work. Her long-term love relationship with the actress Ada Russell, for example, is minutely detailed in the poems of *Pictures of the Floating World*. Lowell's encoding was less hermetic than Stein's—she merely changed the gender words that referred to the speaker of her love poems, but she recorded a faithful picture of Russell and their life together. Because they disguised their subject matter, Stein and Lowell escaped not only the censors and prejudice but also polemical obligations in dealing with lesbianism. They were free to treat the material without a requisite political message.

But writers who did not use the device of encoding found it difficult to escape the polemical obligation either to affirm the male-engendered European lesbian images or to contradict them. Elaine Marks's speculation that "[i]t may well be that only a committed lesbian-feminist writer can, within our culture, succeed in transmitting cogent images of undomesticated women [i.e., real lesbians]" (373) emphasizes the point with regard to lesbian writers of the 1970s and 1980s: the cultural images about themselves that they inherited seemed to necessitate conscious and committed lesbian-feminist counterargument from those openly lesbian writers. The obligation dictated what they could create. The literature itself was thus circumscribed, almost as much as pre-lesbian-feminist literature has been—though it was unarguably more palatable to most lesbian readers.

Such circumscription has produced a narrow historical canon if we look at works by women who have openly taken lesbianism as their subject. There are the French aesthete-decadent-influenced poems and novels of Renée Vivien, Djuna Barnes, Violette Leduc, Anaïs Nin, and their emulators; there are works influenced by the German and English sexologists, from Hall's *The Well of Loneliness* to Ann Bannon's Beebo Brinker novels; there is lesbian-feminist literature, which has been primarily American-influenced, frequently taking as a model Rita Mae Brown's highly successful, polemical *Rubyfruit Jungle*.

Only occasionally have works that are specific about their lesbian subject matter, such as Stein's fascinatingly complex psychological study, *Q.E.D.*, transcended the European and American models. Significantly, Stein did not even attempt to publish that novel, perhaps feeling that readers would not know what to make of it, since it showed not a character struggling with her perversity or with the horrifying realization that she was a member of the third sex but, rather, a character whose love for another woman was the manifestation of her trying to come to terms with herself both as an adult and as a sexual being.

Winterson's *Oranges Are Not the Only Fruit*, a novel of the 1980s, has also escaped from the clichés of its day to present a complex study of a character who has functions that transcend her lesbianism. And students of lesbian literature can take heart that, unlike Stein's novel, Winterson's did not have to sit in a drawer for almost fifty years before it could see light. These two works, written eighty-five years apart, focus on the problems of a human being who is a lesbian. They are truly revolutionary because, instead of involving themselves in the debates of their day, which show the lesbian as a victim of, or victor over, congenital or social forces, they show the lesbian as a person coping with a panoply of life's problems. But works that broke away from the limitations the genre seemed to impose have been rare. Their rarity may not pose a problem to the "queer" reader of the 1990s whose interest is in *difference*, but other readers may regret the loss of multifarious lesbian voices.

Their rarity is especially frustrating when one understands that many of the most interesting women writers have been lesbian or bisexual. As Louise Bernikow observes in her groundbreaking anthology of women poets in England and America, *The World Split Open*, "[F]or all obfuscation about it, the truth seems to be that most [women writers] have loved women, sometimes along with loving men" (14–15). Most of these women writers, however, did not write openly about lesbians not only because of censorship and self-censorship but also because they wanted to avoid the restrictions imposed by the genre. Many fine stories seem to have been lost. And yet, perhaps, they have not been lost. Perhaps in the work of many of those writers lesbianism is hidden but not resistant to exposure. Perhaps we can (and need to) expand the canon by considering works in which lesbianism is not the clear center but something encoded within the piece in various ways.

The most obvious clue to such encoding is the author's own sexual orientation, knowledge of which becomes increasingly accessible, even for writers of earlier generations, as archival materials become available and scholars feel less suppressed by social reticence, which, in other eras, served to censor sexual facts. Jane Rule correctly warns in *Lesbian Images* that it is necessary to distinguish between a writer's life, which may be lesbian, and her work, which may not be. But the task is not so daunting.

For instance, Sharon O'Brien has examined some of Willa Cather's papers, sealed until recently, that confirm Cather's lesbianism (which many literary historians earlier suspected from the known facts of her life). If Cather had written only novels such as *Death Comes for the Archbishop*, Rule's warning obviously would be applicable. But she wrote novels in which her encoding is all but inescapable for the attentive reader. In *My Ántonia*, for example, the "male" narrator is clearly an autobiographical character in masquerade. "He" loves women, as Cather did, but something usually prevents him from succeeding with them erotically (as she must have felt prevented with heterosexual women). Nor does "he" have "manly" social relations with other men. Perhaps he is such an unconvincing man because he was modeled on a woman. The narrative consistently undercuts masculinity and even heterosexuality. The book does not portray a single successful heterosexual relationship, although two of the women characters, Lina and Tiny, settle down together in a romantic friendship at the end.

Perhaps we can also expand our canon by viewing work written before the emergence of the European sexologists, those literary depictions of romantic friendship, as one of the few ways that "prelesbian" writers had to depict love between women. For example, we might give Katherine Philips's seventeenth-century poems of romantic friendship a place in the lesbian literary canon. Philips never deals specifically with lesbian sexuality but nevertheless permits her woman speaker to call another woman "all that I can prize, / My Joy, My Life, My Rest" and to say that neither a bridegroom nor a "crown-conqueror" is as lucky as she is, because "They have but pieces of the Earth, / I've all the World in thee" (Faderman). Emily Dickinson, who describes another woman's "sweet weight" on her heart at night and talks about the wedding of two "queens" (Faderman), should also have a place in the lesbian literary canon, though obviously there are no explicit suggestions of lesbian sexual relations in her poems.

Stimpson suggests that feminist critics must listen for "variations, fluctuations, blurrings, coded signals, and lapses into mimicry or a void" (379). That job is particularly crucial to attempts to define lesbian literature of the past, since much has been veiled and what has previously been canonized by default often lacks variations, fluctuations, and so on. The canon is in desperate need of expansion, which will come in time as more writers who escape from orthodoxy, such as Winterson, emerge. But it can come now as well, through what Adrienne Rich calls "re-vision"—"the act of looking back, of seeing with fresh eyes, of entering old texts from a new critical direction" (90).

California State University, Fresno

Works Cited

Alcott, Louisa May. *Work: A Story of Experience.* 1873. New York: Arno, 1977.
Bernikow, Louise, ed. *The World Split Open: Four Centuries of Women Poets in England and America, 1552–1950.* New York: Vintage, 1974.
Brown, Rita Mae. *Rubyfruit Jungle.* New York: Bantam, 1978.
Cather, Willa. *My Ántonia.* 1918. London: Virago, 1980.
Converse, Florence. *Diana Victrix.* Boston: Houghton, 1897.
Damon, S. Foster. *Amy Lowell: A Chronicle, with Extracts from Her Correspondence.* Boston: Houghton, 1935.
Faderman, Lillian, ed. *Chloe plus Olive: An Anthology of Lesbian Writing from the Seventeenth Century to the Present.* New York: Penguin, forthcoming.
Hall, Radclyffe. *The Well of Loneliness.* New York: Doubleday, 1928.
Hemingway, Ernest. *A Moveable Feast.* New York: Bantam, 1969.
Hull, Helen. Helen Hull Papers. Columbia U; Hull Biographical File (photocopy). New York Lesbian Herstory Archives.
———. *Labyrinth.* New York: Macmillan, 1923.
———. *Quest.* 1922. New York: Feminist, 1990.
Larsen, Nella. *Passing.* 1929. Ed. Deborah E. McDowell. New Brunswick: Rutgers UP, 1986.
Lowell, Amy. *Pictures of the Floating World.* 1919. Boston: Houghton, 1924.
Marks, Elaine. "Lesbian Intertextuality." *Homosexualities and French Literature: Cultural Contexts, Critical Texts.* Ed. George Stambolian and Marks. Ithaca: Cornell UP, 1979. 353–77.
McCullers, Carson. *A Member of the Wedding.* Boston: Houghton, 1946.
Morrison, Toni. *Sula.* New York: Knopf, 1974.
O'Brien, Sharon. *Willa Cather: The Emerging Voice.* New York: Oxford UP, 1987.
Rich, Adrienne. "When We Dead Awaken: Writing as Re-vision." *Adrienne*

Rich's Poetry. Ed. Barbara Gelpi and Albert Gelpi. New York: Norton, 1975. 90–98.

Rule, Jane. *Lesbian Images.* New York: Doubleday, 1975.

Smith, Barbara. "Toward a Black Feminist Criticism." *Women's Studies International Quarterly* 2.2 (1979): 183–94.

Stein, Gertrude. "Ada." *The Norton Anthology of Literature by Women.* Ed. Sandra Gilbert and Susan Gubar. New York: Norton, 1985. 1334–36.

———. "As a Wife Has a Cow: A Love Story." Stein, *Selected Writings* 541–45.

———. "Lifting Belly." Stein, *Yale Edition* 3: 63–115.

———. "Melanctha." Stein, *Selected Writings* 337–457.

———. "Miss Furr and Miss Skeene." Stein, *Selected Writings* 561–68.

———. *Q.E.D. Fernhurst, Q.E.D., and Other Early Writings by Gertrude Stein.* New York: Liveright, 1971.

———. "Sacred Emily." *Matisse, Picasso, and Gertrude Stein.* Paris: Plain, 1933. 37–41.

———. *Selected Writings of Gertrude Stein.* Ed. Carl Van Vechten. New York: Vintage, 1972.

———. "A Third." Stein, *Yale Edition* 4: 331–57.

———. *The Yale Edition of the Unpublished Writings of Gertrude Stein.* 8 vols. New Haven: Yale UP, 1951–58.

Stimpson, Catharine. "Zero Degree Deviancy: The Lesbian Novel in English." *Critical Inquiry* 8 (1981): 363–79.

Walker, Alice. *The Color Purple.* New York: Pocket, 1985.

Winterson, Jeanette. *Oranges Are Not the Only Fruit.* New York: Atlantic Monthly, 1987.

Woolf, Virginia. *Orlando: A Biography.* 1928. New York: Harcourt, 1973.

Zimmerman, Bonnie. *The Safe Sea of Women: Lesbian Fiction, 1969–1989.* Boston: Beacon, 1990.

Teaching the Postmodern Renaissance

Stephen Orgel

My ultimate topic in this essay is gender construction in the Renaissance, but since that subject, as I have learned about it and as I teach it, is related to, and indeed develops out of, postmodern critical perspectives, I wish to begin with those instead. It is often claimed that nobody in Renaissance studies is much interested in reading literature anymore, and the author-centered close reading that I was taught as the basis of my literary training certainly doesn't have much place in the current scholarly work in my field. But close reading is nevertheless practiced, with a fierceness and attention to detail that no New Critic could have matched. The key enabling figures have been Jacques Derrida and Roland Barthes, though Barthes has received little credit in recent years. And though Derrida has come in for some fairly hysterical criticism as an enemy of literature, standards, and values, in Renaissance studies his work has spurred a salutary and extraordinarily fruitful attention to both the text and the history and nature of language. In fact, Derridean language and assumptions have been so subtly naturalized in the past decade that most works in my field consider deconstruction an essential element in the practice of criticism, and *différance* has replaced ambiguity as the thing to find in literary texts.

Derridean and Barthesian readings are subversive in the way they tend to decenter the author and to operate against the idea of the poem, novel, or play as a work of individual genius, the product of a series of conscious choices. They see the work instead as a social artifact or even as a weirdly autonomous linguistic phenomenon. In this respect, such readings work against notions of instrinsic merit and of a literary canon based on it. These ideas have been, for me, simply the substance of scholarship: the close reading I now

find myself doing generally has no reason to privilege canonical literature over anything else—documents, ephemera, legal texts, proclama-
tions, whatever. These texts require, and repay, the same degree of
analysis and close attention that literary texts do; the claims they make
are different from those of poetry, drama, or romance, but they are no
more neutral and objective than literary texts are, and their claims and
assumptions, and the agendas of their authors, need no less to be taken
into account. The classic statement here, coming from a different direction, is Michel Foucault's essay "What Is an Author?" Radical in its
time, the essay has become so much a part of the critical landscape that
one almost need not read it anymore.

   For those who still require a defense of Derrida and Foucault I suppose
no defense will be sufficient, but there can be no disputing the fact that
they have been extraordinarily enabling figures for Renaissance studies
in the past decade—extraordinarily so because Derrida is often accused
of being antihistorical. The most recent, and for me the most striking,
example of how brilliantly enabling Derridean concepts can be for work
in this field is Jonathan Goldberg's *Writing Matter*. It is not simply
about writing in the Renaissance but precisely about the act of writing
itself in the period: how you learned to write and why, what your
handwriting signified socially and sociologically, and most of all how,
historically, your handwriting became your character, the one thing
that could prove that you were really you. All these things that we take
for granted are historically locatable, and they have everything to do
with the particular kind of investment that the early modern period
placed in writing, whether literary or utilitarian. The analysis starts
with, and is continually informed by, Derrida's work and indeed would
be impossible without it.

   I have found such developments not frightening but exciting and
provocative and certainly healthy for the profession. For all the famous
impenetrability of postmodernist theory, my students have a great deal
less trouble with Derrida, Lacan, and Irigaray than I have; passages that
I find hopelessly confusing can usually be explained to me by any number of my graduate students. And even if we don't buy into the whole
Derridean system, it can only be good that we examine our assumptions;
ask what's basic and essential to aesthetic criteria, what's great about
great books; ask how canons get formed, whose interests they serve,
where our notions of value in literature come from and how and why
and when they change—as they demonstrably do. It's the smugness of
William Bennett or Allan Bloom that seems dangerous to me, not because they have different answers to these questions but precisely because they want to prevent such questions from being asked.

   I recently found out something interesting about such attitudes. Two essays of mine, "What Is a Text?" and "The Authentic Shakespeare," discuss the radical instability of Shakespearean texts in particular, and of Renaissance texts (not only theatrical ones) in general, and argue that this instability is a historical phenomenon based on the nature of manuscript and print cultures in the period and on attitudes toward the book generally. I won't try to summarize the analysis here, but I got panicky reactions from several distinguished friends in the field, who clearly felt that I was threatening the very essence of the discipline. Shortly afterward, members of the rare-books section of the American Library Association asked me to address the annual convention. I did a version of the same argument and found that they were not outraged or even surprised but delighted and, moreover, that they were with me all the way. As rare-books people have known all along, texts are unstable, and every copy of a Renaissance book is unique. (This is not hyperbole: every Shakespeare folio is different from every other Shakespeare folio; the same is true, to a greater or lesser degree, of all books published in the period. The variations have to do with the way Renaissance printing houses worked and the way proof corrections were incorporated into the text.) This instability is, indeed, what their work is all about. I also found, to my surprise, that Derrida is their natural language. I had thought of rare-books people as conservatives, but on these matters they are not merely radical: they are the original radicals of the deconstruction of texts—in a real sense, they got there first. The point of this anecdote is simply to observe that whether Derrida, Foucault, and Barthes are destructive or enabling depends on where one's own intellectual capital is invested. Needless to say, it is a good idea to reassess one's investments from time to time.

Such questions, as I try to deal with them, are historical ones, though they also assume that we are involved in history and therefore that there are discoverable reasons why I (I won't presume to say *we*) read the past the way I do. The issues I try to confront are also logically addressed through what can broadly be called Marxist readings. Marxist analyses that undertake to show how Shakespeare participates in the class struggle are a little passé in the United States, though cultural materialists in England are raising that issue in some interesting ways. I certainly would not call myself a Marxist, but my work since *The Illusion of Power* has developed alongside the work of Stephen Greenblatt, Jonathan Goldberg, and Louis Montrose and has been ultimately enabled by the historical work of Hayden White. All these authors are obviously informed by Marxist assumptions about the material basis of artistic production. The most interesting recent Marxist discussions in my field deal, on a broadly cultural level, with the commodification or materiality of literary works. With respect to Elizabethan theater, these critiques see drama as part of a market economy and ask where the text of a Shakespeare play fits, for example, in the *business* of theater: how it was marketed, who the consumers were, what demands it had to satisfy, and what constraints were put on it by patrons, censors, or the theatrical company itself—Shakespeare's spokesmen and collaborators in the production. The best and most elegantly articulated versions of the argument are by young scholars: Jean-Christophe Agnew's *Worlds Apart*, Steven Mullaney's *The Place of the Stage*, and a brilliant book by Douglas Bruster, *Drama and the Market in the Age of Shakespeare*.

Such issues help to historicize Shakespeare in two ways: they present the act of creation as something not autonomous or separate from the conditions of creation; and they see the text—specifically, that figment of the editorial imagination, Shakespeare's original manuscript, Shakespeare's foul papers—not as the play but as only the first step in a process that eventuates in the play or, more precisely, in a particular version of the play. The play, then, is a process, not a product, and the script—the text—is not the play but only where the company started. This view enables us to ask the much larger question, essential for our sense of Shakespeare, of how, historically, we have constructed this continuous and continuing process into a literary phenomenon—of what happens when a script turns into a book.

In relation to nondramatic work, such an analysis would ask a different set of questions: To whom is the text addressed? What is its function in relation to its audience? Did it circulate, like Sidney's *Arcadia* or Donne's poetry, in manuscript to a fairly limited and coherent group? Or, like the quartos of Nashe and Greene and the Shakespeare of *Venus and Adonis* and *The Rape of Lucrece*, to a broad book-buying public? Or, like the folios of Jonson and the posthumous Shakespeare, to a group of wealthy and literate collectors? It would ask again: What happens when the manuscripts of Donne's poems, those bids for patronage, a secretaryship, a career in government, become a book—something Donne did not want—and thereby circulate outside the audience for whom they were intended? Furthermore—certainly most interesting from our point of view—where the author is in the whole operation? What, in other words, is the author's relation to the system that commodifies the work: the patron on the one hand and, on the other, the printer, publisher, and bookseller, the people who make money out of it? Authors in the latter system become primarily selling points and as such can be, and often are, easily detached from their work. The best way to sell the quarto of a play for much of the seventeenth century was to claim that it was by Shakespeare; and for the generation after Shakespeare, the names Beaumont and Fletcher got to be a catchall to attach to new plays, even those written long after Beaumont's death.

So how do we construct an author? I am always fascinated by the way literary histories claim that there is very little fifteenth-century English literature because the Wars of the Roses left no time for poetry. In fact there is an enormous amount of fifteenth-century English literature, but for literary historians it has two fatal flaws: much of it is anonymous, and much that is not anonymous is in Latin or French. We deal with this problem by saying that the works do not exist, and such statements have everything to do with what we will accept as constituting both an author and English literature. Once again Foucault and Barthes are underlying, deeply enabling figures, but more particularly I would cite D. F. McKenzie's fascinating studies in the sociology of texts, the revisionary bibliographical work of Randall McLeod, and Richard Newton and Joseph Loewenstein on Jonson and the book.

My own interests in recent years have focused on an aspect of the Renaissance stage that has received almost no attention whatever: the fact that the Elizabethans maintained a transvestite public theater when no other European society did. Why did the English stage take boys for women? In a way, the most interesting aspect of the question is that it has never seemed a question before; theater historians have treated it as a simple practical matter, with no implications beyond its utility in disguise plots. But it surely has broad implications, both cultural and sexual, that have nothing to do with practicality and everything to do with the way societies conceive and construct gender. Obviously, the issues raised by this question affect the way I find myself reading Shakespeare's plays, but equally obviously, the issues aren't limited to the interpretation of dramatic texts. To ask how the culture constructs women is also to ask how the culture constructs men, how it conceives of the interaction between men and women, and perhaps most important, where we locate ourselves in relation to those issues.

The texts that we use to teach Shakespeare are all but silent on these matters. One extreme example is that no edition of *As You Like It* discusses the implications of the choice of the name Ganymede for Rosalind as a boy. But for a Renaissance audience, the name was explicitly and inescapably allusive, and it made clear that the model for Orlando's wooing was a homosexual flirtation. This allusion is quite unproblematic in the play; the silence of editors indicates, however, how intensely problematic it has been for us. Nevertheless, in the past five years or so, I have found that undergraduate students ask about it. It has become a question: Why invoke the classic name not merely of an attractive youth but also of the beautiful boy for whom Jove abandons his marriage bed? Why is this inescapable allusion to the attraction of men for boys a part of Orlando and Rosalind's wooing? Why do the sexual dynamics of Orlando's love include not simply a boy but also the one boy capable of incapacitating his marriage? And why do the sexual dynamics of Rosalind's love involve her not merely in disguising herself as the dangerous alternative but also in maintaining her disguise as Ganymede even after she knows Orlando loves her as Rosalind? "Alas the day," she says to Celia in the middle of act three, when the play is less than half over, "what shall I do with my doublet and hose?" (3.2.208). What is the point, that is, of her male clothing now? It is a real question, one that the play is willing to confront but that editors have been shy of without exception.

A similarly invisible moment occurs in *Twelfth Night*, when Viola says she will present herself to the duke, Orsino, as "an eunuch" and "sing, / And speak to him in many sorts of music" (1.2.56–58). She then dresses herself in male clothing, gives herself a male name, and enters Orsino's service, acting as his page, confidant, and the agent of his love. The question here is not how this moment functions dramatically, since in any practical sense it scarcely functions at all: Viola does not, in fact, claim to Orsino that she is a eunuch, nor does she do any singing in the play. Precisely because the claim is unique, the question is, What cultural implications lie behind it? That single moment when Viola conceives herself as a eunuch has received little editorial attention, and students who ask about it, as I find they now regularly do, get no help from their textbooks. The word *eunuch* is always glossed as if it were simply a term for a male treble voice, with no underlying history of surgical procedures.

This definition, however, is a pure editorial fantasy; there is no such usage recorded in English. As with the later term *castrato, eunuch* only meant "singer" if the singer was a eunuch. We ought therefore to confront the implications of Viola's conceiving herself not simply as a youth in disguise but also as a surgically neutered one. Here is an example of how we might begin anatomizing those implications.

Viola seems to be proposing a sexlessness that is an aspect of her mourning, that will effectively remove her, as Olivia has removed herself, from the world of love and wooing. This solution in itself, however, is problematic. As Shakespeare's eunuch Mardian complains, the surgery incapacitates only sexual performance; the desire remains as intense as ever: "Yet have I fierce affections, and think / What Venus did with Mars" (*Antony and Cleopatra* 1.5.17–18). If Mardian is to be our guide, Viola has with a single word created for herself a character in whom frustrated sexual desire is of the essence—she has created, in fact, the role she performs in the play. But there is a peculiar overtone as well: being a eunuch, a sexually incapacitated male, is conceived as an equivalent, or an alternative, to being a woman. This fantasy is an old one: Chaucer, expressing his doubts about the Pardoner's sexuality, describes him as "a gelding or a mare" (General Prologue 691). Cleopatra makes the same point even more explicitly, inviting Mardian to play billiards with her: "As well a woman with an eunuch played / As with a woman" (2.5.5–6). Missing from their play are what billiards is played with, a rod and balls; the essential element in sexuality is, in this formulation, male potency. The moment acts out a classic Freudian fantasy, whereby gender difference is a function of castration. *Twelfth Night* makes the fantasy all but explicit in its puns on "cut" and "cunt" (2.5.80–83)—another moment that editors don't want to touch with a billiard cue. If a eunuch is an alternative to a woman, and either is the opposite of a man, then the assumptions behind Viola's disguise desexualize women too.

Or do they? A brief look at the history of castrati complicates the question. The most famous eunuch singers in Shakespeare's time were the choirboys of the Roman Catholic Church, who were used first in Spain from the early sixteenth century and subsequently, most notoriously, in the Vatican. The paternal decision to castrate a son to make him eligible for choir school sounds like a particularly radical and invasive instance of patriarchal authority in action, but it is worth considering whether it is in fact much more radical than the absolute right exercised by fathers in arranging their children's marriages. (It hardly needs to be said that I am not minimizing the outrageousness of castration here but emphasizing the constraints of the Renaissance marriage system.) In a Renaissance Catholic society, good arguments could be produced in favor of castrating your son—the same good arguments as those involved in deciding that he was going to have a career as a priest or a monk or in sending your daughter into a convent.[1] Such decisions guaranteed the child a secure and, in the case of castrati, often lucrative career, and celibacy, if you were serious about your religion, was a virtue. Castration had the disadvantage of being irreversible (marriage was usually irreversible too), but the advantages, in income and security, were correspondingly large. These considerations sound appalling to us, but the practice continued through the eighteenth century. The Vatican castrati quickly started playing secular roles as well as religious ones: like the boys on the English stage, they played the romantic women's parts in entertainments for the exclusively male society of the Catholic hierarchy. In this respect the boys were not at all desexualized; on the contrary, they enabled the introduction of overt sexuality, simultaneously heterosexual and homosexual, into the world of ecclesiastical celibacy.

Viola as eunuch, then, both closes down options for herself and implies a world of possibilities for others—possibilities that were, to a post-Reformation Protestant society, particularly (perhaps temptingly) illicit. The possibilities are conceived as sexual alternatives and equivalents, as either and both; thus Viola says to the uncomprehending Orsino, "I am all the daughters of my father's house, / And all the brothers too" (2.4.121–22). Her twin, Sebastian, fresh from his adoring Antonio, says to Olivia, "You are betrothed both to a maid and man" (5.1.255). This double-gendered figure realizes Shakespeare's master-mistress of sonnet 20, the young man who is such a powerfully desirable alternative to a woman: better looking, less deceitful, more faithful. He has all the advantages of women with no disadvantages, except, as the poem ends, one: he is "pricked out," but it is not clear that this is a disadvantage. Sex, as all the sonnets in Shakespeare's sequence imply, is dangerous and destabilizing when you do it with women; but love is what you do with men—and the love between men, even in sonnet 20, is by no means necessarily nonsexual. The poem certainly denies that the speaker and his love are sleeping together, but if men don't go to bed with other men because they have pricks, then the need for the denial is more significant than the denial itself. Whatever the speaker is doing with the master-mistress of his passion, Shakespeare's disclaimer insists on the reality of sex between men.

A third Shakespearean moment that has only recently become visible, in large measure because students have begun to ask about it, is Portia and Nerissa's ring trick at the end of *The Merchant of Venice*. This moment was largely ignored in critical treatments until the 1980s when Leonard Tennenhouse, Lisa Jardine, and Karen Newman each built around the episode readings that effectively overturn a critical history in which the play concludes with divine harmony and the joys of marriage (see esp. Tennenhouse 58–61; Jardine 13–18). The episode is, once one notices it, genuinely disruptive, pitting friendship against love and leaving the conflict significantly unresolved. Its consistent elision from the history of criticism is not a matter of simple de-emphasis or dismissal. It has been, like Viola the eunuch and Rosalind the catamite, all but invisible.

Here, briefly, is the plot: At the conclusion of the trial scene, Portia and Nerissa, disguised as young men, demand as their recompense for saving Antonio's life the rings they have given Bassanio and Gratiano as love tokens and promises of marriage. Bassanio objects: they have sworn to wear the rings. Portia produces some heavy rhetoric about the monstrousness of ingratitude, Antonio lends his support, and the men unhappily give up the rings. When they return to Portia and Nerissa, who are now in their own persons, and reveal that the rings have been given to two youths as the price of an overwhelming debt of gratitude, the women feign outrage, accuse the men of faithlessness, and declare that they will consider themselves thenceforth relieved of the burden of fidelity to their husbands. The men apologize abjectly, but the issues raised remain unresolved, having to do not with rights and wrongs but with conflicting goods.

What is the point of this strange and discordant conclusion to a play that seemed to have resolved its problems in the containment of Shylock and the marriages of Portia and Bassanio, Lorenzo and Jessica? It could be a salutary point, reminding us that in this world there are no absolutes, that however steadfast we believe we will be to our vows, there are situations in which we will inevitably break them. In the circumstances of Antonio's trial, Bassanio was not wrong to give up the ring; Portia set up a test for him that she knew he was bound to fail. The failure could lead the play to a great humane moral: it might remind us that there are always extenuating circumstances and that the good isn't single or isn't always clearly visible; it might urge us to be patient with our own and others' failings; or it could demonstrate to us, as nothing else in the play does, that the quality of mercy is not strained. But the revelation of Portia and Nerissa's disguise evokes no such reassurance. The play ends not with the heavenly harmony that opens the final act but, in its last moments, with threats and fears of a justified cuckoldry, combined, moreover, with a startling pederastic fantasy. In another invisible moment, Gratiano conceives of spending his wedding night in bed with the young man to whom he gave Nerissa's ring:

> . . . were the day come, I should wish it dark
> Till I were couching with the doctor's clerk.
> Well, while I live I'll fear no other thing
> So sore as keeping safe Nerissa's ring—.
>
> (5.1. 304–07)

"Ring" is not simply the love token but also a word for both the vagina and the anus (of which "ring" is a literal translation): even sexually, Nerissa and the doctor's clerk are equivalents and alternatives. These are the last lines of the play: the women's charade has given Portia and Nerissa something to hold over their husbands forever, something to ensure that, in marriage, the men can never be certain of their wives' chastity and the women always have the upper hand.

If we resist the impulse to dismiss this episode as a joke that the women play on the men, with no larger implications, and focus instead on the anxieties it expresses, as criticism has begun to do, it is part of a fantasy of female sexual power that is difficult to read as humane or benevolent. It sets the demands of love not only against those of friendship but also, more dangerously, against those of gratitude. In a culture of clientage like Shakespeare's, ingratitude is the primal sin—as it still is in Milton's version of the Fall, that exemplary case of a man required to choose between loyalty to his wife and loyalty to his patron. The domineering—or, as the age significantly put it, *masculine*—woman was both a figure of fun and deeply destabilizing. People who are offended by the depiction of Portia in this episode—if we take it seriously, it can be seen as powerfully misogynistic—dislike the extent to which the women in this play are represented as acting like men. Indeed, Tennenhouse maintains that, in *The Merchant of Venice*, "Shakespeare has created a problem which can only be resolved by a transvestite" (59).

If we read Shakespeare through the material world of the Renaissance stage, if we stop ignoring the moments that have, historically, made us uncomfortable, the plays unquestionably look unfamiliar, but they also respond to us in new ways, revealing as much about our own preconceptions and resistances as they do about Shakespeare's cultural milieu. The most exciting and provocative recent work for me, therefore, examines, on the one hand, the material bases of literature and drama and, on the other, the margins of social discourse—the setting of margins being the way the culture defines its center. Neo-Freudian work, particularly that of Jacques Lacan and Luce Irigaray, and theoretical work on gender construction have proved invaluable (and, usually, maddeningly difficult). Often enough these investigations have little to do with literature, but at the same time they show how much literature has to do with everything else. Donna Haraway's astonishing work on the fictions and politics of biological notions of gender is a revelation for me, as are Thomas Laqueur's, Audrey Eccles's, and Ian Maclean's accounts of the history of gynecology—works that consider how, historically, science has constructed, and continues to construct, gender. Feminist and gay studies are obviously relevant; the feminist work has tended to be more adventurous theoretically, despite a certain inevitable tendentiousness, at least in the first generation of critics of both persuasions. Here I have found Teresa de Lauretis, Judith Butler, and Barbara Gelpi invaluable, if sometimes confusing, guides. In gay studies, John J. Winkler's and David Halperin's recent books, though they are about classical culture, turn out to be indispensable, as are the pioneering works of Alan Bray and Eve Kosofsky Sedgwick (especially the opening chapters of *Between Men*) and Gayle Rubin's classic essay "The Traffic in Women."[2] All these examples can serve, if not invariably as models of theoretical and critical practice (unlike several of my guides, I prefer to be readily comprehensible), at least as an indication of just how interdisciplinary such work needs to be.

I have cited a great many critics from a wide range of critical perspectives, and I am perfectly well aware that many of my authorities will not feel at all happy to find themselves in the company of the others.

Probably only those of us who think of ourselves as guides, rather than as theorists, can afford to be so cheerfully ecumenical, and anyone who accuses me of having a less than fervent commitment to theory will get little argument from me. But it is the interplay of methods and perspectives, not any particular doctrine, that I have found most valuable. And finally, the material I have been describing seems to me the indispensable, cautionary next step after Lawrence Stone, Christopher Hill, E. P. Thompson—what we, as literary critics, have tended to think of as simply "history," as if historians had no agendas, no vested interests. And underlying all these perspectives for me has been, once again, Foucault, in *The History of Sexuality*, along with the scholar whose work I consider perhaps the most basic of all, Norbert Elias. He brings into the world of critical and historical discourse the whole range of subjects that were, when I was being trained, not so much unmentionable as invisible: subjects that have been, quite simply, the stuff of our lives.

Stanford University

Notes

[1] The practice of castration to produce singers was forbidden in canon law but was nevertheless specifically authorized and encouraged by Sixtus VI in a papal bull of 1589.

[2] See also the important critiques of the essay by Stuard and by Orgel ("Mankind Witches").

Works Cited

Agnew, Jean-Christophe. *Worlds Apart.* Cambridge: Cambridge UP, 1986.

Bray, Alan. *Homosexuality in Renaissance England.* London: Gay Men's, 1982.

Bruster, Douglas. *Drama and the Market in the Age of Shakespeare.* Cambridge: Cambridge UP, 1992.

Butler, Judith. *Gender Trouble.* New York: Routledge, 1989.

de Lauretis, Teresa. "Sexual Indifference and Lesbian Representation." *Theatre Journal* 40 (1988): 155–77.

Eccles, Audrey. *Obstetrics and Gynaecology in Tudor and Stuart England.* Kent: Ohio State UP, 1982.

Elias, Norbert. *The History of Manners.* Trans. Edmund Jephcott. New York: Pantheon, 1982.

———. *Politics and Civility.* Trans. Edmund Jephcott. New York: Pantheon, 1982.

Foucault, Michel. *The History of Sexuality.* Trans. Robert Hurley. 3 vols. New York: Vintage, 1980–86.

———. "What Is an Author?" *Textual Strategies: Perspectives in Post-structuralist Criticism.* Ed. Josue V. Harari. Ithaca: Cornell UP, 1979. 141–60.

Gelpi, Barbara. *Shelley's Goddess.* Oxford: Oxford UP, 1993.

Goldberg, Jonathan. *Writing Matter.* Stanford: Stanford UP, 1990.

Halperin, David M. *One Hundred Years of Homosexuality and Other Essays on Greek Love.* New York: Routledge, 1990.

Haraway, Donna. *Primate Visions.* New York: Routledge, 1989.

———. "Situated Knowledges: The Science Question in Feminism and the Privilege of Partial Perspective." *Feminist Studies* 14 (1988): 575–99.

Jardine, Lisa. "Cultural Confusion and Shakespeare's Learned Heroines." *Shakespeare Quarterly* 38 (1987): 1–18.

Kastan, David Scott, and Peter Stallybrass, eds. *Staging the Renaissance.* New York: Routledge, 1991.

Laqueur, Thomas. *Making Sex.* Cambridge: Cambridge UP, 1990.

Loewenstein, Joseph. *Responsive Readings.* New Haven: Yale UP, 1984.

———. "The Script in the Marketplace." *Representations* 12 (1985): 101–14.

Maclean, Ian. *The Renaissance Notion of Woman.* Cambridge: Cambridge UP, 1980.

McKenzie, D. F. *Bibliography and the Sociology of Texts.* London: British Library, 1985.

———. "The London Book Trade in the Later Seventeenth Century." Unpublished essay.

———. *Stationers Company Apprentices 1641–1700.* Oxford: Oxford Bibliographical Soc., 1974.

McLeod, Randall [Random Cloud]. "Editing Shak-speare." *Substance* 33–34 (1982): 26–55.

———. *Material Shakespeare.* Forthcoming.

———. "Tranceformations in the Text of Orlando Furioso." *Library Chronicle of the University of Texas at Austin* 20.1–2 (1990): 60–85.

———. "The Very Names of the Persons: Editing and the Invention of Dramatick Character." Kastan and Stallybrass 88–96.

Mullaney, Steven. *The Place of the Stage.* Chicago: U of Chicago P, 1988.

Newman, Karen. "Portia's Ring." *Shakespeare Quarterly* 38 (1987): 19–33.

Newton, Richard. "Jonson and the (Re-)Invention of the Book." *Classic and Cavalier: Essays on Jonson and the Sons of Ben.* Ed. Claude J. Summers and Ted-Larry Pebworth. Pittsburgh: U of Pittsburgh P, 1982. 31–55.

Orgel, Stephen. "The Authentic Shakespeare." *Representations* 21 (1988): 1–25.

———. *The Illusion of Power.* Berkeley: U of California P, 1975.

———. "Mankind Witches." Forthcoming.

———. "What Is a Text?" Kastan and Stallybrass 83–87.

Rubin, Gayle. "The Traffic in Women." *Toward an Anthropology of Women.* Ed. Rayna R. Reiter. New York: Monthly Review, 1975. 157–210.

Sedgwick, Eve Kosofsky. *Between Men: English Literature and Male Homosocial Desire.* New York: Columbia UP, 1985.

Stuard, Susan. "The Annales School and Feminist History." *Signs* 7 (1981): 135–43.

Tennenhouse, Leonard. *Power on Display.* Methuen: New York, 1986.

Winkler, John J. *The Constraints of Desire.* New York: Routledge, 1990.

Lesbian Modernism: (Trans)Forming the (C)Anon

Karla Jay

In recent years, feminist critics have begun to document the way in which many modernist writers, including lesbians and gay men, nongay women, and people of color, have been marginalized, trivialized, and omitted from the canon by powerful white Eurocentric critics and cultural theorists who have attempted to prioritize their own values and to central-ize their place in literature at the expense of the rest of hu-manity. While there is no simple, generally agreed-upon, exact definition of modernism, the major anthologies of "great works" all include James Joyce, T. S. Eliot, Ezra Pound, D. H. Lawrence, and Virginia Woolf among the moderns, but they usually omit Vita Sackville-West, Gertrude Stein, Djuna Barnes, and Zora Neale Hurston. Are these omissions an accident, or have misogynist, racist, and anti-Semitic critics consciously sought to carve out in the arts the same firm monopoly that they have on morality, politics, religion, and social agency? Gay male modernists, such as E. M. Forster, Thomas Mann, and D. H. Lawrence (a closet case), conformed to the canon makers' ideals by recapitulating the same sexual hegemony in the modern novel that they saw in the society around them; surely, by the turn of the century, sexual differ-ences had been firmly categorized, and gay people were al-ready relegated to being not only the third sex but third-class citizens as well. Thus, in the same way that gay male and lesbian media censors later ferreted other homosexuals out of sensitive jobs and removed homoerotic innuendos from celluloid footage, the gay literati helped create and cement a homophobic canon that has still not been entirely restored to a more just interpretation.

There are many modernisms. Most of them include at least one gay male writer and one woman (sexuality irrelevant); a few have even added some members of the Harlem Renaissance. What is missing from traditional literary explorations of modernism is a recognition of the important role lesbians had in formulating it. I interpret literary modernism—for it would be impossible here to go into music, art, and dance as well—as a movement fueled to a great extent by lesbian writers. While male and nongay female modernists certainly challenged some of the institutions that embody the gender system (the church, the legal system, language, marriage, and the family, among others), they embraced the gender system itself, which lesbian modernism attempted to disrupt.[1]

To understand that modernism may be as much a shift in thematic material as it is in form and language opens up the canon in a new way. Lesbian modernists encoded lesboerotic content and language and foregrounded issues of gender identification in content as well as in experimental language. These writers sometimes lulled us with conventional forms, persuading us to read works that undermined the power system and transformed the gender roles that allow the system to operate. In other words, some lesbian modernists hid revolutionary sexual themes in traditional genres. Others experimented with form and language but used them to attack patriarchy and the traditional literature it endorsed. If we shift the definition of modernism in this way, the works of Willa Cather, Radclyffe Hall, Natalie Clifford Barney, Renée Vivien, and Elizabeth Bowen, among others, seem more related to modernism than we have been led to believe.

In reviewing critical sources for a seminar I taught entitled Modernism and Gender, I realized that most of the major scholarship canonized a single set of "modernist" principles as if they were necessarily true. Jane Lilienfeld aptly calls these ideas "early male modernism—fiction that is experimental, audience-challenging, language-focused rather than story or character-focused" (49). Although none of the critics defined modernism in precisely the same words, in the end all of them, including Sandra Gilbert and Susan Gubar, focused intensely on Joyce and Eliot, even if their critical intent was to excoriate the misogyny of the male modernists as Gilbert and Gubar do in epic proportions in the two-volume *No Man's Land*. Still, the men get the scrutiny and the foregrounding. Gilbert and Gubar explicitly attack Stein, make fun of Amy Lowell, and so continue the hegemony of men. Lesbian modernists like Barnes continue to lurk on the fringes while Hall, Vivien, Barney, Cather and others are discounted as modernists entirely. By referring to a few commonly taught and widely read novels to illustrate my points here, I attempt to undo, to a small extent, the damage that has been wrought by embracing "early male modernism" or by viewing the movement through a nongay lens. I turn first to the way lesbian modernists differed from their canonized brothers and quietly undermined and re(de)fined generally accepted modernist principles.

FREUD

Most of the lesbian modernists (HD being a notable exception), including Woolf and Stein, rejected Freud; in fact, some of the women went out of their way to deny that they had read Freud. For example, as Elizabeth Abel points out, Freud's work was well-known in the Bloomsbury circle, where psychoanalysis had found an "intellectual home." Adrian Stephen, Woolf's brother, was trained as a psychoanalyst, and the Hogarth Press published Freud's International Psycho-Analytical Library, including his *Collected Papers*, in 1924 and 1925. Woolf, however, "claimed to have avoided reading Freud until 1939." James Strachey, brother of the Bloomsburyist Lytton, wrote to Alix Strachey on 14 May 1925 that "last night . . . Virginia made a more than usually ferocious onslaught on psychoanalysis and psychoanalysts, more particularly the latter." When Woolf had a nervous breakdown, she was not treated by a psychoanalyst "for fear that it might endanger her creativity." While the male members of the Bloomsbury circle, and some of the nongay women too (for example, Karin Stephen, Adrian's wife), championed psychoanalysis and gave it a literary slant, Woolf felt queasy about "the psychoanalytic simplification of character" (Abel 13, 14, 17).

Stein also denied that she had read Freud, and she never mentions him in her notebooks.[2] Members of Stein's circle in Paris did not view Freud in so literary a fashion as their English counterparts did; Stein contemplated and rejected Freud, as she had other boring "scientists," when she was studying medicine at Johns Hopkins University in Baltimore. The enthusiasm her brother Leo had for Freud probably further encouraged Stein to reject Freud and his teachings. For one thing, Stein didn't believe in an unconscious (or so she frequently said). She didn't think that automatic writing was at all connected to psychoanalytic thinking, and her ideas on repetition predated Freud's *Beyond the Pleasure Principle* (Ruddick 93, 99).

Freud's theories, however, were more threatening to Stein as a lesbian than as a writer. They put

> Stein in a classic double bind. On the one hand, the scientific belief that lesbianism was pathologically determined indicated that those "afflicted" with this "disease" were passive victims, yet societal fears [some of them based on psychological developmental

theory] that sexual behavior in fact, was voluntarily chosen resulted in the stigmatization of homosexuals as "social outlaws."
(Blackmer 236)

Here we come to the heart of the issue. If homosexuality could be altered through psychoanalysis, then it was malleable behavior, for which the participant was largely responsible. Any voluntary practice could be abandoned or, at the very least, repressed. The Victorian and post-Victorian emphasis on moral control supported Freudian assumptions, which helped reinforce notions of women's roles as wife and mother. Conversely, the essentialist model posed by Havelock Ellis in particular (and to a lesser degree by Krafft-Ebing) was much more attractive to Stein, Barnes, Barney, Vivien, Hall, and other lesbians. According to that theory, the born invert, that natural member of the third sex, could not possibly change her behavior, any more than true heterosexuals could force themselves to become homosexuals. Biological destiny is not only unalterable but also guilt-free. Thus, Stein's Melanctha "wanders" in her sexual attention because it is her nature, just as Rose is inherently "lazy" and "careless": "Rose had the simple, promiscuous unmorality of the black people" ("Melanctha" 85–86).[3] Jeff Campbell, by trying to emulate white morality, experiences unhappiness and a certain loss of identity. The word *unmorality* is crucial here, for Stein chooses it over *immorality* and all that the latter implies. For Stein, people are the products of nature, environment, and native intelligence: morality is irrelevant.

Likewise, in Barnes's *Nightwood*, Nora Flood is doomed to fail in her attempt to alter Robin Vote's promiscuity (though of course Nora would not dream of eliminating Robin's lesbianism!), and Matthew O'Connor, while practicing his transvestism in the privacy of his bedroom, guiltlessly reveals this secret side to Nora, because his female side is as much a part of his being as his logorrhea is. In *Ladies Almanack*, Barnes insists that Evangeline Musset was a lesbian at birth: "For she had been developed in the Womb of her most gentle Mother to be a Boy, when therefore, she came forth an Inch or so less than this, she paid no Heed to the Error . . . and set out upon the Road of Destiny" (7). Clearly, Evangeline has no control over this path before or after birth.

Among the members of the Parisian lesbian set, Barney, the model for Evangeline in *Ladies Almanack*, was the most adamant that she was "naturally unnatural." Noting the overpopulation that the world suffers from, she suggests in her essay "Predestined for Free Choice" that lesbianism is a "perilous advantage" as well as a pleasant relief from the conformity of the heterosexual masses. She, too, cites Ellis and Krafft-Ebing and avoids mention of Freud.

Like Barney, Hall defended lesbianism as a biological given. She had corresponded at some length with Ellis, who came to her defense at the obscenity trial of *The Well of Loneliness*. Hall considered her lesbianism a " 'condition of nature,' a fact of her existence no different from race or height or lineage" (Glasgow). A devout Catholic, Hall threw in some theology to bolster her essentialism. She declared to her lover Euguenie Souline that she was exactly as God had created her; therefore, her "inversion," as she called it, could not possibly constitute a sin: "There is a God, make no mistake, and I have my rightful place in His creation" (qtd. in Glasgow).

Barnes, of course, satirizes Barney, Hall, and their circle in *Ladies Almanack* but concurs with their essentialist position. Barnes was not interested in Freud; in fact, Margaret Anderson once noted that Barnes "was not on speaking terms with her own psyche" (qtd. in Broe 36).

EXILE

Lesbian modernists did not always disagree completely with other modernists, but their views of modernist writing were distinctly shaded by their sexual preference and their gender. In migrating to Paris and sometimes elsewhere (Capri, Rome, North Africa), for example, lesbian writers and artists seemed to be embracing Stephen Dedalus's dictum of "silence, exile, and cunning" (247). For the sapphic expatriate set, however, the expression of alienation in their lives and works was very different from that of nongay (especially the straight male) modernists. For one thing, Joyce and others who felt estranged from their homelands, families, and religions voluntarily exiled themselves. Some, like Eliot, left one patriarchal religion only to embrace a similar one. As an Irishman, Joyce felt colonized by English culture, yet he wrote in English, not in Gaelic or in the languages of any of the countries he lived in. Though he felt a great deal of anger at the Catholic Church, he married Nora Barnacle in a religious ceremony, and he was not excommunicated for grievous sins or for any of his writings, though they were certainly on the Church's list of banned books. As Shari Benstock has laid out for us, women had more at stake than the flight from puritanical values (including a general rejection of Anglo-American Victorian and post-Victorian values) and the lure of European currencies devaluated after the war. To put forward the early male modernists as "rebels" and "exiles" overlooks the deep conservatism of Pound, Eliot, and Wyndham

Lewis, among others ("Expatriate" 20–21). Perhaps the traditional fore-grounding of form over content diverts us from the politics embedded in the text. Benstock recognizes that the expatriate woman "is driven away under penalty of the law that supports the patriarchal; by defini-tion—that is, by genre and in her gender—she exists outside the law, beyond the reaches to which that law has driven her." Benstock goes on to suggest, without noting the obvious homoerotic message, that these lesbian expatriates traveled to Paris, a city that "has consistently been imaged as female" ("Expatriate" 25, 27).

Even in London, expatriates such as HD felt doubly exiled by their femaleness and their lesboerotic proclivities. In her roman à clef *Paint It Today*, Josepha and Midget feel that in England they are "separated from the separated" (20). As Susan Stanford Friedman has pointed out, "They discover that they are exiled even from the exiles—separate as women in love with each other from both American and European norms" (95).

Others, such as Woolf, while not expatriates, were exiles in the broader sense of the word, as Mary Lynn Broe and Angela Ingram suggest in *Women's Writing in Exile*. Women were exiled from male-oriented language, mainstream culture, publication, and serious review atten-tion. Sometimes women were discouraged from pursuing certain genres. They may have been doubly or triply ostracized because of their class, race, or sexual preference. And as is often true, they were exiled individu-ally within their homes.

The lesbian writers were also exiled by the growing sense of danger they felt from the legal systems and moral climates in England and the United States. The imprisonment of Oscar Wilde made the worst possibilities all too clear, even though his trial was supposedly a message aimed at deviant men and even though lesbianism was technically legal. While most of the lesbians felt no common cause with Wilde, it was now apparent that what they were doing was not just rebellious but possibly politically dangerous as well.

As a result, many English-speaking lesbian modernists decided to remain in France, where foreign lesbians were left alone, and some felt it was safest or wisest to write of the "love that dare not speak its name" from the grave, which at least offered refuge from the law. It is no accident that Stein's *Q.E.D.* and HD's *Paint It Today* were posthu-mously published, while Barnes's *Ladies Almanack* was privately printed in France and sold by subscription, not only to raise capital for the publication but also to ensure that the copies landed in the right hands. Even Barney privately printed *The One Who Is Legion; or, A.D.'s After-life* in a limited run of a few hundred copies so that she could strictly control the distribution of the book. Woolf embedded her love letter to Sackville-West in the life of the androgynous (but ostensibly straight) Orlando. Clarissa Dalloway's love for Sally Seton can seem less important, to a nongay eye at least, than her musings over Richard Dalloway and Peter Walsh. In part, lesbian modernism has often gone unnoticed because its central texts have been hiding in the closet for far too long. Some writers, including Stein, Vivien, and Barney, further exiled themselves and estranged their works from their native (and perhaps primary) audiences by writing in French.[4]

SILENCE AND CUNNING

Although Hall's work has been consistently omitted from modernist considerations, the obscenity trials about *The Well of Loneliness* affected lesbian modernists who knew Hall by foregrounding the dangers of their subject matter. Because Hall's work is a lesbian text, the trials about it seemed far more relevant—and threatening—than did similar persecutions of Joyce and Lawrence. As Jane Marcus points out in "Sapphistory," Woolf altered *A Room of One's Own* in response to Hall's British trial and encoded the lesbian material so that a theme of lesbian seduction runs as a subtext while still allowing the text to pass as straight for the uninitiated reader.

Barney felt equally uneasy about Hall's persecution. For one thing, she was the model for Valérie Seymour in *The Well of Loneliness*, a characterization so thinly altered that anyone who knew, or knew of, Barney recognized her immediately. Valérie is the only character in the novel who is unapologetic about lesbianism. During the 1920s, Barney's unrepentant lesbian proselytizing created no end of possible enemies, especially in the wake of antifeminist backlashes in the United States and England after the success of the suffrage movement. If Stephen Gordon's groveling apologies for her inborn "inversion" still did not exonerate *The Well of Loneliness* from legal persecution, then Valérie, who encourages her entourage to celebrate their sexuality, must have seemed particularly threatening and offensive.

At the very least, the obscenity trial of *The Well of Loneliness* signaled to Barney, Woolf, Barnes, and other lesbians that the era of studied blindness to sapphism had drawn to a close and that they were as likely as any other group was to suffer the consequences of public pressures for conformity. That Hall was not imprisoned was of little comfort to them, for the thought of a public trial was horribly distasteful whatever the verdict. As in contemporary times, the notoriety of a trial serves as punishment in and of itself.

As a result, lesbian modernism exercised the ultimate in what Joyce had referred to as "silence . . . and cunning." Not only Woolf but also Barney resorted to the use of dashes and ellipses to signify lesboeroticism that could not be blatantly eulogized in works intended for a general audience.⁵ Lesbianism, which Woolf alludes to several times in *Mrs. Dalloway* (1925) as Clarissa reflects on her relationship with Sally Seton, is totally encoded by the time of *A Room of One's Own* (1929). Barney, who wrote passionate love poems to other women in *Quelques portraits-sonnets de femmes* (1900), encoded her love affair with Vivien in *The One Who Is Legion* (1930), a Gothic nightmare through which a gynandrous narrator floats, no longer entirely fixed in her or his own body. After the 1928 trial, Barney replaced the direct style of her early poems, plays, and "scatterings" with a murky blend of symbolism and surrealism, through which the narrative thread—and its lesbian content—can barely be grasped. Stein so successfully disguised her relationship with Alice B. Toklas that most readers of the *Autobiography* (1933) thought that Toklas was Stein's secretary or paid companion. Or modernists like Stein wrote about something else, something that was not lesbianism except by its absence. Interestingly, only Barnes, perhaps because she so doggedly defined herself as a heterosexual, felt free to continue pursuing all sorts of deviant characters in *Nightwood*.

Yet even *Mrs. Dalloway* has been read through the years as a novel about Clarissa's failed relationship with Peter, a response to *Ulysses*, and a reaction to World War I. For many readers—and critics—the lesbianism remained as invisible as the incest that Woolf had survived as a child. Only when Louise DeSalvo's work pulled the veil away from the readers' eyes were the references to incest all too apparent. The same is true for the lesbian modernists: the lesboerotic themes are there, but they are perceptible only to those with the same magical vision. One has to start out being different and trying to find others like oneself in order to search out lesbian characters and themes in purportedly straight texts.⁶

SUBVERSION OF THE POWER SYSTEM

The most daring possibility of lesbian modernism is that it exists right under the collective nose of patriarchy. Perhaps it is not always encoded in hermetic language or stylistic theatrics. Instead, it boldly poses in conventional clothes. It denies its modernism. It wears the style and other trappings of the traditional novel in order to undermine its very conventions. It is a literary transvestite, a saucy trompe l'oeil.

Let us take, for instance, *The Well of Loneliness*. Stephen Gordon sacrifices Mary, the woman she loves, so that Mary may lead the life of a "normal" married woman. This act encompasses a courtly gesture that the audience should easily recognize and greatly appreciate, since it is embedded in many literary romances. But men, not women, are supposed to behave in such a chivalrous fashion. Stephen's altruism makes her nobler than the husband who accepts Mary's hand in marriage at the expense of another human being's happiness. Unfortunately for Hall, the audience could not savor the essence and depth of Stephen's renunciation of her dream, for readers never got beyond the two women's romantic involvement.

Similarly, Barney and Vivien each rewrote the life of Sappho so that the tenth muse leaps over the Leucadian cliffs because one of her disciples is in love with Phaon.[7] The transformation is much more than a twist on the legend that Sappho committed suicide because her beloved Phaon betrayed her for another. Her death is not so much a tragedy as it is a refusal to accept the status quo of marriage. When Vivien's Prince Charming marries the lovely princess, the nobleman turns out to be the prince's sister in drag. The two women elope and hide in Venice, but their happiness subverts the very church and legal system that united them when the bride and groom were believed to be of different genders.

In a later work, Woolf's Orlando loves an androgynous Russian woman named Sasha (a male Slavic nickname and a use of the orientalism that was dear to the male modernists as well) who he at first thinks is a boy.[8] Later, Orlando does love a man, but his body is that of a woman. Yet Sackville-West posed for Orlando as both man and woman. What then is Orlando's gender? The answer might lie in the language, for Orlando's speech is transformed along with his or her gender, and though the two appear to be exactly the same to those who know them (everyone from Mrs. Grimsditch to Orlando's dogs), they certainly don't speak alike.

The divergence of lesbian writers from the fragmented, experimental language and thematic material of the early male modernists is clear. While Joyce, Eliot, and Pound may at times question the meaning of religion, nationality, and morality, they hold firmly to their (en)gendered power. Male modernists explore exile while on leave from their home and church, but not from their manhood, not from their native tongue. Bloom, Dedalus, and Prufrock are all men—make no mistake about it. When Bloom is made to play the part of a woman in Nightown, it is part of a perverse fantasy, set in the proper milieu of a red-light district. Bloom's impotence with his wife, Molly, is a crucial problem in their marriage, not the catalyst for other sexual practices.

*   *   *

To begin to re(de)fine modernism in this way does more than allow an additional lesbian or two to creep into the canon or to stand poised at its fringes. It foregrounds lesbians as revolutionary literary thinkers of the twentieth century and proposes for some of the early male modernists a form of exile that they never envisioned.

Queer theory and lesbian feminist scholarship are suggesting new ways to read literary modernisms, ways that foreground texts and writers marginal to the grand récit of Western culture. What was once deviant is now central to the concerns of readers (gay or nongay), and even Eliot, Lawrence, and Joyce are being read with attention to encoded instances of writing that connect them to lesbian and gay modernism.

Pace University

Notes

I would like to thank the following individuals for their helpful comments on this essay as it developed: Joanne Glasgow, Mark Hussey, Ruth Johnston, Jane Marcus, and Bonnie Zimmerman. I would also like to thank the Scholarly Research Committee at Pace University, Sherman Raskin, and Charles Masiello, who have all generously helped make space for me to write over the years. Finally, I would like to thank Joanne Glasgow for permission to quote from her unpublished work.

[1] I have intentionally thrown down a tremendous gauntlet here and obliterated almost all modernist criticism. To support my position fully would certainly require more space than I have in this essay, for I would need to challenge every critical work that I have ever read on modernism, including my own writings.

[2] Ruddick demonstrates how Stein used Freud's work in *The Making of Americans*. It is somewhat paradoxical, however, to claim that Stein was silent about such a major figure because she "was selectively taking in his ideas" (94).

[3] The racism in "Melanctha" remains a thorny problem, in part because most critics have ignored its implications when discussing Stein's work. Stein had clearly internalized negative stereotypes of black people, despite her daring in foregrounding Melanctha, an African American woman, as her protagonist and her later collaboration with Virgil Thomson on *Four Saints in Three Acts*, the first opera written especially for black singers. There is also the perhaps less obvious sexism of calling Melanctha by her first name while giving Jeff Campbell the authority of a surname. Moreover, Stein casually tosses out anti-Semitic remarks in *The Autobiography of Alice B. Toklas*, where she complains that a stranger at her salon "looks like a Jew" (11), even though Stein was Jewish herself. In "Wrestling Your Ally," Saldívar-Hull begins to grapple with Stein's attitudes toward race and class. Barney's anti-Semitism has been discussed in

several works (Benstock, *Women*; Jay; Livia), but the general hegemonic assumptions of patriarchal power need to be addressed at length, not only for Stein and Barney but also for Barnes and others.

[4] It is commonly overlooked that Stein wrote her essays on Picasso and a few other works in French. *Picasso* was translated into English by Alice B. Toklas, who didn't receive credit for her work in the book.

[5] Woolf and Barney used ellipses earlier, of course, but I believe the device took on different connotations after 1928. Marcus points out that male texts about lesbians, including Mackenzie's *Extraordinary Women*, also use ellipses and unfinished sentences (personal communication). Mackenzie may have noticed this grammatical usage in the works of the women he was satirizing and decided to imitate it.

[6] This searching is what some today call "gaydar"—gay people trying to figure out which movie stars and sports figures might be "one of us."

[7] See DeJean for a discussion of the literary contest to define Sappho's reputation.

[8] At this period of history, many Western Europeans still considered Russians to be "Orientals."

Works Cited

Abel, Elizabeth. *Virginia Woolf and the Fictions of Psychoanalysis*. Chicago: U of Chicago P, 1989.

Barnes, Djuna. *Ladies Almanack*. 1928. New York: New York UP, 1992.

———. *Nightwood*. New York: New Directions, 1937.

Barney, Natalie Clifford. *The One Who Is Legion; or, A.D.'s After-life*. London: Partridge, 1930.

———. *A Perilous Advantage: The Best of Natalie Clifford Barney*. Trans. Anna Livia. Norwich: New Victoria, 1992.

———. "Predestined for Free Choice." Barney, *Perilous Advantage* 91–94.

———. *Quelques portraits-sonnets de femmes*. Paris: Société d'Editions Littéraires, 1900.

Benstock, Shari. "Expatriate Modernism: Writing on the Cultural Rim." Broe and Ingram 19–40.

———. *Women of the Left Bank: Paris, 1900–1940*. Austin: U of Texas P, 1986.

Blackmer, Corinne E. "African Masks and the Arts of Passing in Gertrude Stein's 'Melanctha' and Nella Larsen's *Passing*." *Journal of the History of Sexuality* 4 (1993): 230–63.

Broe, Mary Lynn, ed. *Silence and Power: A Reevaluation of Djuna Barnes*. Carbondale: Southern Illinois UP, 1991.

Broe, Mary Lynn, and Angela Ingram, eds. *Women's Writing in Exile*. Chapel Hill: U of North Carolina P, 1989.

DeJean, Joan. *Fictions of Sappho, 1546–1937*. Chicago: U of Chicago P, 1989.

DeSalvo, Louise. *Virginia Woolf: The Impact of Childhood Sexual Abuse on Her Life and Work*. Boston: Beacon, 1989.

Friedman, Susan Stanford. "Exile in the American Grain." Broe and Ingram 87–112.

Gilbert, Sandra M., and Susan Gubar. *No Man's Land: The Place of the Woman Writer in the Twentieth Century.* 2 vols. New Haven: Yale UP, 1988–89.

Glasgow, Joanne. "Ad/dressing the Lesbian Body: Radclyffe Hall's Style." Unpublished ms., 1992.

Hall, Radclyffe. *The Well of Loneliness.* 1928. New York: Pocket, 1974.

HD [Hilda Doolittle]. *Paint It Today.* New York: New York UP, 1992.

Jay, Karla. *The Amazon and the Page: Natalie Clifford Barney and Renée Vivien.* Bloomington: Indiana UP, 1988.

———. Introduction. *Adventures of the Mind.* By Natalie Clifford Barney. New York: New York UP, 1992. 1–17.

Joyce, James. *Portrait of the Artist as a Young Man.* 1916. New York: Viking, 1973.

Lilienfeld, Jane. "Willa Cather (1873–1947)." *The Gender of Modernism: A Critical Anthology.* Ed. Bonnie Kime Scott. Bloomington: Indiana UP, 1990. 46–53.

Livia, Anna. "The Trouble with Heroines: Natalie Clifford Barney and Anti-Semitism." Barney, *Perilous Advantage* 180–92.

Mackenzie, Compton. *Extraordinary Women: Theme and Variations.* London: Secker, 1928.

Marcus, Jane. "Sapphistory: The Woolf and the Well." *Lesbian Texts and Contexts: Radical Revisions.* Ed. Karla Jay and Joanne Glasgow. New York: New York UP, 1990. 164–79.

Ruddick, Lisa. *Reading Gertrude Stein: Body, Text, Gnosis.* Ithaca: Cornell UP, 1990.

Saldívar-Hull, Sonia. "Wrestling Your Ally: Stein, Racism, and Feminist Critical Practice." Broe and Ingram 181–98.

Stein, Gertrude. *The Autobiography of Alice B. Toklas.* New York: Vintage, 1933.

———. "Melanctha." *Three Lives.* New York: Liveright, 1939. 83–236.

———. *Q.E.D. Fernhurst, Q.E.D. and Other Early Writings by Gertrude Stein.* New York: Liveright, 1971.

———. *Picasso: The Complete Writings.* Boston: Beacon, 1970.

Vivien, Renée. "Prince Charming." 1904. *The Woman of the Wolf.* Trans. Karla Jay and Yvonne M. Klein. New York: Gay, 1983. 23–28.

Woolf, Virginia. *Mrs. Dalloway.* London: Hogarth, 1925. New York: Harcourt, 1985.

———. *Orlando.* London: Hogarth, 1928. New York: Harcourt, 1985.

———. *A Room of One's Own.* New York: Harcourt, 1929.

Race, Homosocial Desire, and "Mammon" in *Autobiography of an Ex-Coloured Man*

Cheryl Clarke

READING FOR HOMOSEXUALITY

In 1977 the black lesbian-feminist critic Barbara Smith read Toni Morrison's second novel, *Sula*, as a "lesbian novel" in her controversial essay, "Toward a Black Feminist Criticism."[1] Smith was claiming not that genital homosexuality lies at the root of the relationship between the dual protagonists, Sula and Nel, but, rather, that Morrison's narrative opens what Marilyn Farwell calls a "disruptive space of sameness" in an overtly heterosexual text. In *Sula*, that "disruptive space of sameness" (lesbianism) is revealed, according to Smith, through the centrality of the women characters, Nel and Sula's passion for each other, and "Morrison's consistently critical stance towards the heterosexual institution of male/female relationships, marriage, and the family" (33). In Afro-American narrative, that disruptive space demands a questioning of white power just as "inscribing female desire in a plot demands a questioning of heterosexuality" (Farwell 95; see also Farwell's essay in this volume).

In " 'That Nameless . . . Shameful Impulse': Sexuality in Nella Larsen's *Quicksand* and *Passing*," Deborah McDowell uncovers the lesbian subtext in Larsen's 1929 novel *Passing*. McDowell, as a strong reader of Afro-American literature, opens that disruptive space and names that impulse in a way that Larsen could not and previous critics would not. *Passing*, a novel whose "surface theme and central metaphor" is "the safe and familiar plot of racial passing" (160), tells a riskier story of the dangerous Irene Redfield's repressed sexual desire for the duplicitous Clare Kendry.

A similarly disruptive space of sameness opens in James Weldon Johnson's *Autobiography of an Ex–Coloured Man*, a perplexing narrative of a man of mixed ancestry who poses and passes on both sides of "the color line" (DuBois, *Souls* 122) and ultimately passes as white. By exploiting nineteenth-century slave narrative conventions and by creating a racially dubious, painfully ambivalent narrator and protagonist, Johnson allows more complex and dangerous subtexts to disrupt the familiar tradition of Afro-American narrative. Johnson—an exemplar of "black distinctiveness" (Bruce 232)—experiments as fluently, though not as directly, with modernist concepts of sexuality as he does with the psyche of a person of color in a white supremacist world.

Robert B. Stepto's penetrating and male-centered study of Afro-American literature, *From behind the Veil*, discusses Johnson's narrative strategies as quests that do not result in the narrator's self-knowledge. Thus, Johnson's narrator, cast against earlier narrators, "misreads" their "canonical images" (104). Johnson synthesizes the rhetorical and pedantic strategies of Booker T. Washington's *Up from Slavery*, the geographic symbolism of W. E. B. DuBois's *The Souls of Black Folk*, the homosocial desire and heroic communalism of Frederick Douglass's *The Life and Times*, and numerous other tropes signifying nineteenth-century black narrative. He then misreads the canonical images to generate "energies that propel beyond synthesis into a new narrative realm" (97), within which developed the modernist black fiction of the 1920s, 1930s, and 1940s.

In a similar vein, Lucinda McKeithan argues that Johnson's *Autobiography* is a "satire organized around the use of a persona who is incapable of self-knowledge," which "makes him, in his white mask, the agent of Johnson's attack on white society's values" (141). Further, in his black mask, Ex–Coloured Man is the agent of Johnson's ambivalence toward the values of post-Reconstruction, fin de siécle black society, primarily the "third class" of "coloured people—the independent workmen and tradesmen . . . and well-to-do and educated" (*Autobiography* 78).

McKeithan, like Stepto before her, reads Johnson's strategies as "inversions of the narrative arrangement of the slave narratives; in Johnson's reworking, every scene exhibits the protagonist's regression into slavery" (141; see Stepto 122). The title of the novel sets Ex–Coloured Man against all the "ex-slaves" who tell their stories in nineteenth-century black narratives. The narrator's refusal to name himself in the narrative is set against the willingness of all those who have named themselves. The narrator's reticence in naming others who would be "connected with this narrative" (3) to protect himself is set against the conventional slave narrator's wish to protect those not named. The ambiguity of miscegenation is set against the knowing of blackness, the constant "misreading" against the struggle for literacy, the flight from autonomy against the flight for freedom. All the tropes of knowledge and freedom, which characterize the most outstanding nineteenth-century (female and male) black narratives, are revised and ironized to tell a modernist story of unknowing, alienation, and the inability to see within the "veil" (DuBois, *Souls* 209), to be "within the circle" (Douglass, *Narrative* 57). DuBois's veil metaphor and Douglass's circle metaphor signify spaces of racial and sexual sameness in the black male world.

This new narrative realm allows the reader to perceive dimensions of sameness—of the homosocial—that transgress white supremacist patriarchal and heterosexual codes and disrupt traditional sacred and ritual spaces of Afro-American culture. In Afro-American literature, disruptive spaces of sameness are racial and sexual. Ex–Coloured Man is ultimately unable to occupy either. Through this tragic mulatto, Johnson articulates some of the most profound and prophetic musings on the color line and some of the most profane. Ex–Coloured Man is perhaps the first antiheroic narrator in Afro-American literature.

In *Between Men*, an illuminating study of "male homosocial desire," the feminist theorist Eve Kosofsky Sedgwick examines a spectrum of social bonds between men in certain eighteenth- and nineteenth-century British narratives. Her purpose is not to prove that sex between men is the root of male homosociability but, rather, to examine the continuum of male homosocial relationships, including homosexual ones, and to uncover disruptions of the continuum between the homosocial and the homosexual. For Sedgwick those spaces of sameness, those homosocial spaces, are political and erotic, homosexual and homophobic, disruptive and affirming of patriarchal codes, masculinized and feminized, culturally contingent, and most often representative of the power over, and subordination of, women.

Homosocial relationships give Ex–Coloured Man his agency. In every chapter of the work a man or a male network gives him safe and sometimes sorry passage. Usually, these homosocial bonds are struck with men of color. Except for the ephemeral bond with his absent white father, the adolescent bond with his piano teacher (ch. 2), and an erotic triangle that results in murder, his homosocial desire is unmediated by women. The relationships with women, though intense, are valorizing foils for his homosocial desire. Ex–Coloured Man's homosocial (including homosexual) desire, however, is ultimately disrupted by racist, heterosexist, capitalist patriarchy.

In chapter 8, his first sojourn in New York City, Ex–Coloured Man is on an unacknowledged quest for sexual awareness; in chapter 10, his return to the southern homeland, he is on an inauthentic quest for blackness. Both chapters configure him on the brink of knowledge, of a literacy of self and blackness, posing/passing within and outside the veil. Both chapters signify the disturbing consequences of sexual and racial autonomy through culminating scenes of violence. The satire and the parody rupture in these scenes and give way to a horrific realism that Ex–Coloured Man cannot interpret correctly, because of his racial ambiguity and sexual ambivalence. Each quest reveals Ex–Coloured Man in a radically different place in his reading or misreading of black culture—and life.

RACE AND THE "HOMOSOCIAL DESTINATION OF DESIRE"

Chapters 8 and 10 are pivotal to Johnson's strategies of racial and sexual unknowing. Having become habituated to his New York City environs and its undergrounds—the gambling house, an exclusively male homosocial space, and the "Club," a place "well known to both white and coloured people of certain classes" and both sexes (103)—Ex–Coloured Man moves with facility between the two. He also describes the Club as a place of black male culture: "the walls were literally covered with photographs and lithographs of every coloured man in America who had ever 'done anything' " (104). Stepto calls the Club "an Afro-American ritual ground where responses to oppressing social structures are made and in some measure sustained by 'tribal' bonds, as they are in DuBois' Black Belt" (123). Johnson's construction of the Club signifies his departure from the antecedent black narratives.

The "oppressing social structures" of segregation and the patriarchal code of heterosexual monogamy are transgressed and disrupted in the Club by racial mixing and illicit sexuality, including interracial homosexuality and bisexuality. In the Club, Ex–Coloured Man first hears and then learns to play the classic American music form ragtime. He also learns about the sexually illicit, though he withholds this information from the reader through an announced silence, what Stepto calls "rhetorical omission" (105), a gap that serves as a space of transgressive sexuality. After revealing to the reader that "the widow"—one of the Club's most striking white female habitués—paid for her black companion's clothes and diamonds, Ex–Coloured Man cryptically observes, "More that I learned would be better suited to a book on social phenomena than to a narrative of my life" (109).

There is sparse mention of *Autobiography* in Johnson's own dense and uplifting 1933 autobiography, *Along This Way*.[2] He does tell us, though, that in publishing the novel anonymously in 1912, he intended to create the illusion of "human document" instead of affixing his name to the work as a "frank piece of fiction" (238). Was Johnson, in 1912, inverting the reader's sense of the authorial authenticity of antecedent black narratives? Or was he hiding his identity as fiction writer because the subjectivity of his narrator was too dangerous even as a "frank piece of fiction"?

Unable to specify his narrator's homosocial desire as homosexual, Johnson filters it through the safe convention of the narrative gaze. Most notable are the sensual and densely descriptive gazes: at his black schoolmate Shiny, who "strongly attracted" his attention (14); at himself as he narcissistically inventories his facial beauty (17); again at the "positively handsome" Shiny, whose valedictory speech was like "touching an electric button" (45); at his Cuban landlord in Jacksonville, who was "redeemed from insignificance" by "a handsome black mustache and Spanish eyes" (67); at the "always faultlessly dressed" black companion of the widow (108); at his "clean-cut, slender, athletic" patron (116). All these gazes culminate in two devastating visual confrontations: he witnesses the murder of a white woman by a black man and the lynching of a black man by a white mob. These two incidents, both over the presumption of transgressive sexuality, result in a disruption for Ex–Coloured Man of the sexual and racial spaces of sameness.

It is in the Club that Ex–Coloured Man meets his "benefactor"—a word that at once disguises the homoerotic subtext of their relationship, which Ex–Coloured Man misreads as "familiar and warm," and serves as a euphemism for its inequality (121). His versatility at exploiting black cultural forms—at translating a black aesthetic into a white one— draws Ex–Coloured Man into a homosocial liaison with a white millionaire, "who was the means by which [he] escaped from this lower world" (115). Johnson, as a writer and strong reader and "misreader" of black culture, carefully separates the gambling house and the Club, where no gambling is allowed and where the liquor is kept in a closet (104). Ex–Coloured Man, the unconscious misreader, however, conflates the Club and the gambling house as "this lower world" and distorts the major nineteenth-century black narrative trope of "escape" to draw a misconceived parallel to slavery.

In explicating Ex–Coloured Man's relationship with the benefactor, McKeithan vigorously suggests that it is a parody of the master-slave relationship, sans the erotic (143). Stepto, hardly concerned about the relationship, suggests in passing that a father-figure transference occurs in Ex–Coloured Man's relationship with his benefactor (126). Though both critics distance their arguments from the sexual subtext of the relationship, I have no argument with either reading. The relationship can also be read, however, as a revision of the relationship between Ex–Coloured Man's mother and her white benefactor, Ex–Coloured Man's father. Each of these explanatory narratives conceals, as McDowell says of *Passing*, the telling of the more dangerous and transgressive story of homosexual interracial concubinage—or each tells it "slant."

Describing his benefactor, Ex–Coloured Man reports, "He gave me a card containing his address and asked me to be there on a certain night" (116). This statement marks Ex–Coloured Man's entrée in to a new kind of bondage, Mammonism.[3] On the appointed evening, Ex–Coloured Man enters this new patriarchal and homosocial space much like the slave who is brought to the house of a new master, and—unlike most slaves—he is given a cordial escort to the kitchen and is fed "without being asked whether [he] was hungry or not . . ." (117). "I was called in to begin my work," he continues, for the gathering of guests, whom he describes:

> The men ranged in appearance from a girlish-looking youth to a big grizzled man whom everybody addressed as "Judge." None of the women appeared to be under thirty, but each of them struck me as being handsome. I was not long in finding out they were all decidedly blasé. (118)

The language Johnson chooses here can be read as a code for the homosexual dimension of male or female homosociability. He uses the gender-switching terms "girlish-looking youth" and "handsome" women, as well as the term "blasé," which in French means "to be surfeited" but in English, at that time, presupposed a surfeiting of transgressive experiences—women smoking cigarettes, racial mixing, the sexually illicit, and so on.

When the blasé guests leave, the benefactor appropriates the pleasure Ex–Coloured Man has provided with his inauthentic ragtime. "Well, I have given them something they've never had before," says the benefactor. When Ex–Coloured Man accepts the glass of wine the benefactor "made [him] take," along with twenty dollars and a cigar, he in effect bonds himself to his "friend" and "readily" accepts the "proposition" to play only for his benefactor and at engagements his benefactor will secure for him (120).

The parody of the slave master's hiring out of the slave's labor is obvious here, but the word "proposition" may also signal a sexual subtext in the transaction. Admittedly, sex is more elliptical in *Autobiography* than in *Passing*. But just as McDowell reads Irene Redfield's "buried sexual desire" for Clare Kendry in Larsen's use of fire imagery (157), so the eroticism between Ex–Coloured Man and the benefactor in chapter 8 is displaced onto the piano playing. The benefactor would "drive" Ex–Coloured Man "mercilessly to exhaustion" with his demands for piano playing. Sexual codes are once again embedded in Ex–Coloured Man's reading of his employer's abusiveness: "The man's powers of endurance in listening often exceeded mine in performing" (121). Ex–Coloured Man, already "drunk with the wine" ("Lift Ev'ry Voice," Johnson, *Along This Way* 155) of Mammon, only rarely allows himself to feel "a sort of unearthly terror" at this peculiar and sadistic treatment. "[B]esides," he comments, the benefactor "paid me so liberally I could forget much. . . . On my part, I looked upon him at that point as about all a man could wish to be" (121).

The Club then becomes the setting of Ex–Coloured Man's most startling sexual misreading. Earning a handsome benefaction from his millionaire friend, Ex–Coloured Man no longer "depended on playing [ragtime] at the 'Club' to earn [his] living." Taking "rank with visiting celebrities," he puts on his heterosexual mask: "[A]mong my admirers were several of the best-looking women who frequented the place," one of whom was "the widow" (122).

When a male friend warns that the widow's "black companion" is a "bad man," Ex–Coloured Man rationalizes his sexual attraction to the widow as "native gallantry and delicacy" that "would not allow [him] to repulse her." The "finer feelings" that he claims "overcame [his] judgment" are a purposeful misreading of the situation of intrigue he has constructed by inserting himself into an erotic triangle with the widow and the "surly black despot who held sway over her deepest emotions" (123). On the surface, the reader is made to think that the black companion kills the widow because of the homosocial rivalry between himself and Ex–Coloured Man.

Because of Ex–Coloured Man's earlier rhetorical omission about the "social [read sexual] phenomena" in the Club and his understatement of his own motives concerning the widow, it is quite possible that the widow, who is in the company of a woman when Ex–Coloured Man joins her that fateful evening, is engaging in a bit of homosocial bonding herself. Perhaps Ex–Coloured Man and the black companion were conscious or unwitting foils for her *homosexual* desire. And, perhaps, Ex–Coloured Man was attempting to use the widow as a foil for his own homosexual proclivities for the "surly black despot."

The images of "the jet of blood pulsing from" her "beautiful white throat" coupled with the "indelible red stain on my memory" suggest both a male and a female castration as the consequence of transgressive sexuality, even in a space like the Club, disruptive as it already is of patriarchal codes (125). In any event, this scene of naked violence propels

Ex–Coloured Man's escape from, and rejection of, the "ritual ground" of the Club into the arms of Mammon and European culture (Stepto 122).

The father-figure transference, suggested by Stepto, is implied in Ex–Coloured Man's ultimate rejection of his white benefactor's patronage (ch. 9), though neither Ex–Coloured Man nor Johnson explicitly connects this rejection to the earlier scene at the opera in which Ex–Coloured Man sees but is not recognized by his white father. After being remade into a "polished man of the world," Ex–Coloured Man, determined to become a race man, leaves Europe and his homosocial liaison to set out on his second sojourn South, "to live among the people, to drink in [his] inspiration firsthand" (143, 142). He receives money and a cautionary farewell from his benefactor, who shows him "the first physical expression of tender regard" (144). This dissembling statement reveals Johnson's inversions of the master-slave relationship, father-figure transference, and heterosexual concubinage. Ex–Coloured Man books his passage back to the United States, but still "drunk with the wine" of Mammon, he is mainly interested in the commodification of black culture, not in an authentic quest for blackness.

RACE, SEX, AND PATRIARCHAL CODES

Aboard the ship back to the United States, Ex–Coloured Man uses the pronoun *we* to impress his racial affiliation on the "gigantic," "well-dressed," "distinguished" black doctor, another object of Ex–Coloured Man's numerous homosocial interludes. Chapter 10, more than any other in the novel, shows Ex–Coloured Man's passing strategies on both sides of the veil. Increasingly aware of his ambiguous appearance, Ex–Coloured Man passes as white on the train to Macon, Georgia, in a car with four white patriarchs whom he overhears pontificating on the "Negro question" (158). Each expresses a decidedly divergent viewpoint. The Texas racist enunciates a major southern patriarchal code in his question to the more liberal patriarch, a Civil War veteran: "Do you want to see a mulatto South? To bring it right home to you, would you let your daughter marry a nigger?" (163).

Unable to appreciate the consequences of breaking this code in the South, Ex–Coloured Man merely reflects on "this perplexity of southern character" that dreads "racial intermixture . . . worse than small pox, leprosy or the plague" and ponders its contradictions in southern history (171). Traveling the southern interior and posing on both sides of the color line, he approaches black culture like an exoticizing white anthropologist, "trying to catch the spirit of the Negro in his relatively primitive state" (173). Unlike the Club, the South has a disruptive space of sameness only in the segregated site of the "big meeting," where a more primal and authenticating sacred black culture thrives. In the ritual of the big meeting, Ex–Coloured Man witnesses the powerful preaching of John Brown and a "wonderful leader of singing, who was known as 'Singing Johnson' "—two "black and unknown bards" and exponents of black folk culture (174). The scene mirrors one at the Club (ch. 6), where Ex–Coloured Man first sees "a young fellow singing a song, accompanied on the piano by a thickset, dark man" playing ragtime (98). In the detailed commentary on the big meeting—and in the earlier narrative on ragtime and the cakewalk (ch. 5)—the satire ruptures; through Ex–Coloured Man, Johnson provides a critical reading of what Stepto cites as "the 'sacred' bond of Afro-America's music and its tribal integrity" (122), even as Ex–Coloured Man misreads the tribal integrity as "crude," "vulgar," and "primitive" (99, 173).

Circumscribing the ritual ground of the big meeting are white supremacist patriarchal codes, which have historically inscribed black people as sexually depraved and manipulated their sexual speech. Unlike the bonding in the exclusive male homosocial space of the gambling house and in the sexually illicit space of the Club, the bonding in this space of racial sameness is heterosexual and contained within the veil, where "much rustic courting . . . is indulged in" (174).

Inspired by the big meeting, Ex–Coloured Man is "anxious to get some place" where he can "settle down to work, and give expression to the ideas which were teeming in [his] head" (182). Once again, however, he follows the "homosocial destination of his desire" (Sedgwick 56) and accepts an invitation from a young male teacher he has met at the meeting on its closing Sunday. The two drive back to the town where the teacher, who is very much a race man, works. The young man has been educated at a Negro college and even knows Ex–Coloured Man's boyhood friend Shiny. Typically, Ex–Coloured Man asserts his facility at misreading yet another signifier of racial (and, perhaps, sexual) knowledge. He perceives that the young man is "too much in earnest over the race question" (183).

Ex–Coloured Man expresses a rather dismissive attitude toward racial progress—unlike "the majority of intelligent coloured people"— because of his ability to be taken for white on both sides of the veil. His antidote for the "overserious" among what Dubois calls the "talented tenth" is "a slight exercise of humor" that "save[s] much anxiety of soul" (183).[4]

The self-authenticating, "overserious" schoolteacher is an object of Ex–Coloured Man's homosocial desire. If we extend Stepto's argument about ritual spaces (i.e., the Club and the southern interior, DuBois's

"Black Belt" [*Souls* 91–110], Washington's Tuskegee) to ritual people (i.e., the ragtime players, Singing Johnson, the preacher John Brown), the schoolteacher could potentially teach Ex–Coloured Man as much about race as any of the other three could. Presumably, Ex–Coloured Man accepts the teacher's invitation because of this potential. But viewed in the context of Ex–Coloured Man's numerous experiences of male bonding—outnumbering similar experiences with women—his surface racial attraction is a cover for his unacknowledged sexual preference. Ex–Coloured Man promises to spend the night and to visit the young man's school the next day.

The tranquil scene of the schoolteacher asleep in bed and Ex–Coloured Man in the same room, "poring over" his notes and "jotting down" (184) ideas is soon disrupted by the encroaching hoofbeats of white supremacy. Paying no more heed to the schoolteacher, who pleads with him not to go out, than he paid to his friend in the Club who warned him not to rouse the ire of the widow's surly black companion, Ex–Coloured Man follows the mob: "Perhaps what bravery I exercised in going out was due to the fact that I felt sure my identity as a coloured man had not yet become known in the town" (185).

Ex–Coloured Man's nightmarish description of the lynching of the black man is bereft of any connection to the victim's humanity. The reader must wonder whether Ex–Coloured Man sees the "degeneracy" of the victim as cause or outcome of the lynching. Though he seems to feel some discomfort at the sight of the victim's "eyes bulging from their sockets . . . appealing in vain for help," he is more grimly and gruesomely reminded of his own black maleness and what it could mean (187). In fleeing the southern interior, as he fled Jacksonville (ch. 7) and as he fled the Club, Ex–Coloured Man leaves his schoolteacher friend with little ceremony. In the murder of the widow and the lynching of the black "wretch," Johnson links sex and race as transgressive awarenesses that can potentially result in destruction. The widow is murdered because she transgresses unstated racial and sexual codes; the black man is lynched for actually or presumedly transgressing the South's prohibitions against miscegenetic unions. With the first murder, which occurs in a racially mixed black ritual space, Johnson commits what McDowell sees as "a banishing act" in *Passing*, a refusal to bring homosexuality to "full narrative fruition" in the Club (160). Johnson banishes homosexuality, along with Ex–Coloured Man and his white benefactor, to Europe. The second murder occurs outside the ritual ground of the big meeting but within the circumscription of white patriarchal codes, and Johnson inscribes on his unknowing narrator the full horror of being black and being sexual outside the racial space.

Johnson's *Autobiography* is as much a narrative of illicit sexuality

(including homosexuality) as it is a revision of antecedent black narratives, a satire of the conventional slave narrator, a "fictionalized rendering of *The Souls of Black Folk*" (Baker 24), "a study of race and music
in the world of Mammon" (Stepto 122), and a confession containing
"the true discourse of sex" (Foucault 63). Ex–Coloured Man, the child
of a white southern aristocrat and a black former slave and servant,
repeatedly transgresses the color lines. The patriarchal code that is being
argued in chapter 10, from the scene on the train to the scene of the
lynching, and indeed throughout the narrative, is the prohibition against
the "intermixture of the races," the "anti-intermarriage laws," miscegenetic unions, and sexual relations between black men and white women
(171, 164). The "surly black despot" would have suffered the fate of the
"poor wretch" had he showed up in the south with the widow (186).

JOHNSON'S INDEBTEDNESS TO DOUGLASS

Johnson is as indebted to Douglass's *The Life and Times* (1892) as he
is to DuBois's *Souls* and Washington's *Up from Slavery*. In fact, *Autobiography*'s final chapter, in which Ex–Coloured Man crosses over to the
white side of the color line, is a direct parody of "Escape from Slavery,"
the final chapter of the first part of Douglass's narrative. In that dramatic
chapter, Douglass reveals for the first time how he passes as a free man,
a sailor, to escape slavery. Johnson is also indebted to Douglass for the
construction of male homosocial desire in *Autobiography*. Particularly
in *The Life and Times*, as in all his narratives, Douglass creates, constructs, and reconstructs a world of male homosocial relations. This
homosocial bonding gives him the agency to engineer his first unsuc-
cessful escape from the patriarchal bondage of slavery. In reflecting on
his feelings for his brother slaves, Henry and John Harris, who were
also involved in the failed escape, Douglass says, "[T]hey were brave,
and . . . fine-looking. . . . I never loved, esteemed, or confided in men
more than I did in these. . . . I felt a friendship as strong as one man
can feel for another, for I could have died with and for them" (153, 156).
"As strong," indeed.

The heterosocial group of free blacks and others that Douglass associated with in Baltimore formed his triumphant escape network. Within
this circle is Douglass's first wife, Anna Murray, a free woman, whose
own flight from Baltimore to Philadelphia to join and marry Douglass
receives scant mention in *The Life and Times*, as does the story of the
schoolteacher fiancée in chapter 6 in *Autobiography*. In revising the communal structure of Douglass's narrative, Johnson embeds the possibility

of homosexual desire in the conventional depiction of the male slave's homosocial world.

Ex–Coloured Man cannot authenticate himself as a race man in the New York City Club, where an underground authenticating black culture thrives, or in rural Georgia, the land of violent racism, where a "mine of [black folk] material" can be found (173). Johnson's narrator represents the political and aesthetic arguments Afro-Americans would take on more fully during the Harlem Renaissance and beyond. Yet Ex–Coloured Man fails to be either an artist or an interpreter of black culture. Blackness is not congruent with Mammonistic patriarchal codes, nor are the intermixture of the races, illicit sexuality, authentic art forms, and bohemian "lower worlds." He cannot give up the wine of materialism to live the life of the rag pianist or Singing Johnson or even his schoolteacher friend:

> I had made up my mind that since I was not going to be a Negro, I would avail myself of every possible opportunity to make a white man's success; and that, if it can be summed up in any one word, means "money." (193)

Johnson commits another banishing act in Ex–Coloured Man's final flight back to the North. He disrupts the continuum between the homosocial and the homosexual in Ex–Coloured Man's final rejection of racial and sexual ritual spaces for the pursuit of whiteness, Mammon, and obligatory heterosexuality (Sedgwick 3). At the narrative's end, Ex–Coloured Man, a father of two and a widower, states his bitter regret at having sold his "birthright for a mess of pottage" (211).

The homosocial spaces that Ex–Coloured Man moves through are a means to self-gain. Unlike Douglass's narrator, Ex–Coloured Man sustains no emotional or affectional bonds within either the homosocial or the black cultural spaces he inhabits. He is always dissociated, gazing from some other space that perpetuates his unkowing and his alienation. He gains only a surface understanding of the life he sees and the books he reads; he takes some notes, writes some scores but never goes into the mine of black culture. He develops no communal sense of the ritual spaces, no sense of their palpable history, as earlier narrators did.

The narrative strategy of inversion in *Autobiography* enables Johnson to tell the story of illicit sexuality (including sexual inversion), just as Larsen's ostensibly heterosexual plot and "safe" theme of racial passing enable her to tell a story of latent lesbian desire in *Passing*. Larsen, a more discontented member of the "talented tenth," could not talk any more openly about female homosexuality in 1929 than Johnson could talk openly about male homosexuality—latent or otherwise—in 1912 or 1927. This tradition of covert, subtextual discourse on transgressive sexuality has persisted in black narratives of all kinds. Students— whether they are black, white, gay, straight, feminist, queer, or lesbian— must read those disruptive spaces of sameness, especially when there are no narrative strategies to prevent the psychic or physical destruction of the characters who pass into them.

Rutgers University

Notes

This essay is part of a longer work on Afro-American modernism and homosexual texts that I began in Donald B. Gibson's 1991 graduate seminar Nineteenth-Century Black Autobiography at Rutgers University. I am indebted to Deborah E. McDowell's searching and daring reading of the lesbian subtext of Nella Larsen's *Passing*. Her work serves as a model for many of us trying to revise and enrich our understandings of the sexual discourse within our ancestral texts. Finally, I would like to thank George Haggerty for his generous help in editing this essay.

[1] Classifying *Sula* as a lesbian novel raised the eyebrows of the black literary community. McDowell articulates some of the problems with Smith's formulation, challenging Smith's reading as lacking precision in terms of what constitutes both a lesbian novel and black feminist criticism ("New Directions").

[2] Johnson's novel was published anonymously by the New York company Sherman, French as *The Autobiography of an Ex–Colored Man* in 1912, though Johnson had shown the first two chapters to his friend and teacher, the Columbia professor Brander Matthews, around 1905. Johnson, then thirty-four, had lived a rich and adventurous life by the time he tried his hand at fiction. In 1927, Knopf reprinted the novel under the same title but changed the spelling of *Colored* to *Coloured*. In *Along This Way*, Johnson questions the wisdom of his earlier choice to remain anonymous. The 1927 edition gives Johnson's name and includes an introduction by Carl Van Vechten, the legendary white patron of the Harlem Renaissance and the author of *Nigger Heaven*, who informs readers that the fictional *Autobiography* is not the story of Johnson's life. I quote Hill and Wang's reprint of the Knopf edition throughout.

[3] DuBois defines "Mammonism" in his revised parable, "The Wings of Atalanta," which is based on the myth of Atalanta and Hippomenes. He cautions black people against losing touch with their "spiritual strivings" in striving for the "dream of material prosperity as the touchstone of all success" (66).

[4] In "Of the Training of Black Men," DuBois provides a narrative history of the formal education of black people since the close of the Civil War. He argues for a training that goes beyond that of the industrial school, a training that would open "the outer courts of knowledge to all, display its treasures to many,

and select the few to whom the mystery of Truth is revealed" (77). This select few, this "appreciable number of Negro Youth . . . capable by character and talent to receive that higher training, the end of which is culture" (not "bread-winning"), is DuBois's "talented tenth," who would guide the "black lowly" out of the mire of ignorance (89).

Works Cited

Baker, Houston A., Jr. *Singers of Daybreak: Studies in Black American Litera-ture.* Washington: Howard UP, 1974.

Bruce, Dickson D. *Black American Writing from the Nadir: Evolution of a Literary Tradition, 1877–1915.* Baton Rouge: Louisiana State UP, 1989.

Douglass, Frederick. *The Life and Times of Frederick Douglass.* 1892. New York: Collier, 1962.

———. *Narrative of the Life of Frederick Douglass.* 1845. *The Classic Slave Narratives.* Ed. Henry Louis Gates, Jr. New York: NAL, 1987. 243–332.

DuBois, W. E. B. "Of the Training of Black Men." DuBois, *Souls* 74–90.

———. *The Souls of Black Folk.* 1903. New York: Penguin, 1989.

———. "The Wings of Atalanta." DuBois, *Souls* 63–73.

Farwell, Marilyn R. "Heterosexual Plots and Lesbian Subtexts: Toward a Theory of Lesbian Narrative Space." *Lesbian Texts and Contexts: Radical Revisions.* Ed. Karla Jay and Joanne Glasgow. New York: New York UP, 1990. 95–114.

Foucault, Michel. *An Introduction.* Trans. Robert Hurley. New York: Vintage, 1980. Vol. 1 of *A History of Sexuality.*

Johnson, James Weldon. *Along This Way.* 1933. New York: Penguin, 1990.

———. *The Autobiography of an Ex–Coloured Man.* 1912. New York: Hill, 1981.

Larsen, Nella. *Quicksand [and] Passing.* Ed. Deborah McDowell. New Bruns-wick: Rutgers UP, 1987.

McDowell, Deborah. "New Directions for Black Feminist Criticism." *Black American Literature Forum* 14 (1980): 186–99.

———. " 'That Nameless . . . Shameful Impulse': Sexuality in Nella Larsen's *Quicksand* and *Passing.*" *Black Feminist Criticism and Critical Theory.* Vol. 3 of *Studies in Black American Literature.* Ed. Joseph Weixlman and Houston Baker, Jr. Greenwood: Penkevill, 1988. 139–67.

McKeithan, Lucinda H. "Black Boy and Ex–Coloured Man: Version and Inver-sion of the Slave Narrator's Quest for Voice." *CLA Journal* 32 (1988): 123–47.

Sedgwick, Eve Kosofsky. *Between Men: English Literature and Male Homosocial Desire.* New York: Columbia UP, 1985.

Smith, Barbara. "Toward a Black Feminist Criticism." *Conditions* 1.2 (1977): 27–52.

Stepto, Robert B. *From behind the Veil.* Urbana: U of Illinois P, 1979. 95–127.

Washington, Booker T. *Up from Slavery.* 1901. New York: Penguin, 1986.

Lesbian Poetry in the United States, 1890–1990: A Brief Overview

Paula Bennett

One does not have to be a perfervid constructionist to acknowledge that, as an ontological entity, "lesbian poetry" does not exist. At best, the term represents a critical category that includes, without in any way defining, the writing of a heterogeneous group of women poets, many of whom have nothing but their presumed sexual preference—and, with respect to this essay, their nationality—in common. Is there any point, then, in speaking of lesbian poetry at all?

I believe that there is, but only if we accept sexual preference as a site for poetic invention, a locus for productive as well as reproductive play. In this essay, I describe some of the ways in which women who identify as lesbians, or who have been identified as lesbians by scholars, have exploited possibilities related to their preference in their verse. For the poets I discuss, physical attraction to members of their own sex has, in one way or another, been a significant, indeed, an enriching, element in their writing. But, like any quality, it is also only one of many. In stressing differences as well as similarities among these poets, I hope to demonstrate just how various and flexible the category "lesbian poetry" is and must be. (On attempts to define lesbian literature and the lesbian narrative, see the essays of Faderman and Farwell, respectively, in this volume.)

From Aristotle, who as a scientist came by the notion legitimately enough, we inherit a biological concept of inherent natural forms in art—a tendency to define artistic genres in ontological terms (tragedy "is," etc.). But, as E. H. Gombrich has demonstrated, the shape that style and form take in art has far more to do with changes in convention (or, dread word, fashion) than it does with the fulfillment of innate essential characteristics. However important a poet's sexual preference may be to her as an individual, or as a writer, the way in which she writes, as well as what she writes, is determined by the historical and cultural moment in which she comes, as an artist, to be. A "lesbian" poem written in the 1990s is, therefore, likely to have more in common formally and even thematically with a poem written by a heterosexual male contemporary than it will with a poem written by a lesbian living a hundred years before.

What is true of artistic style is true of "lifestyle" as well. Our conception—or construction—of ourselves as lesbians is subject to the same temporal and cultural constraints. Even if lesbianism existed, as indeed it did, before the invention of homosexuality, artifacts such as Anne Lister's diary make clear that earlier lesbians did not and could not see themselves as we see ourselves today. Too much history has passed; too many cultural and psychological changes have occurred. The need to create separation between the generations—for each generation to make its mark in its own way—is too great. One has only to look at the controversy swirling around the definition of the butch-femme couple before 1969 and after 1980 to see what I mean.

Because of these factors, we should not be surprised that the poetry lesbians have produced is as various as the women are who have written it, particularly when one adds in differences created by race, class, ethnicity, and a woman's positioning of herself with respect to the sexual mores of her group and day. But before I discuss these differences, what, if anything, can be said of lesbian poetry generally as it has come down to us over the past hundred years?

Aside from the fact that lesbian poetry exists at all, the most striking feature of the genre in the United States is the extraordinary number of "major" voices included within this category. With only a few exceptions (I think immediately of Marianne Moore, Gwendolyn Brooks, Sylvia Plath, and Anne Sexton), to list lesbian or bisexual American women poets is to provide a roll call of the most influential women poets of the last century, together with many others who, although less well-known outside feminist circles, have helped make American women's poetry what it is: Emily Dickinson, Amy Lowell, Gertrude Stein, HD, Alice Dunbar-Nelson, Angelina Weld Grimké, Elizabeth Bishop, Muriel Rukeyser, May Swenson, Adrienne Rich, Audre Lorde, Judy Grahn, Susan Griffin, June Jordan, Irena Klepfisz, Olga Broumas, Cherríe Moraga, Robin Morgan, Pat Parker, Paula Gunn Allen, Gloria Anzaldúa, and Kitty Tsui, to name only a few.

The significance of this list becomes apparent when one realizes that one cannot draw up a similar list for lesbian novelists. Again, with a few exceptions (most obviously, Djuna Barnes and Willa Cather), the major voices in American women's fiction have historically been straight, and our new openness has, to date, not changed this fact.[1] Poetry is the literary genre in which lesbian writers have flourished and to which they have contributed the most. Indeed, I would argue that where lesbian novelists have been at their strongest (as in Barnes, Virginia Woolf, and Monique Wittig), they have also written something closer to poetry than prose. I would put a number of recent prose-poet theorists into this ambiguous category as well, together with those poets who also tried their hands at fiction—Stein, HD, and Lorde, in particular.

And ambiguity may well be the key to why poetry, including prose poetry, has traditionally proved so much more amicable to lesbian writers than has prose. As Rachel Blau DuPlessis has argued, novelists— that is, prose fiction writers—must either work with, or find subversive ways around, the ineluctable drive of the marriage plot that has historically dominated the novel as a genre, a plot that institutionalizes heterosexuality in fiction in the form of the "happy ending" (21). In the well-known phrasing of one of the most famous female capitulations in literature: "Reader, I married him."

But the lyric voice of the lesbian poet has never been so bound. From the time of Sappho on, the "master" narrative that dictates heterosexuality has existed outside the poet's lyric world and does not have to be brought explicitly into it. Not only is the lyric poet free to devote her poems to many things beside romance but also, when writing love poetry, neither the speaker nor the object of her affections need be specifically gendered. And in this ambiguity lies the possibility of freedom, freedom that poets writing before 1969 could—and did—exploit. It is, I believe, this freedom, combined with the thematic flexibility poetry offers, that has made it, rather than fiction, the rich resource for lesbian writers that a brief survey of American poetry written by lesbians over the past century proves it to be.

For the purposes of this overview, I divide the history of lesbian poetry in the United States into four basic periods: early modernism as exemplified in the romantic lyrics of Lowell, Grimké, Elsa Gidlow, and in her own way, HD; modernist poetry proper, as in the writing of Stein, Bishop, Swenson, and Rukeyser; the poetry of identity politics, the dominant poetry of the 1970s, which is characterized by its articulation of a lesbian-feminist position; and finally, the poetry of our own poststructuralist, postfeminist era, a period of what I would call creative stock taking and diversification. Limitations of space make it impossible for me to do more than sketch the salient characteristics defining the poetry of each period. By establishing this framework, however, I hope to facilitate future studies of lesbian poetry that will give the differences as well as the similarities among these writers their full due.

THE EARLY MODERNIST ROMANTIC LYRIC

Despite Lowell's disclaimer in "Sisters," the first readily identifiable lesbian poetry in the United States emerged directly from nineteenth-century women's poetic traditions (Bennett 150–84). Far from repressing their sexual desires or, even more improbable, living in utter ignorance of them, nineteenth-century American women dwelt on the issue of sexual passion obsessively in their writing (as, indeed, Foucault might have predicted). And, however "sentimental" or conventional the terms they used, as often as not, they owned what they felt. From this women's tradition, which stretches from Maria Gowen Brooks to Lizette Wood-worth Reese and which, like so much romantic poetry in the West, employs imagery drawn in equal parts from Sappho and the Bible (the Song of Songs), came the erotic lyrics not only of Dickinson but also of a number of other lesbian poets writing just before or after the turn of the century.

In the hands of poets such as Lowell, Grimké, and HD, this imagery, usually based in nature and conventionally "romantic" in every respect, made possible the articulation of a richly nuanced lesbian, woman-centered sexual subjectivity. Despite the disparateness of these poets' lives (one a Brahmin, known for her cigar smoking; one an isolated and closeted member of the Harlem Renaissance; the last a bisexual torn between worlds), each woman was able to use the erotic tradition of her female precursors to give vivid expression to her own sense of lesbian agency and desire. Each had, in effect, been bequeathed a "language of love" by the poets who had gone before, and because of the ambiguity of poetic reference, each was able to turn this language to her own less socially acceptable ends. Here, for example, are the opening lines from Lowell's "The Weather-Cock Points South":

> I put your leaves aside,
> One by one:
> The stiff, broad outer leaves;
> The smaller ones,
> Pleasant to touch, veined with purple;
> The glazed inner leaves.
> One by one
> I parted you from your leaves,

Until you stood up like a white flower
Swaying slightly in the evening wind.
                    (211)

And here is the first stanza of Grimké's "A Mona Lisa," a poem whose
lesbianism has been established on biographical grounds by Gloria Hull
(140–41):

I should like to creep
Through the long brown grasses
    That are your lashes;
I should like to poise
    On the very brink
Of the leaf-brown pools
    That are your shadowed eyes;
I should like to cleave
    Without sound,
Their glimmering waters,
    Their unrippled waters;
I should like to sink down
    And down
        And down . . .
            And deeply drown.
                    (Honey 147)

In both these poems, the authors have used the familiar but highly
erotic female sexual imagery of natural objects, of flowers, grasses, and
water, of colors and intoxicating sensations, to express not the love of
man for woman or of woman for man but the love of one woman for
another. They have been able to do so by leaving the sex of their speakers
unspecified, thus carving out, as it were, a lesbian space. In this space,
the excess of lesbian love, its intensity and physical vigor, as well as
its strong sense of agency and subjecthood, can be delineated, precisely
because the authors place themselves, however equivocally, in the traditional "male" role: the role of he who speaks, who desires, who drowns.
It is only by resituating these poems within their authors' biographies
that we can understand them for the powerful articulations of lesbian
sexuality they are. Their imagery may be conventional, but it is lesbianism that made these poems possible, just as it is lesbianism that
motivates and accounts for the profoundly woman-centered revision of
the classical erotic tradition in HD's far more extensive and complex

(yet in some ways, surprisingly similar) work (Grahn, *Highest Apple* 27–29, 60–62, 102–09; Laity; Gregory).

MODERNIST POETRY

With the triumph of modernism between 1910 and 1930, the richly articulated discourse, or language, of love that I have just described was lost. Whatever else modernism was, it represented the rejection of presumably hackneyed and outmoded nineteenth-century poetic conventions, conventions that were labeled not just sentimental but effeminate by such authorities as Ezra Pound and T. E. Hulme (Gilbert and Gubar 154). No conventions came under greater attack than did those used by nineteenth-century women to express desire.

As Joanne Feit Diehl has demonstrated through her brilliant analysis of Moore's drafts for "Octopus," modernist aesthetics encouraged women poets to eliminate from their texts not just the sentimental but also, with it, the personal and the explicitly sexual (71–90). What was true of Moore was, I believe, true of poets such as Stein and Bishop as well. It was less the unacceptability of their sexual preference that led these poets to obscure their sexuality in their writing than it was their fear of being seen as "poetesses" in the nineteenth-century vein. Succinctly, if they wished to be poets of their time, they had to separate themselves not just from their female precursors but also from the language these writers used. Since women's sexuality had traditionally been figured in this language in Western literature, women modernists had two choices: they could eliminate sexuality from the writing they published, as Moore and Bishop did, or, like Stein, they could invent new, if frequently obscure, ways in which to express desire. In its playful if distanced approach to its subject (the love between Stein and Alice B. Toklas), Stein's "Lifting Belly" is a delicious example:

> Lifting belly sings nicely.
> Not nervously.
> No not nervously.
> Nicely and forcefully.
> Lifting belly is so sweet.
> Can you say you say.
> In this thought.
> I do think lifting belly.
> Little love lifting.
> Little love light.

> Little love heavy.
> Lifting belly tight.
> (Grahn, *Really Reading* 190)

This situation does not mean, however, that lesbianism ceased in other respects to influence the poetry of lesbian modernist writers. On the contrary, as the burgeoning "science" of sexology was increasingly rendering lesbianism a pathological subject position, lesbian poets may well have been drawn to modernist doctrines and rhetorical strategies that could help them articulate their growing alienation from society and their disillusionment with the patriarchal order. (In psychoanalytic terms, of course, modernism also gave these poets a way to separate themselves from their nineteenth-century poetic "foremothers.")[2]

Thus, for example, Grahn has argued eloquently that lesbianism was fundamental to Stein's entire achievement. According to Grahn, Stein's dismantling of the hierarchies of grammar and plot made room for a completely new—and thoroughly lesbian—way of writing, not because Stein celebrates her lesbianism explicitly in her content but because she enacts it in the most basic elements of her verse:

> By unifying the internal and the external viewpoints, and by assigning equal value to each component of her work, each letter of the word, each word of the sentence, each image being described, Stein enabled a nonlinear, democratic and powerfully female landscape of the mind; she literally dis-enchanted the mythic "sleep" ... of Western patriarchal literature, and she did this primarily through her approach to language.   (*Highest Apple* 69–70)

Grahn believes that by "[l]ooking at the outside from the inside and at the inside from the outside, Stein fulfilled her function of Lesbian poet to the highest degree" (*Highest Apple* 67).

What is true of Stein is also true of Bishop, in spite of their stylistic differences. Like Stein, Bishop wrote consistently from the position of one who was marginalized, on the "outside" looking in, on the "inside" looking out. Like Stein, although with a good deal more subtlety, Bishop set herself against a dominant Western poetic tradition that she gendered male (cf. Stein's "Patriarchal Poetry" and Bishop's "The End of March").[3] For both, their sense of personal, sexual, and social alienation, symbolized and made manifest by their expatriate status, was their point of sympathetic entrée into modernist aesthetics. But for both, the potential of these alienated aesthetics to sustain a protofeminist "political" position, whether in opposition to women's oppression (Stein's "The Mother of Us All") or in relation to their own eccentric position as lesbians and women poets (Bishop's "Pink Dog"), allowed them to make modernism distinctively their own. As Bishop says of her protagonist in "Crusoe in England," neither poet was at home on an island were people drank only "real tea" (166).

THE POETRY OF IDENTITY POLITICS

If modernism represented a rejection of nineteenth-century romantic or sentimental conventions, the highly politicized poetry written to accompany the liberation movements of the 1970s represented a rejection of modernism and its academic explicator, the New Criticism. In insisting that their writing was explicitly political, minority poets of this period were not only attempting to define what was unique and valuable in themselves outside the dominant structures of their culture (one of the most imperative tasks of this era). They also wanted to flush out the hidden politics of what had gone before, to demonstrate that modernism, in its misogyny, elitism, and erasure of alternative and competing voices, was no less "political" or personal than any other kind of writing was, despite its explicators' claims to the high ground of "universal" and objectively practiced nonsentimental art.

These poets (including lesbian poets) wished, in fact, to make their poetry everything modernist poetry was not: not just overtly political but also direct, personal, openly emotional, and above all, accessible. One of the primary reasons so much poetry was produced in these years was that poets, waving before them the banner of Walt Whitman—or that of the black activists and Vietnam protesters—had gone into the streets. Poetry, of all things, had become a grassroots movement, and to feminists, the words of poets like Grahn, Brown, Rich, and Lorde—appearing on posters, T-shirts, and broadsides, as well as in books—became the revolutionary shibboleths of a new and politically aroused generation. Having been engaged in writing and editing poetry myself in this period, I can only say that it was a heady time. The exhilaration it produced is, in my opinion, one of the most striking features of the poetry that appeared, poetry such as Brown's ringing call to battle in "Sappho's Reply":

> My voice rings down through thousands of years
>
> . . . .
> An army of lovers shall not fail.
> (Bulkin and Larkin 136)

or the marvelously gothic and defiant conclusion of Grahn's "A Woman Is Talking to Death":

> wherever our meat hangs on our bones
> for our own use
> your pot is so empty
> death, oh death
> you shall be poor
>   (Bulkin and Larkin 80)

There was or, as it turned out, there seemed to be nothing off-limits to lesbian poets at this time, not their sexuality, not their outrage, not their dreams. In the brief span of ten or fifteen years—between the publication, say, of Grahn's "Common Woman" poems in 1969 and Elly Bulkin and Joan Larkin's *Lesbian Poetry: An Anthology* in 1981— the history of lesbian poetry in the United States was completely rewritten. No longer hiding in the shadows of ambiguity or isolated by their alienation, lesbian poets had become the voices of a powerful and seemingly undauntable social movement that would reform not just the relationship between women and men but also the entire social and political fabric of the United States. As the title of Rich's eighth book, *The Dream of a Common Language,* indicates, these poets were determined to reform language and culture at once.

The names of the poets included in the Bulkin and Larkin anthology and printed, appropriately enough, on its cover, tell the story: Gloria Anzaldúa, Sharon Barba, Robin Becker, Julie Blackwomon, Alice Bloch, Joyce Kim, Irena Klepfisz, Ana Kowalkowska, Audre Lorde, Honor Moore, Cherríe Moraga, and so on. Despite the differences of race, class, ethnicity, and religion that divided these poets, lesbian feminism seemed, however momentarily, to have brought them together under one roof in the service of one cause, the cause, they believed, of women everywhere. As later events made clear, this sense of unity in purpose was illusory, but it was an illusion that made the lesbian-feminist revolution in poetry one of the most productive and exciting periods in the history of American women's literature.

POSTSTRUCTURALIST, POST-LESBIAN-FEMINIST POETRY

The division between pre- and post-1980s lesbian poetry that I have made here is probably more evident on a theoretical level than it is on a practical level at this time. I believe, however, that developments occurring in theory, especially poststructuralist and postfeminist theory, are in the process of affecting lesbian poetry as well—as, indeed, they inevitably must. Three important areas are the increasing emphasis on difference, the conflicts over sexuality, and the possible shift from pure poetry to poetically heightened prose.

As I have noted, it did not take long for lesbian feminism's claim to commonality to prove itself vulnerable to the multitude of differences that in fact separate one lesbian from another. These differences are increasingly reflected not just in the way we think about ourselves but also in the poetry we write. Thus, for example, lesbian poets writing today are as (if not more) likely to write about their ethnic, racial, or class differences as they are to dwell on the joys—or politics—of lesbian love. Indeed, since the early 1980s there has been an inundation of anthologies and journal issues devoted exclusively to the work of lesbians from various ethnic, racial, and religious minorities: Native American, Latina, African American, Italian, Jewish, and so forth, all reflecting the growing multicultural awareness of the culture at large and the need to situate oneself in complex interacting and sometimes competing subject positions (Martin and Mohanty). While this literature is in some sense the logical outcome of the 1970s insistence on respecting the rights and needs of the "other," it also points to the end of Rich's—and lesbian feminism's—"common" dream.[4]

If ethnic, racial, and class differences divide us, sexual differences do as well. Lesbian sexuality is now the site of contending discourses, as sexual minorities who believed themselves to have been disenfranchised by lesbian feminism's drive toward a politically correct notion of mutual "woman-identified" sex now give voice to their "unacceptable" desires (Nestle). No better measure of the distance that separates many lesbians today from their precursors—not just Lowell but also Rich—can be found than Pat Califia's remarkable "Gender Fuck Gender," from which I quote the following stanza:

> On your belly,
> You make me hurt to have a cock,
> To wrap my arms around
> Your boy-slender waist,
> Bite into the cords of muscle
> That bind your broad shoulders.
> I want to cover the grapefruit-curved
> Cheeks of your ass
> With my broader hips
> And take you

> Up the ass,
> Cockhead against the tight sphincter
> Until my words in your ear,
> Whispered but sharp as spears,
> Opens it up
> To the shove and thrust and hump.
>
> (1)

If, as Califia might argue, a lesbian-feminist journal such as *Conditions* would not have published this poem in 1976, the year in which *Conditions* first appeared, it is just as unlikely that Califia would have written it then.[5] Yet while "Gender Fuck Gender" is a superb example of "lesbian" poetry, not every lesbian will—or should feel obliged to—relate to it. As Eve Kosofsky Sedgwick observes in the introduction to *Epistemology of the Closet*, where sex is concerned, nothing is axiomatic (22–27). In a way that recalls the poems by Lowell and Stein already cited or even Rich's famous "floating poem," Califia's poem is a product of her engagement with her time, her period, and the rhetorical strategies available to her (that is, the poetry of gay—and straight—men). That her poem will not appeal to many readers is part of what makes it so completely a poem for today. In its self-imposed limitedness, Califia's poem shows where we are in our relation to difference and in our understanding of the enormous complexity and diversity of our sexual lives as well as of "lesbianism" itself.

"Gender Fuck Gender" was the leadoff poem in the final issue of *Conditions*, and the death of this prestigious literary journal may mark the end of the literary revolution that lesbian feminism inspired as well. Whether poetry will cease to be the premier genre through which lesbian sensibility finds literary expression in the United States is more difficult to say. Certainly, among women writers generally, some of the most ardent and richly complex voices writing today seem to be gravitating toward the prose poetry of the poststructuralist novel and poststructuralist theory. I think, for example, not only of Toni Morrison, Maxine Hong Kingston, and Leslie Marmon Silko but also of writers such as Hélène Cixous, Luce Irigaray, and Monique Wittig. As the poetry of Nicole Brossard, Michelle Cliff, and Jeffner Allen indicates, lesbian poets will generally follow suit, using the rhetorical strategies available to them, as they always have, to reenvision or refashion themselves in new and challenging ways, ways that both reflect and help shape the times in which they live.

So the story "ends" here: not with a conclusion but with a set of possibilities, for lesbianism and poetry both are sites for invention. They are loci where we produce and reproduce ourselves in ever-changing forms that mirror, and help bring to pass, transformations in the culture at large as it constructs, deconstructs, and reconstructs the values, dreams, and conventions by which we live. By which we write.

Southern Illinois University, Carbondale

Notes

[1] The roll call of lesbian novelists cited on the flyleaf of Zimmerman's *Safe Sea of Women* (Rita Mae Brown, Monique Wittig, Kate Millett, June Arnold, Jane Rule, Bertha Harris, Sally Gearhart, Paula Gunn Allen, Camarin Grae, and Audre Lorde) is instructive here. Of these novelists, the five who have been the most influential also best qualify either as poets or as prose poets (Wittig, Millett, Harris, Allen, and Lorde), while the remaining five, however solid their virtues, are not major players in contemporary women's fiction.

[2] In a recent study of early modernist women poets, Walker argues that a Bloomian pattern of generational conflict between women poets has been unduly ignored in feminist criticism (19–22). I agree, but instead of using Bloom's Oedipal pattern, which privileges male experience, I prefer to frame women poets' need to reject their precursors as an adolescent drive to separate from parents, a drive that afflicts sons and daughters alike.

[3] Here, as throughout this paragraph, I am deeply indebted to Diehl's discussion of Bishop (91–110).

[4] The recent agonized defense of the sobriquet *common* by the editorial collective of the lesbian-feminist journal *Common Lives/Lesbian Lives* is one example.

[5] Ironically, the deconstructive, poststructuralist approach I use in this essay is itself an example of this phenomenon. As Gombrich observes, the way we organize experience is a direct function of the culturally inherited categories we employ (320–29). These categories are themselves subject to constant revision. See, for example, Carruthers's different thematic approach to lesbian poetry.

Works Cited

Bennett, Paula. *Emily Dickinson: Woman Poet.* Iowa City: U of Iowa P, 1990.

Bishop, Elizabeth. *The Complete Poems: 1927–1979.* New York: Farrar, 1984.

Bulkin, Elly, and Joan Larkin, eds. *Lesbian Poetry: An Anthology.* Watertown: Persephone, 1981.

Califia, Pat. "Gender Fuck Gender." *Conditions* 17 (1990): 1–3.

Carruthers, Mary J. "The Re-vision of the Muse: Adrienne Rich, Audre Lorde, Judy Grahn, Olga Broumas." *Hudson Review* 36 (1983): 293–322.

Diehl, Joanne Feit. *Women Poets and the American Sublime.* Bloomington: Indiana UP, 1990.

DuPlessis, Rachel Blau. *Writing beyond the Ending: Narrative Strategies of Twentieth-Century Women Writers.* Bloomington: Indiana UP, 1985.

Friedman, Susan Stanford, and Rachel Blau DuPlessis, eds. *Signets: Reading H.D.* Madison: U of Wisconsin P, 1990.

Gilbert, Sandra M., and Susan Gubar. *No Man's Land: The Place of the Woman Writer in the Twentieth Century*. Vol. 1. New Haven: Yale UP, 1988.

Gombrich, E. H. *Art and Illusion: A Study in the Psychology of Pictorial Representation*. New York: Pantheon, 1961.

Grahn, Judy. *The Highest Apple: Sappho and the Lesbian Poetic Tradition*. San Francisco: Spinsters, 1985.

———. *Really Reading Gertrude Stein: A Selected Anthology with Essays by Judy Grahn*. Freedom: Crossing, 1989.

———. *The Work of a Common Woman: The Collected Poetry of Judy Grahn, 1964–1977*. New York: St. Martin's, 1978.

Gregory, Ellen. "Rose Cut in Rock: Sappho and H.D.'s Sea Garden." Friedman and DuPlessis 129–54.

Honey, Maureen, ed. *Shadowed Dreams: Women's Poetry of the Harlem Renaissance*. New Brunswick: Rutgers UP, 1989.

Hull, Gloria T. *Color, Sex, and Poetry: Three Women Writers of the Harlem Renaissance*. Bloomington: Indiana UP, 1987.

Laity, Cassandra. "H.D.'s Romantic Landscapes: The Sexual Politics of the Garden." Friedman and DuPlessis 110–28.

Lister, Anne. *I Know My Own Heart: The Diaries of Anne Lister (1791–1840)*. Ed. Helena Whitbread. London: Virago, 1988.

Lowell, Amy. *The Complete Poetical Works of Amy Lowell*. Boston: Houghton, n.d.

Martin, Biddy, and Chandra Talpade Mohanty. "Feminist Politics: What's Home Got to Do with It?" *Feminist Studies/Critical Studies*. Ed. Teresa de Lauretis. Bloomington: Indiana UP, 1986. 191–212.

Nestle, Joan. "The Fem Question." *Pleasure and Danger: Exploring Female Sexuality*. Ed. Carole S. Vance. London: Pandora, 1989. 232–41.

Rich, Adrienne. *The Dream of a Common Language: Poems 1974–77*. New York: Norton, 1978.

Sedgwick, Eve Kosofsky. *Epistemology of the Closet*. Berkeley: U of California P, 1990.

Stein, Gertrude. "The Mother of Us All." *Last Operas and Plays*. New York: Rinehart, 1949. 52–88.

———. "Patriarchal Poetry." *Bee Time Vine and Other Pieces*. Freeport: Books for Libraries, 1969. 249–94.

Walker, Cheryl. *Masks Outrageous and Austere: Culture, Psyche, and Persona in Modern Women Poets*. Bloomington: U of Indiana P, 1991.

Zimmerman, Bonnie. *The Safe Sea of Women: Lesbian Fiction 1969–1989*. Boston: Beacon, 1990.

PART 3

Sameness and Differences

Teaching Differences: Theory and Practice in a Lesbian and Gay Studies Seminar

David Román

The current institutional interest in lesbian and gay studies has created many exciting challenges for teachers in the field. We need to establish curricula that acknowledge the diversity of our scholarship and to question the efficacy of such scholarship as a political praxis for lesbian and gay people both inside and outside the academy. Along with the need to incorporate scholarship that focuses on lesbian and gay issues in traditional courses and disciplines comes the more difficult question facing lesbian and gay studies at large: how to formulate an interdisciplinary field within the academy. In brief, just what is it that we propose to teach in lesbian and gay studies classes? Luckily for all of us, the current wave of lesbian and gay studies is not only reaching across disciplines but also establishing a continually growing network of practitioners within these fields who are concerned with this very question of curriculum and classroom practice. While the rather recent emergence of professional mechanisms of legitimacy for lesbian and gay studies (research institutions, conferences, publications, hirings) continues to inform, and in some ways even to determine, the curricula of our courses, we cannot overlook the need to develop pedagogical strategies that account for the various differences among us.[1]

It is essential to this process, of course, for us to develop methods of interrogating the various theories, scripts, and performances of sexuality that postulate and problematize a lesbian or gay identity. Such a project must take seriously into account the subject positions that we bring into our classrooms both through our syllabi and through our own position(s). The challenge does not end there, however; further work must focus on exploring the ramifications of teaching differences, particularly in relation to the experiences of people of color. Finally, we need to explicate more completely the overall contribution our work holds for those outside our classrooms and professional organizations so that we may initiate and expand the possibilities of personal and political representations.

THEORY, SCRIPTS, PERFORMANCE

In 1991, I taught a lesbian and gay studies seminar at Pomona College to a group of lesbian and gay students.[2] My main interest in the class was to contextualize the notion of a lesbian and gay identity by examining both representations of, and performances by, lesbians and gays in the late twentieth century, primarily in the United States. I also wanted to introduce my students to the theoretical implications of such a project. Overall, my goal throughout the semester was to offer my students a means by which they might interrogate their own subject positions as gays and lesbians and take an active, self-determining role in fashioning their own identities. Our semester readings were drawn from the recent interdisciplinary publications in lesbian and gay studies. The course was loosely structured around various current critical issues within lesbian and gay communities, although the three main areas of investigation were representations and performances of lesbian and gay experience, sexuality, and the vexed relation between theory and practice.

Early in the semester, I raised several questions about representation and its relation to lesbian and gay identities and communities. How, and for what purpose, has the relatively modern notion of homosexuality been scripted by dominant discourses in our society? How have lesbians and gay men responded to such scripts? Where are the moments of resistance, acceptance, negotiation? How are these scripts represented in mainstream and in lesbian and gay venues? Related to this mode of questioning is the idea of performance, of how lesbians and gay men fashion an identity based on sexual orientation. I wanted us to consider the ramifications of lesbian and gay performances—ranging from gay rights tactics to mainstream commodification of gay codes—and to question whether seemingly self-determining performances rupture scripts or, rather, reinscribe them. Thus, for example, we read Sue-Ellen Case's classic study of butch-femme roles and lesbian agency, "Toward a Butch-Femme Aesthetic," to enable students to postulate at once how one dominant cultural script (heterosexism) solicited a related script (butch-femme) and how that same social performance of a butch-femme aesthetic can be read as a political intervention within heterosexist ideology.

The two-week theoretical unit with which the course began established some of the methodologies of the inquiry that we would practice throughout the semester. We read selections from Eve Kosofsky Sedgwick, David Halperin, Judith Butler, and Sue-Ellen Case to establish an analytical base for our semester readings and to set up a critical matrix to hold our discussions. These readings also initiated an unsettled classroom debate that rages, sometimes vehemently, inside and outside the academy, about the political implications of reading "high theory." My students were suspicious of the sometimes "inaccessible" academic writing, questioning its utility outside the classroom and my own investment in explicating the texts. If it takes a PhD to read some of these critics, they wondered, what practical purposes do the texts serve for lesbian and gay people who are not academics? Were they as students being indoctrinated into a critical language that sets them apart because of their privileged access to higher education? In other words, the politics of theory seemed only to duplicate the hegemonic power structures that alienate the disenfranchised. Still, these were not the only responses. Students found useful Halperin's overview of the debates between essentialists and social constructivists; Sedgwick's analysis of the closet as an ideological apparatus that perpetuates certain binarisms about sexuality, politics, and ways of seeing; Butler's contention that gender and sexuality are "sustained social performances" (141); and Case's articulation of a butch-femme aesthetic. Yet these readings set the tone of the class: the interrogation of lesbian and gay identities involved the interrogation of the very means of our inquiry. Lesbian and gay studies classes not only need to teach the debates within the discipline but also must be held accountable for the implications of these debates.

To respond to the "high theory" section of the class, we examined some lesbian and gay lived experiences (what the students quickly identified as practical or "low theory") documented in oral history projects, folklore studies, and independent films. Our discussions followed the call-and-response mode of analyzing dialogue between seemingly divergent fields of subject positions, theoretical methodologies, and political positions. In other words, we read "high theory" in relation to "low theory" to establish the lapses as well as the interstices within various lesbian and gay articulations of identity. What happens, for instance, when one considers differences related to the construction of a self-identity that are drawn from, say, ethnicity, race, gender, class, or spiritual expression? By weighing the implications of such self-fashioning, which is based on a diverse field of difference, we were able to recognize the fluidity of self-constructions, thus questioning the entire phenomenon of historically determined forms of self-presence that are based only on marks of sexuality. Yet instead of tossing out the entire idea of a lesbian and gay identity as a last and nostalgic impulse of prepostmodernist politics, these insights in identity constructions contextualized the practice of lesbian and gay politics from both a historical axis of determination and an epistemological means of self-exploration and knowing. By exploring the historical contingencies of any identity politics based on unauthorized sexual practices, we were able to begin to differentiate the various methods and implications of a lesbian and gay self-fashioning throughout the past hundred years. While sex acts constituted the major mode of gay identity throughout the life stories, the acts themselves, let alone their meanings, were vastly different. Furthermore, the choice of a sexual partner also determined to a high degree one's identity. The terms *lesbian* and *gay* emerged from this unit as dynamic categories rather than as fixed, immutable, transhistorical identifications that imply both a shared script and performance.

By reading the oral histories and gay folklore and viewing the documentary films produced by and about lesbians and gays, we recognized that certain contradictions emerged in seeing lesbian and gay identity as a dynamic process. For example, the emergence of self-identified gays and lesbians, instead of opening up possibilities for gays and lesbians and offering up alternative lifestyles, often produced hegemonic scripts that were as stifling as compulsory heterosexuality was. This problem was especially true of sexual desire, sexual practice, and conventional attitudes toward gender, as an example from *Walking after Midnight: Gay Men's Life Stories* (Hall Carpenter Archives) illustrates. One man, John Alcock, recounts his sexual impulses and self-identification as a "queer" or "sissy boy" whose desire was manifested only with "real" men best exemplified by those in the military. "Tootsie trade," or sex between "queer boys," as one of his contemporaries, Bernard Dobson, explains, "was not the proper thing" (45). If the ruling sexual ideology for "queers" in the twenties was "trade," or sex with masculine ideals, imagine Alcock's dilemma when, after serving time in the military, he became his own masculine ideal. His entire scripted sexual identity was ruptured by his own "deviance" from the sissy norm. Was he a "queer boy" or was he a military man? Years later, and now "gay" instead of "queer," he recalls how sexuality was reconfigured by gay males who eroticized sex between gay-identified men; tootsie trade was in.

The lesbians interviewed in the Hall Carpenter Achives women's oral history project, *Inventing Ourselves: Lesbian Life Stories,* recalled how the dynamics of the butch-femme paradigm often led women entering a lesbian space to face an immediate rigidity. As Laura Jackson explains, the question "Are you a butch or a femme?" permeated lesbian and gay clubs and determined certain "unwritten rules" that shaped the interpersonal relationships between working-class women in the late sixties. Citing various contradictions in her sexual experiences with women, Jackson posits that, despite the insistence on a butch-femme model, "there may have been more flexibility in roles behind the scenes" (128). The hegemony of scripts introduced and perpetuated by gays and lesbians, while often providing the codes by which to identify other gays or lesbians, also determined to a large extent the limited performances of lesbian and gay identity in pre-Stonewall society. As the semester progressed, we continued to probe the dynamics of such a phenomenon in areas ranging from direct expressions of sexuality to current fads and fashions.

TEACHING DIFFERENCES

Differences determined by ethnicity and race, while evident in the selections of subjects interviewed in the oral history projects, were still, for the most part, instances of how "whiteness" allowed lesbians and gay men a certain privileged access denied to people of color within the dominant discourses of societal organization. For us to begin to comprehend the experiences of gay and lesbian ethnic minorities in the United States, including their alliances with a larger gay and lesbian community as well as a separate construction of identity and community, I found it useful to select texts that articulated the experiences from a minority population; continued the dialogue between theory and practice; and presented the problems of such a dialogue as expressed between majority lesbian and gays and gays and lesbians of color. In preparing my course, I tried to respond to my own annoyance with projects promising reflections on racial difference and racism that offer only obligatory calls for inclusion. Instead of setting up an impossible hierarchy of oppression, I problematized the construction of a singular, linear development of the gay and lesbian identity or movement that the oral histories seemed to posit.

The task at hand demanded a critical practice that considered the heterogeneity of sexual identities and demonstrated, or at least began to come to terms with, the issues at stake within any claim of identity based on marks of difference. My own position—that of a Latino gay male academic whose intellectual and political formation is grounded in feminism—highlighted all the more the complexities of speaking from *an* ethnic minority experience without being perceived by my students as speaking from *the* ethnic minority experience. I used this moment in the class to examine our own specific subject positions in relation to a lesbian and gay identity. What connecting points were we willing to negotiate in order to arrive at a sense of community? With whom, if anyone, did we feel aligned? And, finally, what purpose did these alliances serve? For my students this discussion was a welcome break from the academic field in which we had immersed ourselves. For lesbian and gay undergraduates especially, the chance to be authorized to apply theoretical models of inquiry based on sexuality to their own lives, moreover, was a novel experience.

The first "minority" position we examined outside those in the oral history anthologies was that of the black gay filmmaker Marlon Riggs. Our discussion of his film *Tongues Untied* avoided the pitfalls typical of readings of minority artists who are perceived as speaking for an entire community. Instead, fueled in part by our previous discussion, we viewed *Tongues Untied* as a film that spoke *from* and not *for* the black gay male experience. We raised questions that focused on alternatives to the social scripts posited by an African American heterosexist ideology, as well as on alternatives to the racist implications of many dominant lesbian and gay discourses. We also explored the possibility that Riggs's film might serve as a means to educate black men struggling with coming out issues. One of the strengths of *Tongues Untied* lies in its various representations of black gay men expressing their sexuality among themselves and thus performing a process of community articulation—one whose premise is based on separate, diverse experiences. In other words, the film does not allow for a monolithic black gay male "identity"; instead, it demonstrates how various men negotiate sexuality among themselves and in relation to a white gay majority. In this sense, Riggs's film disturbs the comfortable chronology of a lesbian and gay historiography by unsettling the idea of a shared political agenda for a post-Stonewall lesbian and gay community. Rather than uphold a static conception of gay identity that focuses on urban white gay male experiences, Riggs, like many other gay people of color, articulates a complex constellation of socially constituted differences and their limits within dominant culture. Thus it becomes difficult to continue to conceive of a lesbian and gay culture based on simply the sameness of erotic choice.

Tongues Untied also inaugurated discussions on the common misconception that materials by gay and lesbian people of color are scarce.

While material conditions and institutional practices often hinder the production of, and access to, works by lesbians and gays of color, the works do exist, although often outside established mainstream venues. If we are seriously interested in diversifying our curricula, we need to look creatively to small presses, independent film distributors, and alternative performance spaces and galleries to broaden our own awareness of the vastness of the artistic and social contributions of gay and lesbian people of color.

Along with the idea of disturbing the progression of a lesbian and gay culture, the course syllabus included works that spoke to the issues of difference between and among various subject positions. I chose Jeffner Allen's anthology, *Lesbian Philosophies and Cultures*, primarily for this reason.[3] Women of color have gained some prominence within women's studies programs, especially since the 1981 publication of Cherríe Moraga and Gloria Anzaldúa's anthology, *This Bridge Called My Back*, and have thus instigated an entire reevaluation of women's experience to include issues of class, race, ethnicity, and sexuality. The dialogues between white lesbians and lesbians of color, however, have only begun to take shape. Although *Lesbian Philosophies and Cultures* includes essays by lesbians of color, older lesbians, working-class lesbians, and differently abled lesbians, the dialogues within the anthology continued our own speculations about the efficacy of theory for the material reality of lesbian lives, a concern highlighted throughout the anthology. Essays from lesbians who "inhabit multiple cultures" poignantly depicted the experience of marginality within white, middle-class, and abled lesbian "cultures" (2). While these essays focused on racism, ageism, and access, students were quick to note that the other more theoretical or philosophical essays in the anthology showed little response to, or engagement with, these issues.

Lesbian Philosophies and Cultures also raises important questions of desire and sex that, of course, are central to gay and lesbian studies. How do lesbians (and by extension gay men) construct, articulate, and express desire? What constitutes desire, and how is lesbian desire, in particular, manifested within a patriarchal and phallocentric ideology? Susie Bright's *Susie Sexpert's Lesbian Sex World* and essays from *Lesbian Philosophies and Cultures*, along with the performance pieces of Holly Hughes, anchored our discussions, while our previous accounting of differences informed our speculations and assumptions based on such limited accounts. Nonetheless, our discussions opened up a series of (unanswerable) questions on desire and sexuality, especially relating to the discourses by which these questions take shape. Once more, by challenging the notion of sexuality, we disrupted the very methods we use to think of desire and sexuality. Such texts and discussions also raised important concerns about the implications of my assigning works geared to a specifically lesbian audience, to say nothing of how the students are implicated in reading them.

A class excursion to see Hughes's play *The Well of Horniness* at a lesbian and gay theater in Los Angeles helped bring this debate to the forefront of our discussions. We read essays by lesbian performance theorists, on lesbian representation and the ramifications of a nonlesbian spectatorship, to contextualize our participation in these dialogues and debates (see Davy; Dolan; de Lauretis; Case, Letter; Hughes, Reply). Still, the issue of "theoretical tourism," which occurs when "outsiders" claim the authority to travel through highly charged and personally invested debates within a marginalized population, was not easily resolved.[4] What, for example, are the implications of perpetuating, in the classroom, the debates of performance theorists and artists if the very nature and venue of these debates might reposition the lesbian subject as fetishized object within mainstream discourse? Discussions about commodification and appropriation helped clarify these issues, but overall we remained aware of our own incrimination in the processes we were critiquing. Such recognition, of course, does not absolve participants, but it did force each of us to examine our investment in the issues we talked about during the semester.

The discussions on sexuality included perspectives by gay men and concluded with a unit on AIDS. Most of the essays I chose by gay men were written in the past decade and were thus informed to varying degrees by AIDS. Although the available writings on AIDS are voluminous, the course was not about AIDS alone, so I limited my selections to writings that addressed the issues introduced earlier in the semester. The essays focused on AIDS among gay men and lesbians, but I made it clear that we would not be studying AIDS as a gay disease. Rather, we would explore its ramifications for gays *and* lesbians and the ways in which it informs lesbian sexuality, identity, and politics. Anthologies like Douglas Crimp's *AIDS: Cultural Analysis/Cultural Activism* and Tessa Boffin and Sunil Gupta's *Ecstatic Antibodies: Resisting the AIDS Mythologies* demonstrate, for example, how various writers and activists target their cultural strategies to distinct constituencies and yet form a coalition of positions to counter AIDS. Furthermore, a second outing to see *Sex/Love/Stories*, by the performance artist and cultural activist Tim Miller, helped focus these issues.

The issues of representation became a central concern during our discussions of the anthologies and Miller's performance. We examined dominant constructions depicting gay men as innate embodiments of AIDS and gay male responses to such mythologies, and we questioned the popular media's lack of attention to gay men of color and lesbians and AIDS and the problems inherent in such invisibilities. I hoped to access the strategies that gay men and lesbians have engendered in response to the epidemic, to consider how these responses complicate the various agendas of diverse gay and lesbian populations, and to look critically at the cultural productions of gay and lesbian artists in response to AIDS.

While many texts could serve this agenda, I found Sarah Schulman's 1989 novel *People in Trouble* an excellent example of how AIDS issues are interrelated and dependent on a cultural politics that recognizes them as such. Schulman's bildungsroman charts the political awakening of a young white lesbian in New York City who becomes involved with various women and the emerging AIDS activist movement. Along with providing the focus for our discussions on AIDS, *People in Trouble* brought to the surface issues of how "high" theory works in gay and lesbian and AIDS activist politics, how "low" theory can intervene in dominant ideological mythologies differently, how people construct and negotiate sexuality at different times and for different purposes with astoundingly dissimilar results, and finally, how any articulation of a lesbian and gay political formulation must present these debates. The novel's protagonist struggles with these issues as she encounters people who represent other, often contradictory, positions. Thus Schulman's reader is drawn into the debates and forced to think through the issues along with the central character.

Although *People in Trouble* speaks eloquently about the suffering and loss caused by AIDS (as do the selections we read from Klein's collection *Poets for Life*), my goal was for students to see how activists— in this case a prominent lesbian writer—choose to engage in critical practices that pose direct challenges to AIDS. In other words, we focused less on the literary merits of *People in Trouble* than we did on Schulman's use of popular fiction as a strategy for political change. We questioned the capabilities of such a cultural production as a response to AIDS. Of all our semester readings, *People in Trouble* invoked the strongest reactions and the most heated discussions. Students were drawn to the issues in *People in Trouble* and, because of our earlier readings, were able to engage critically with the implications of Schulman's project. Schulman concludes her novel with an indictment by a surviving character: "We are a people in trouble. We do not act" (228). Our semester ended with these words and our own responses to them. I'm not quite sure whether our readings and discussions are symptomatic of this syndrome or whether this current wave of gay and lesbian inquiry constitutes a minor, albeit important, intervention in a larger and divergent cultural politics of difference moving us into the twenty-first century. My gut reaction is that the work we do as academics in gay and lesbian studies does seep out of the insular world of academia, if mainly through the students in the classroom.[5]

University of Washington

Notes

[1] For a discussion on the implications of the recent institutional interest in lesbian and gay studies, see Cohen.

[2] This essay attempts to theorize my own goals for the class, highlighting only certain moments in the semester rather than providing a weekly breakdown of our discussions.

[3] Trujillo's more recent anthology, *Chicana Lesbians*, was not yet available. As Gonzalez notes, Trujillo provides an exciting "forum" for Chicana lesbians (82). For essays that explore Jewish lesbian philosophies and cultures, see Beck's groundbreaking and now indispensable collection, *Nice Jewish Girls*.

[4] I'm indebted to Bravmann's remarkably honest and provocative essay on lesbian and gay studies, which quotes Kaplan's phrase "theoretical tourism."

[5] I want to thank the students in the seminar—Brian Smith, Wendy Stark, Jennifer Willis, and J. Aaron Jacobs—for helping me think through these issues and for sharing their ideas honestly and often. I also thank Joe Boone, Susana Chavez Silverman, and Yvonne Yarbro-Bejarano for reading earlier drafts of this essay. This essay is dedicated to Evie Beck, my teacher and friend, whose theory and practice helped shape my own.

Works Cited

Allen, Jeffner, ed. *Lesbian Philosophies and Cultures.* Albany: State University of New York P, 1990.

Beck, Evelyn Torton, ed. *Nice Jewish Girls: A Lesbian Anthology.* 1982. Rev. ed. Boston: Beacon, 1989.

Boffin, Tessa, and Sunil Gupta, ed. *Ecstatic Antibodies: Resisting the AIDS Mythology.* London: River Oram, 1990.

Bravmann, Scott. "Telling Stories: Rethinking the Lesbian and Gay Historical Imagination." *Out Look* 8 (1990): 68–74.

Bright, Susie. *Susie Sexpert's Lesbian Sex World.* Pittsburgh: Cleis, 1990.

Butler, Judith. *Gender Trouble: Feminism and the Subversion of Identity.* New York: Routledge, 1990.

Case, Sue-Ellen. Letter. *Drama Review* 33 (1989): 10–14.

———, ed. *Performing Feminisms: Feminist Critical Theory and Theatre.* Baltimore: Johns Hopkins UP, 1990.

———. "Toward a Butch-Femme Aesthetic." *Making a Spectacle: Feminist Essays on Contemporary Women's Theatre.* Ed. Lynda Hart. Ann Arbor: U of Michigan P, 1989. 282–99.

Cohen, Ed. "Are We (Not) What We Are Becoming? 'Gay' 'Identity,' 'Gay Studies,' and the Disciplining of Knowledge." *Engendering Men: The Question of Male Feminist Criticism.* Ed. Joseph A. Boone and Michael Cadden. New York: Routledge, 1990. 161–75.

Crimp, Douglas, ed. *AIDS: Cultural Analysis/Cultural Activism.* Cambridge: MIT P, 1987.

Davy, Kate. "Constructing the Spectator: Reception, Context, and Address in Lesbian Performances." *Performing Arts Journal* 10 (1986): 74–87.

de Lauretis, Teresa. "Sexual Indifference and Lesbian Representation." Case, *Performing Feminisms* 17–39.

Dolan, Jill. "Lesbian Subjectivity in Realism: Dragging at the Margins of Structure and Ideology." Case, *Performing Feminisms* 40–53.

Gonzalez, Deena. "Masquerades: Viewing the New Chicana Lesbian Anthologies." *Out/Look* 15 (1992): 80–83.

Hall Carpenter Archives Gay Men's Oral History Group, ed. *Walking after Midnight: Gay Men's Life Stories.* New York: Routledge, 1989.

Hall Carpenter Archives Lesbian Oral History Group, ed. *Inventing Ourselves: Lesbian Life Stories.* New York: Routledge, 1989.

Halperin, David M. *One Hundred Years of Homosexuality and Other Essays on Greek Love.* New York: Routledge, 1990.

Hughes, Holly. Reply to letter of Sue-Ellen Case. *Drama Review* 33 (1989): 14–17.

———. *The Well of Horniness. Out Front: Contemporary Gay and Lesbian Plays.* Ed. Don Shewey. New York: Grove, 1988. 221–51.

———. *World without End. Out from Under: Texts by Women Performance Artists.* Ed. Lenora Champagne. New York: Theatre Communications, 1990. 3–32.

Kaplan, Caren. "Deterritorializations: The Rewriting of Home and Exile in Western Feminist Discourse." *Cultural Critique* 6 (1987): 187–98.

Klein, Michael, ed. *Poets for Life: Seventy-six Poets Respond to AIDS.* New York: Crown, 1989.

Miller, Tim. *Sex/Love/Stories.* Performance piece. Highways Performance Space, Santa Monica. 8–24 Mar. 1991.

Moraga, Cherríe, and Gloria Anzaldúa, eds. *This Bridge Called My Back: Writings by Radical Women of Color.* Watertown: Persephone, 1981.

Riggs, Marlon, dir. *Tongues Untied.* Frameline, 1989.

Schulman, Sarah. *People in Trouble.* New York: Penguin, 1989.

Sedgwick, Eve Kosofsky. *Epistemology of the Closet.* Berkeley: U of California P, 1990.

Trujillo, Carla. *Chicana Lesbians: The Girls Our Mothers Warned Us About.* Berkeley: Third Woman, 1991.

Expanding the Categories of Race and Sexuality in Lesbian and Gay Studies

Yvonne Yarbro-Bejarano

The increased visibility of lesbians and gays on the political scene in the 1980s and 1990s (the organized response to NEA censorship, the public activities of ACT UP and Queer Nation) has been accompanied by the emergence of lesbian and gay studies within academia. While this is an exciting time for people in our field in general, the stakes in the establishment of lesbian and gay studies as an academic discipline are particularly high for lesbians and gays of color, given the exclusionary politics of domination that characterize the histories of women and American ethnic studies. Many lesbians and gays of color remained on the fringe of 1960s and 1970s feminist and civil rights struggles or paid the high price of alienation, ostracization, and closeting for doing political work that demanded the privileging of race, gender, or class over sexual identity (Saalfield and Navarro 353, 354). While sexual identity prohibited lesbians of color from feeling completely at home in racially based social movements, cultural and class experiences led to a far-reaching critique of categories such as "women" that universalized white middle-class women's experience.

As the 1980s progressed, the critique became an ongoing process, exposing the ways discourses on "difference" have been appropriated by white feminists, addressing new forms of racism (for example, in Anzaldúa's anthology *Making Face, Making Soul/Haciendo Caras*), and calling attention to the "inclusion without influence" of women of color in women studies programs and research (Uttal). Within American ethnic studies, debates have emerged about gender, but lesbian and gay issues continue to be marginalized. For example, Rosa Linda Fregoso and Angie Chabram, in their introduction to a special issue of *Cultural Studies,* call for an interrogation of cultural nationalism's notion of a singular Chicano identity (204), yet they too fail to engage questions of lesbian Chicana and gay Chicano subjectivities. For many complex reasons, heterosexual women of color can clearly see that they are marginalized because of race, gender, and class origins, but they may not realize that they occupy the center of heterosexual privilege. The need for a multiple critique of racial and ethnic identity is greater than ever, given the recent resurgence of cultural nationalism in communities of color, accompanied now as in the 1960s and 1970s by misogyny and homophobia (Hemphill).

Another example from a Chicano context, the area within American ethnic studies that I am most familiar with, documents a shift away from the heterosexual male dominance of earlier times: namely, the increasing female and lesbian presence within the National Association of Chicano Studies (NACS). As recently as 1990, Chicanas had to fight for women-only space within the institutional structure of NACS conferences. By the 1992 conference, however, the schedule included a lesbian caucus meeting, a lesbian roundtable, and a lesbian panel. Even Chicano gays, less vocal over the last two decades compared with Chicana lesbians, met during the 1992 conference and formed the National Association of Latino Gay Academics (NALGA). These changes were brought about by the continuous pressure applied to the organization by Chicana feminists and the refusal of Chicana lesbians to remain silent and invisible.

There is reason to be hopeful that this history of debate about exclusionary practices and the current climate of increased multicultural and multiracial awareness can prevent the establishment of programs that might as well call themselves "white lesbian and gay studies." Proposals for the formation of lesbian and gay studies should build in a pervasive multicultural emphasis, and people of color and antiracist white people should be on the committees for lesbian and gay studies, including the steering committees. Yet in spite of precautionary measures put in place during the process, the outcome will be affected by institutional constraints that determine the availability of resources, radically reducing the possibility of hiring people whose work involves an analysis of race.

The small, and dwindling, number of faculty members of color forces a contrast between concrete, material reality and what Hazel Carby calls the fashionable "politics of difference." As she points out, while university syllabi become integrated, apartheid continues to reign in the cities and educational systems of the United States. Although universities express their commitment to diversity, ninety percent of faculty members in this country in 1990 were white, while the number of students of color at all levels declined and Latino and black communities sank deeper into poverty (84). The university is part of the power structure underpinned by pervasive racism. In twenty years, we will have degree-granting programs in lesbian and gay studies, but there are no guarantees that they will be headed by people whose work incorporates an awareness of race. Lesbians and gays of color and their allies need constant vigilance, networking, and organizing to ensure that lesbian and gay studies will be a site for what it purports to do: study lesbians and gays (not just white, middle-class lesbians and gays).

It would be difficult to overemphasize this fact: lesbians and gays come in all colors, from all cultures and classes. In other words, the problem of recognizing diversity—for example, the diversity of women within women studies or of people of color within American ethnic studies—has surfaced within the gay liberation movement. Charles Fernández critiques the gay movement's privileging of a white, middle-class, and often male subject that stands in opposition to heterosexual categories (21), since, as Norma Alarcón and others have pointed out, subjectivity is formed in opposition to *multiple* categories. The dominance of the privileged white male subject in the gay movement marginalizes lesbians and gays of color as well as white lesbians and represents the greatest drag on the development of a nonhierarchical lesbian and gay studies. Richard Mohr's statement that the struggles of "other" groups are not "our" struggles is merely the transparent centering of the privileged white male subject as the norm of the gay movement (qtd. in Fernández 22). Catherine Saalfield and Ray Navarro analyze the exclusionary connotations of the pink triangle as a symbol of queer identity, noting the "oppressively iconic 'flesh tone' " that excludes lesbians and gays of color, as well as the disappearance of the black triangle, historically used to designate lesbians and other "anti-social" elements (347–48). The absorption of specifically lesbian histories of oppression within the pink triangle parallels the disappearance of lesbians (and women) within the term *queer*. Saalfield and Navarro document how within ACT UP, which was "originally dominated by white gay male sensibilities, women and people of color have created coalitions and their own style of participation in order to negotiate their own agendas" (351). Bringing to bear a knowledge of historical instances of discrimination based on race and gender in relation to disease and science, women and men of color and white women have insisted on an analysis of the "specific manner in which sexism and racism, as well as homophobia, have been used to perpetuate the AIDS crisis" (351). In this way, space for a more far-reaching critique has been opened up in what is already perceived as a radically subversive sphere, much as I proposed that lesbian and gay studies should be expanded.

In the light of current discussions of the exclusionary and homogenizing tendencies that inhere in the concept of "nation," the absorption of
differences under the rubric of "queer nation" also needs to be addressed.
While supporters point out that the term is meant to be oxymoronic,
counterposing the difference of *queer* to the sameness of *nation* (Berubé
and Escoffier 14), this works only if *queer* is articulated within an awareness of the heterogeneity of racialized and gendered sexual identities.
If, however, it cloaks the privileging of the white, middle-class gay male
subject, *queer nation* can become multiply exclusionary for lesbians
and gays of color. Natasha Gray's "Bored with the Boys: Cracks in the
Queer Coalition" exposes the persistent gender and class inequalities
in the queer movement from a white lesbian perspective, revealing the
pitfalls in the promise of any "unifying identity":

> [T]he only lesbians who really interested gay men were those who
> were fighting for gay male lives, on gay male turf and on gay male
> terms. . . . [N]o matter how much we wrap ourselves in a queer
> identity, it is our status as women that will define the way we
> live.   (27–28)

At the root of these problems is the focus on one issue, whether it
be gender, race, class, or sexuality, as if it existed separately from the
others. The insistence on keeping these analytic categories discrete indicates white people's resistance to perceiving their own gender or sexuality as racially constructed and their tendency to assign the category of
race exclusively to people of color (Gordon 105), as well as the resistance
of people of color to perceiving their own gender or heterosexual privilege. The rigid separation of these categories reveals that people generally resist acknowledging that they experience racial and cultural
identity inseparably from gender and sexual constructions of the self.
The emphasis on gender alone or sexual identity alone reaffirms white
dominance (Gordon 105), just as the exclusive emphasis on race and
culture reaffirms male and heterosexual dominance.
The solution to this problem is not one of "inclusion." It just doesn't
work. Theorists who reinscribe the politics of domination within discourses on "difference" (of gender, race, class, or sexual identity) tend
to see difference within a paradigm that implies a norm and the tolerance
of deviance from it (Gordon 100; Spelman). The "additive" model of
"including" previously excluded categories in an attempt at correction
maintains power in the hands of those who constitute the "norm,"
graciously inviting the "different" in. It also works against an understanding of the relations among the elements of identity and the effect
each one has on another (Spelman 115; Uttal).

Critics of the additive model have proposed a relational theory of difference that examines identity formation in the dynamic interpenetration of gender, race, sexuality, class, and nation (Mohanty 2). The problems in producing this relational theory not only have to do with sins of omission resulting from racism, homophobia, and heterosexism and sexism but also point to a profound "conceptual and theoretical difficulty" (Gordon 101–02). It is a tremendous challenge to replace old ways of thinking, old paradigms, with a new consciousness. We need a paradigm that permits analytic categories to expand, giving expression to the lived experience of the ways race, class, sexuality, and gender converge (Childers and Hooks). Notions of *simultaneous* oppressions are not entirely successful in capturing the ways these categories interact and interdefine one another, while conceptualizing the *intersection* of these categories may communicate an excessively static, rather than a dynamic, understanding of the process. The required new paradigm would allow the kind of categorical expansion we need to understand "sexualized racial identities," or "racialized sexual identities," as Linda Gordon suggests in her discussion of the complex interdefining of racial and gender categories (105).

Because of the current shifts in thinking about identity, it would be a step backward to consider the experiences of lesbians and gays of color as "different" or to merely "include" their experiences under the auspices of lesbian and gay studies. The fluidity and heterogeneity of forms of sexual identity exemplified in the emergence of Queer Nation speak for the possibility of more complexity than a binary gay-straight dichotomy would indicate. In spite of the dangers of exclusionary definitions of queerness alluded to above, the term points to an awareness of plural sexual identities. Similarly, the debate on ethnicity has moved from an us-them dichotomy underpinning a unitary notion of identity and experience to a recognition that terms like *Chicano, black,* or *people of color* are constructed and political. This movement has carved out a space for "the recognition of the extraordinary diversity of subject positions, social experiences and cultural identities" that compose these categories (Hall 28). The result of this new way of thinking about identity is the blurring of boundaries among analytic categories that were formerly rigidly separated, a blurring that permits us to perceive the proliferation of racial and sexual identities, to see what Katie King calls the "race of sex" and the "sex of race" (86).

The expansion of the categories of race and sexuality within a new relational paradigm is crucial as we actively produce theory about lesbian and gay sexual identity and its representation. The lack of attention to race in the work of leading lesbian theorists reaffirms the belief that it is possible to talk about sexuality without talking about race, which in turn reaffirms the belief that it is necessary to talk about race *and* sexuality only when discussing people of color and their texts. Elizabeth Grosz's work on lesbian desire, presented at the 1991 MLA convention, does not consider how eroticism and desire—even the desire between two white women—are permeated with racial projections, fears, and tensions. Judith Butler's project of destabilizing categories such as "woman," "lesbian," "identity," and "theory," however, addresses the ways these normative and regulatory categories exclude multiple figurations: they do so "because gender is not always constituted coherently or consistently in different historical contexts, and because gender intersects with racial, class, ethnic, sexual and regional modalities of discursively constituted identities" (*Gender Trouble* 3). Yet her interpretation of gender as a "stylized repetition of acts," assumed through a structure of impersonation or imitation for which there is no original, does not actively factor in how racial formations shape the "performance" of gender and sexual identity (*Gender Trouble* 140; "Imitation" 19). It is not a question of evolving a parallel theory of the performance of racial identity vis-à-vis a phantasmic racial ideal analogous to gender but, rather, one of reading race, and political movement as well, into Butler's performative model.

The absence of a consideration of race in much white feminist theory on lesbian sexuality is particularly apparent in Teresa de Lauretis's "Film and the Visible," in which she omits the subject of race from her analysis of *She Must Be Seeing Things*, a film about an interracial lesbian couple. For de Lauretis, the film's refusal seriously to consider race justifies her exclusive focus on the "use of fantasy and of the film-within-the-film as strategies of lesbian representation and address" (272). This omission is, to a certain extent, understandable, yet even the Asian Canadian videomaker Richard Fung, who remarks on the film's tokenism in "inserting" people of color, makes the important point that "by casting the role of Agatha as a person of color, a whole cultural baggage is invoked" (de Lauretis 270). It would seem worthwhile to examine both how the film racializes desire for the characters and how the film engages the spectators' racial fantasies and identifications.

What assumptions underlie the perception that the introduction of racial issues somehow interrupts or defers the discussion of lesbian sexuality? Is de Lauretis's "Film and the Visible" an example of provisional and strategic privileging of one category in the hopes that the theoretical model thus produced will be useful to others "in thinking about how fantasy may work or may be used in film to address racially as well as sexually different spectators" (270), a position underwritten by the black British filmmaker Isaac Julien? Does the relegation of race to those for whom it is the "central focus of [their] work over time and not superficially" reinforce the artificial boundaries among analytic categories? Should the analysis of race be confined to texts that foreground it in particular ways? De Lauretis does not deny that race is in the film, but it is not there "in such a way that allows [her] to rethink and say something interesting about the relations of race, sexuality, and desire" (273). This impasse seems to point to the limitations of the psychoanalytical model for broaching the interdefining of race and sexuality, in Grosz's and Butler's work as well, with respect to the kinds of questions it can construct as "interesting." Yet Julien, who suggests a reading of the same film within de Lauretis's own theoretical framework, which embraces masquerade, fantasy, and race, would seem to indicate that even within the psychoanalytical model the categories of race and sexuality can be expanded.

Everyone's sex has a race and vice versa, just as everyone's gender identity is constructed in the interplay among race, class, sexuality, and nation. No one becomes who he or she is in relation to only one social category, and no representation of sexuality is free of racialization (even in the absence of people of color). Building on the call of recent cultural critics for an examination of whiteness as an unmarked racial or ethnic identity (Dyer; Frankenberg; Mercer), a consideration of the cultural construction of white sexuality would enrich analyses of the representation of desire and contribute to the destabilization of the separate categories of race and sexuality. In this regard, we must emphasize the contribution of lesbians of color to this theoretical project of categorical expansion, in part because some white feminists have appropriated that contribution[1] and also because lesbians of color have provided a significant piece of the theoretical groundwork that could and should serve as the foundation of lesbian and gay studies.

Jeffrey Escoffier recognizes this contribution in an article on the challenges facing lesbian and gay studies, crediting Cherríe Moraga and Gloria Anzaldúa's *This Bridge Called My Back* (1981), along with Audre Lorde's *Sister Outsider* (1984), the anthology *Home Girls* (1983), edited by Barbara Smith et al., Anzaldúa's *Borderlands* (1987), and Moraga's *Loving in the War Years* (1983) with proposing "a new way of thinking about cultural identity and difference":

> These women of color criticized the impulse . . . to emphasize the essential similarities of all women rather than the differences of race, sexuality, and class among women. . . . These writers' exploration of the overlapping identities of gender, race, and sexuality also implies criticism of "universalistic" conceptions of the making of homosexual identity.   (44)[2]

These writers have been producing what Moraga calls "theory in the flesh" (Moraga and Anzaldúa 23), an embodied theory that emerges from the material reality of multiple oppression and, in turn, conceptualizes that materiality. It would be ironic if the institutionalization of lesbian and gay studies replicated the very politics of domination that these writers of color wrote against within feminist and cultural nationalist enclaves.

As we struggle to expand the categories of analysis in our exploration of our complex identities, histories, and desires, we must avoid being what Fernández calls "beached on the barren rocks of ranked oppressions" (23). Working-class lesbians of color are in a unique position to disrupt excessively discrete categories of analysis. Possessing no privilege in the areas of class, race, culture, gender, or sexuality, the working-class lesbian of color "violates the ranking and abstraction of oppressions" (Moraga 29). Moraga answers her own question, "Do we merely struggle with the 'ism' that's sitting on top of our own heads?" with a qualified yes: "But to fail to move out from there will only isolate us in our own oppression" (29).

Yet Moraga points out a dual danger: "The danger lies in ranking the oppressions. *The danger lies in failing to acknowledge the specificity of the oppression"* (29). While avoiding the appropriation of other struggles of liberation (Fernández 22–23), lesbians and gays must demand the recognition of the specificity of homophobia and heterosexism. Clearly, the establishment of lesbian and gay studies within the university is important because of the enforced invisibility and silence of lesbians and gays in our society, the hatred and violence reflected in recent legislation and the increase in gay bashing, and the need to redress chronic discrimination and underrepresentation. The challenge remains to foreground the specificity of the oppression, subjectivity, and experience of lesbians and gays without reinscribing exclusionary gestures.

A key stance for accomplishing this feat is an awareness of the multiplicity of identity. The contributors to *This Bridge Called My Back* refuse to choose between race and gender, sexual identity and culture, a position recently echoed by the African American filmmaker Marlon Riggs when asked his opinion on the "black gay" versus "gay black" controversy:

> Many of us try to divide ourselves up into part-Black and part-gay and then arrange these parts in some formal kind of hierarchy and decide, "Which am I first?" . . . There is no way to divide myself—I am whole, all of these things are complete and virtuous to me.
> (qtd. in Banneker 18)

This consciousness of the inextricable relations among the various components of identity facilitates a nonhierarchical and temporally determined maneuverability within the framework of identity and coalition politics.

Chela Sandoval has provided a theory that privileges one category of oppression or identity tactically, without abandoning a fundamental sense of identity as multiple and fluid. In her theory of "oppositional" or "differential" consciousness, Sandoval describes a sense of political identity that allows no single conceptualization of a person's position in society. Oppositional or differential consciousness is a skill that those marginalized in the categories of race, sex, or class develop for reading the shifting webs of power. For Sandoval, a new community based on the strength of diversities is the source of new political movements. Her theory legitimates the multiplicity of tactical responses to the mobile circulation of power and a shifting, tactical subjectivity that recenters according to the forms of oppression being confronted.

In *Borderlands*, Anzaldúa theorizes a similar form of consciousness, which she calls "mestiza" (hybrid), or "border," consciousness. Anzaldúa defines mestiza or border consciousness as the activity or process of breaking down dualisms in the production of a third thing, or hybrid element. Mestiza consciousness is not relativism or pluralism but rather the "tolerance for contradictions" (79). It is not a counterstance, which would reposition the subject as "other" or "different" in binary relation to the same, the dominant, the center. The new mestiza is the site or point of the confluence of conflicting subject positions.

The writing and the theory of these Chicana lesbians and others have provided a new paradigm of multiple and shifting identities and identifications, consciousness, and political agency that can form the theoretical framework of lesbian and gay studies. As David Román points out in his essay in this volume, lesbian and gay studies can avoid the production of "hegemonic scripts that were as stifling as compulsory heterosexuality was" by problematizing "the construction of a singular, linear development of a gay and lesbian identity or movement" and acknowledging the "heterogeneity of sexual identities." For Román, the terms *lesbian* and *gay* should be worked with as "dynamic categories rather than as fixed, immutable, transhistorical identifications that imply both a shared script and performance."

Besides informing the ways we study identity and history, the expansion of the categories of race and sexuality has an equally significant effect on the approach to another major area of lesbian and gay studies: the construction of desire. The knowledge that everyone's sexuality is racialized can help us understand the ways in which our desires are racialized in both interracial and intraracial contexts.

In the introduction to *How Do I Look? Queer Film and Video*, members of the editorial collective Bad Object-Choices examine the relations between lesbian and gay sexuality and ethnic and racial difference. They commit themselves to the task of interfering with ethnocentric pressures—which they aptly refer to as the "cultural law of gravity"—to absorb ethnic and racial differences in the privileging of the homogenous white subject, concluding that "the introduction of homosexuality is not, of course, sufficient in itself to subvert racist codes. . . . [T]he troubling of heterosexual difference may in fact be *compensated* by reinforcing standard representations of racial difference" (26).

While it is important to analyze racist elements in the representation and construction of desire across color lines, Kobena Mercer's complex contextualization of Robert Mapplethorpe's work and its reception encourages us to avoid a premature shutdown of the dialogue on interracial desire. Several pieces in the winter 1992 issue of *Out/Look* address interracial relationships under the interrogative rubric "Sleeping with the Enemy?" Are cultural, class, and racial differences insurmountable? Is it inevitable that the attraction of a lesbian or gay of color to a white person be a manifestation of internalized racism or color-blind liberalism? What are the ramifications of wholesale suspicion of interracial connections? Debate continues, in texts such as Julien's films, most recently *Young Soul Rebels* and *Confessions of a Snow Queen* (Belton 18–19).

Besides considering the interplay between race and desire across and within color lines, the general task facing lesbian and gay theory is to question what the African American photographer Lyle Ashton Harris calls "the positioning of sexuality as the transcendental signifier" in analyses of history and identity as well (8–9). The destabilization and expansion of regulatory categories of analysis will help us to produce more complex imaginings of ourselves in the world and the place of race in our lived realities as gendered sexual subjects.[3]

Stanford University

Notes

[1] I refer in shorthand fashion to a complex debate, currently taking place at conferences and in writing, about white feminists' appropriation of the work of women of color, which I cannot detail here. See King's essay and Aanerud's unpublished article on the citation history of *This Bridge Called My Back*.

[2] I quote Escoffier at length, not to privilege a gay white man's validation of the work of women of color, but to call attention to the recognized contribution of lesbians of color to the intellectual development of lesbian and gay studies.

[3] Many thanks to the participants in the lesbian roundtable at the March 1992 NACS conference, to the students in my spring 1992 graduate seminar Race,

Sexuality, and Nation, and to David Román, Ellie Hernández, Ruth Frankenberg, and Lata Mani for their help in thinking through the various stages of this paper.

Works Cited

Aanerud, Rebecca. "*This Bridge Called My Back* and Feminist Theory." Unpublished essay. 1991.

Alarcón, Norma. "The Theoretical Subject(s) of *This Bridge Called My Back* and Anglo-American Feminism." Anzaldúa, *Making Face* 356–69.

Anzaldúa, Gloria. *Borderlands/La frontera. The New Mestiza.* San Francisco: Aunt Lute, 1987.

———, ed. *Making Face, Making Soul/Haciendo Caras: Creative and Critical Perspectives by Women of Color.* San Francisco: Aunt Lute, 1990.

Bad Object-Choices, eds. *How Do I Look? Queer Film and Video.* Seattle: Bay, 1991.

Banneker, Revon Kyle. "Marlon Riggs Untied." *Out/Look* 3.2 (1990): 14–18.

Belton, Don. "Young Soul Rebel: A Conversation with Isaac Julien." *Out/Look* 4.4 (1992): 15–19.

Berubé, Allan, and Jeffrey Escoffier. "Queer/Nation." *Out/Look* 11 (1991): 14–16.

Butler, Judith. *Gender Trouble: Feminism and the Subversion of Identity.* New York: Routledge, 1990.

———. "Imitation and Gender Insubordination." Fuss 13–31.

Carby, Hazel. "The Politics of Difference." *Ms.* Sept.–Oct. 1990: 84–85.

Childers, Mary, and Bell Hooks. "A Conversation about Race and Class." Hirsch and Keller 60–81.

de Lauretis, Teresa. "Film and the Visible." Bad Object-Choices 223–76.

Dyer, Richard. "White." *Screen* 29.4 (1988): 44–64.

Escoffier, Jeffrey. "Inside the Ivory Closet: The Challenges Facing Lesbian and Gay Studies." *Out/Look* 3.2 (1990): 40–48.

Fernández, Charles. "Undocumented Aliens in the Queer Nation." *Out/Look* 12 (1991): 20–23.

Frankenberg, Ruth. *White Women, Race Matters: The Social Construction of Whiteness.* Forthcoming.

Fregoso, Rosa Linda, and Angie Chabram. Introduction. *Chicano/a Cultural Representations: Reframing Alternative Critical Discourses.* Ed. Fregoso and Chabram. Spec. issue of *Cultural Studies* 4.3 (1990): 203–12.

Fung, Richard. "Looking for My Penis: The Eroticized Asian in Gay Video Porn." Bad Object-Choices 145–68.

Fuss, Diana. ed. *Inside/Out: Lesbian Theories, Gay Theories.* New York: Routledge, 1991.

Gordon, Linda. "On Difference." *Genders* 10 (1991): 91–111.

Gray, Natasha. "Bored with the Boys: Cracks in the Queer Coalition." *NYQ* 26 Apr. 1992: 26–30.

Grosz, Elizabeth. "Theorizing Lesbian Desire." MLA Convention. San Francisco, 27 Dec. 1991.

Hall, Stuart. "New Ethnicities." *Black Film/British Cinema.* Ed. Kobena Mercer.

London: ICA Document 7, British Film Institute Production Special, 1988. 27–31.

Harris, Lyle Ashton. "Revenge of a Snow Queen." *Out/Look* 4.1 (1991): 8–13.

Hemphill, Essex. "If Freud Had Been a Neurotic Colored Woman." *Out/Look* 4.1 (1991): 50–55.

Hirsch, Marianne, and Evelyn Fox Keller, eds. *Conflicts in Feminism.* New York: Routledge, 1990.

Julien, Isaac. "Concluding Discussion." Bad Object-Choices 277–84.

King, Katie. "Producing Sex, Theory, and Culture: Gay/Straight Remappings in Contemporary Feminism." Hirsch and Keller 82–101.

Mercer, Kobena. "Skin Head Sex Thing: Racial Difference and the Homoerotic Imaginary." Bad Object-Choices 169–210.

Mohanty, Chandra Talpede. "Introduction: Cartographies of Struggle." *Third World Women and the Politics of Feminism.* Ed. Mohanty et al. Bloomington: Indiana UP, 1991. 1–47.

Moraga, Cherríe. "La Güera." Moraga and Anzaldúa 27–34.

Moraga, Cherríe, and Gloria Anzaldúa, eds. *This Bridge Called My Back: Writings by Radical Women of Color.* Watertown: Persephone, 1981; New York: Kitchen Table Women of Color, 1983.

Saalfield, Catherine, and Ray Navarro. "Shocking Pink Praxis: Race and Gender on the ACT UP Frontlines." Fuss 341–69.

Sandoval, Chela. "A Report on the 1981 National Women's Studies Association Conference." Anzaldúa, *Making Face* 55–71.

———. "U.S. Third World Feminism: The Theory and Method of Oppositional Consciousness in the Postmodern World." *Genders* 10 (1991): 1–24.

Spelman, Elizabeth V. *Inessential Woman: Problems of Exclusion in Feminist Thought.* Boston: Beacon, 1988.

Uttal, Lynne. "Inclusion without Influence: The Continuing Tokenism of Women of Color." Anzaldúa, *Making Face* 42–45.

Explicit Instruction: Teaching Gay Male Sexuality in Literature Classes

Earl Jackson, Jr.

The majority of my courses focus on gay male literature and visual culture, taught within a framework that I conceive as a nonappropriative dialogue with feminist theory, as well as other cultural critical discourses. The degree of sexual explicitness in many of the texts we examine (literary and visual) often puts us in the cross fire of the feminist sex wars, while making us vulnerable to conservative pressure groups. In this essay, I sketch the practical and theoretical issues surrounding cultural representations of gay male sexuality and their place in the classroom. In the first part, I raise questions concerning the appropriateness of given materials, the means of using them, and the risks involved—the external threats of censorship and homophobic or intimidated administrations and the internal complications of classroom dynamics. The theory I sketch in the longer, second part of this essay both informs my decisions of what to teach and emerges from those classes. These theoretical remarks also provide practical suggestions on how to contextualize explicit sexual texts in college courses.

PRACTICE

A 1991 *Rolling Stone* article on the boom in lesbian and gay studies begins, "The subject is fist-fucking." It then goes on to describe the instructor, Martin Duberman, as "Distinguished Professor of History at the City University of New

York Graduate Center, author of fifteen books, recipient of numerous scholarly awards and prizes . . . looking every inch the relaxed, silver-haired senior scholar he is" (D'Erasmo 83). The obvious sensationalism of the opening sentence is only ambivalently eased by the listing of Duberman's credentials and appearance. The shock value of the subject matter is not necessarily ameliorated by this depiction of the instructor; rather, it can serve as another means to delegitimize liberal education. Duberman's accomplishments in the context of his topic can be used to cast suspicion on the university or even on the value of academia itself.

In spring 1991 I taught Literature 1, a "close-reading" course required for all literature majors at the University of California, Santa Cruz, that fulfills humanities requirements for nonmajors as well. It is taught in all three quarters, and the topics and texts vary according to the specialization of the instructor. I focused on lesbian writers of color, but I also included two rather sexually graphic texts: Dennis Cooper's "Square One," an essay-story on gay male porn films, and Robert Glück's "Workload," on masturbating to gay porn magazines. Word of these texts got out to the *Redwood Review*, a conservative campus paper (which receives funding from the same groups that fund the *Dartmouth Review*). The editorial board read the assigned readings, and on at least two occasions staff members attended my class without my knowledge. After one such "visit," the editor introduced himself to me, expressed his paper's "concern" about my course (a clear attempt at intimidation), and requested an interview, to which I agreed. The story and interview were prefaced by the most "obscene" passages from the Cooper and Glück texts, and the headline read, "If Only Mom and Dad Knew . . ." (Lehman). Nothing really came of this episode, but it is easy to imagine what kind of fallout could have occurred on a campus less liberal than Santa Cruz.

These two incidents raise an interesting question: in attempting to establish lesbian and gay studies as "legitimate" disciplines, how careful do we need to be of the sensibilities of the "general public"? Providing ammunition to the enemy is not usually a good strategy. Our legitimacy is determined, however, by the intellectual integrity of our project and the challenges we raise to the dominant moralities that would not accept us in the first place. But we have a moral obligation to the students as well—not only to provide the right kinds of material but also to be sensitive to their needs, backgrounds, and fluctuating relations to sexuality, power, and academic institutions. Giving Jesse Helms a headache is one thing; inadvertently traumatizing students is something else. Obviously, sexuality and the forms it takes are going to be, if not on the front burner, at least on the horizon of every lesbian and gay studies class. After all, isn't sexuality central to the formation of these identities and the major reason for their oppression (and their existence as a site of resistance) within dominant culture? But how much of this material can be taught in literature classes that are not primarily gay-focused? How does one effectively and responsibly teach sexually explicit material in the already erotically overdetermined force field of the classroom?[1]

Among the writers I teach, many are noted for either sexual explicitness or direct relations to pornography: Jean Genet, William Burroughs, Robert Glück, Dennis Cooper, Kevin Killian, and Bo Huston, among others. I also deal with film and other visual media: the filmmakers and video makers Pier Paolo Pasolini, Pedro Almodóvar, Richard Fung, Isaac Julien, Kenneth Anger, and Andy Warhol and the visual artists David Wojnarowicz, Robert Mapplethorpe, Rotimi Fani-Kayode, Pierre Molinier, Nayland Blake, and Jerome Caja. Many of these artists borrow heavily from pornographic traditions. In certain classes, I examine pornographic film as well—especially the work of William Higgins, Matt Sterling, and Jim West. Several of the variables that I keep in mind in attempting to draw out questions inherent in such teaching are the differences between print material and visual material, undergraduate and graduate classes, required and nonrequired courses, and required and optional material.

I see no real problem in sexually explicit print material per se. Since the canonization of Joyce and Lawrence, for example, that debate has been essentially rendered moot; however, the number of sexually explicit scenes in gay male texts tends to be at least statistically higher than the number of such scenes in most heterosexual literary texts and in most lesbian texts (a point to which I return later). Many students (particularly the heterosexual students) are not used to the frequency and intensity of sexual depiction in the works, and this issue should be recognized and addressed with both sensitivity and humor. In my Gay Male Narratives class, I try to make the students more comfortable, and to recontextualize sexually explicit prose, by reading the following passage on the first day of class. I preface it by saying that it may be embarrassing to some students, so I want them to listen to it and then to give me their honest impressions on what it feels like to hear such a text read aloud in a classroom:

> His strong, bronzed hands gripped hard 'round the rubber. Slowly and precisely, his forefinger slipped down the steely shaft till it found a natural resting place. He examined with some pleasure the smooth, almost perfect surface beneath him and that hole,

waiting so invitingly. Then it was time. He pulled his hands backwards and then forwards. And in it went.

After the initial awkward silence, a brave soul or two may say something about its being "harsh" or "unfamiliar" or "cold." I ask the students who they think may have written it. After fielding some of these answers, I tell them the source: it is a description of a putt from the *Scottish Golf Journal* (qtd. in "News around the World"). I ask how many straight men wondered where the "natural resting place" was—a question that usually gets scattered confessional laughter. Then I read the passage again, and the effect is very different. After that, students readily go on to actual explicit texts with little trouble.

Visual materials present a different set of problems, and their deployment requires a variety of different strategies. The history of sexual objectification and exploitation of women through advertising and pornography must be taken seriously and be part of the discussion as well as the decision on whether to use such materials and, if so, how. In my undergraduate class Comparative Transgressions I decided to use the trailer from William Higgins's film *Big Guns* to demonstrate the visual excess of gay male sexuality and to begin a discussion of the technologized body as a framework for reading Burroughs's *The Wild Boys*. I stressed that the screening was voluntary and that any student who didn't wish to view it should simply be five minutes late for class that day. To my knowledge, no one took this option, but it seemed the only reasonable way to conduct this admittedly risky experiment.

In 1992, as an affiliated faculty member of the History of Consciousness program, I presented my research on Almodóvar to the proseminar required for all incoming graduate students in the program. My work focused on Almodóvar's debt to pornographic film, as illustrated in the opening masturbation scene in *Law of Desire* (1986). A screening of *Law of Desire* was arranged, and I prepared a tape for in-class screening of its first scene and the first scene of *Matador*, another film made by Almodóvar the same year. I also provided the coordinator of the proseminar with a taped compilation of gay male pornographic film actors' screen tests—featuring solo masturbation and offscreen directorial voices, that seem to provide a structural model for Almodóvar's scene. Because this seminar was required, I thought it only fair to make this tape available for individual viewing on library reserve and not to screen it in class. The idea of requiring students—particularly women students—to look at erections, seemed too close to a form of sexual harassment. The coordinator of the seminar agreed with me and said he definitely could not show those images in his class. Ironically, no objections were raised by the instructor or the students to the screening of the first scene of *Matador,* which features a man masturbating in shadow while watching a video collage of slasher movie excerpts in which women are violently murdered. These are the kinds of contradictions that are opened up when we confront the cultural and political implications of sexual representation.[2]

Given the risks involved, what are the intellectual and theoretical justifications of teaching such material in university classes? I address these issues through three areas of inquiry: the historical relations between gay male subcultures and pornography; sexual practices as discursive practices; and comparative transgressions, a dialogic investigation of lesbian and gay sexualities and their representations.

THEORY

The Historical Relations between Gay Male Subcultures and Pornography

Gay pornographic texts were the first nonapologetic expressions of homosexual desire. The homosexual male sought in pornography "a means to self-ratification through self-gratification" (Yingling 6). The graphic description of sexual acts served not only as erotic entertainment but also as information otherwise unavailable (Blanchford). Like other late-nineteenth-century gay diaries, homosexual male pornographic texts served to document lives led in virtual isolation—both literally and culturally. In the 1920s Samuel Stewart began to write his legendary pornographic fiction under the name Phil Andros, initially as a defense against the isolation he felt in heterosexual society (Preston 5).

The real epistemological break came with the introduction of other technologies—namely, pornographic photography and film. These media also engendered radical transformations in the communities within which these materials circulated and in the subject as constituted and envisioned in these new representational possibilities. The cultural and psychological significance of gay male pornography for its intended audience cannot be understood within normative heterosexual morality. In its role as a medium for self-understanding within a repressive social regime, gay pornography configures visibility in its erotic and political senses.

We must remember that even the most benign and nonsexual representations of lesbian and gay lifestyles as positive alternatives have been legally deemed inherently pornographic (Bronski 160–64). Furthermore, hard-core pornography is often the only venue through which individuals learn the possibilities and parameters of their sexual preferences. Some artists and activists use sexually explicit images to reinscribe their sexuality into a culture that has erased it (Wojnarowicz 142–49). Since the AIDS pandemic, porn has taken on a new critical role, providing clear safer sex information and serving as a conduit through which the body and its actions can be reeroticized to create healthy and fulfilling sex lives that do not contribute to the spread of the disease (Patton 377–79).

We cannot afford to dismiss the contention that gay male pornography promotes male superiority over women much in the same way that straight porn does. But this objection should be considered an opportunity for dialogue rather than the closing of the discussion. While I have complete sympathy for the argument that certain pornographic materials and the industry behind them constitute violence against women and reflect patriarchal modes of oppression, I also wish to distinguish the case of gay men from that specifically heterosexual context and tradition.[3]

Antiporn activists often make a methodological error common to cross-cultural comparisons. For example, when Western theater scholars note that Brechtian techniques produce the "alienation effect" in Western audiences, they often assume that similar practices in Asian theater forms (the original models for Brecht and Piscator) have similar effects within their own spectatorial situations. Nothing could be farther from the truth (Jackson, "Kabuki" 469–70). When Kathleen Barry states that "homosexual pornography acts out the same dominant and subordinate roles of heterosexual pornography" (206), she falls into a similar error, in failing to account for the differences in cultural contexts within which the two forms circulate and in eliding the history of sexual difference, compulsory heterosexuality, and the "biologically authorized" rhetoric of unilateral penetration that inform and condition heterosexual pornography. When feminists accuse gay male pornography of reduplicating the sexualized exploitation of its straight counterpart by placing a male in the "feminized position" (Steinem 250), they are in fact affirming the very ideology that they seek to contest: the identification of the "objectified" sexual partner with "the feminine." Imposing a heterosexually defined gender disequilibrium onto gay porn also detracts attention from a problem inherent in gay porn: the effects of objectification, fragmentation, and sexual roles in images of men of color (see Mercer, "Imaging" and "Skin Head"; see also Fung).

The assumption that power differentials in sex are gender-determined and static is the founding myth of compulsory heterosexuality (the heterosexual contract). Through cultural interventions, lesbians and gay men expose as contingent the purported inevitability of the formulas male = subject = active and female = object = passive. A blanket condemnation of straight and gay porn is particularly unfortunate because our sexual practices and their representations are the most likely means of liberating heterosexuality from its own ideologies. Lesbians, gay men, and bisexuals have a civilizing influence on heterosexual culture in this regard and many others. Furthermore, while in the confines of compulsory heterosexuality the erect penis, wielded like a weapon, often becomes the icon of absolute power, if we include gay and lesbian sexual practices in the discussion, we find that the penis is definitely a sliding signifier. In gay male contexts, it is often merely a spectrum of opportunities for pleasure, an exclamation point within the discourse of the body of mutualizing bliss whose interactional dynamics are empathetic rather than competitive, worked out within the politics of ecstasy rather than within the terrorism of mastery.

Sexual Practices as Discursive Practices

In our readings of gay male literature and culture, we examine the role sexuality plays in the constitution of the subject, but we also define the subject in both psychoanalytic and social senses and thus define how the articulation of that sexuality becomes a mode of cultural agency and resistance. Psychoanalysis is useful because "it conceives sexuality . . . as a highly mobile psychical reality that is organized symbolically, and so is always in excess of the realm of biological needs and the cultural functions it is made to serve" (Fletcher 94) and because it elucidates how "sexuality [is] at work in all practices of the sign," including literature (Rose 229). When we deploy psychoanalysis, we oscillate between using it as a critical tool and reading its texts as symptomatic of the way Western capitalist culture has historically constructed phallocentric definitions of gender and sexuality.

The boundaries of the psychic and the social blur in the sexual practices of gay men as they assert their desire in specially adapted environments and networks; in so doing, they create themselves in what Michel Foucault has called a "homosexual askesis" (Lotringer 206; for a synopsis of Foucault's elaboration of this gay self-fashioning in his later interviews, see Cohen). Discursive expressions of gay male sexuality further reconfigure the relations between psychoanalytic and social constructions of the contested subject, both in building communities and in resisting the dominant order. Sex as practice and potential forms the terms of gay discourse: "[T]hese terms carry an urgency that has more to do with directing one's subjectivity than emptying the libido. These images invite and exclude much the same as the semiotic vocabulary of experimental writing" (Glück, "Who Speaks" 4).

Discourses are not freely chosen options but sites of contestation for interpretative priority. Repressive discourses cannot ensure their effects; in fact, "homosexuality" is Foucault's principal illustration of the instability of discursive power. Nineteenth-century medical and legal conceptions of homosexuality created means for social oppression and "made possible the formation of a 'reverse' discourse: homosexuality began to speak in its own behalf, to demand its legitimacy . . . often in the same vocabulary, using the same categories by which it was medically disqualified" (Foucault, *Introduction* 100–01).

Of course, both the repressive and the reverse discourses were virtually exclusively concerned with male homosexuality, a focus that greatly ramified the organic relations between male homosexuality and phallocentricism. Since its conceptual origins, male homosexuality has been elaborated within the internal contradictions of male heterosexuality and its thematized anxieties over sexual difference. In Freud's histories of the (male) sexual subject, it is often difficult to distinguish the heterosexual male from the homosexual: at times, the traumatic discovery of the woman's "lack" of a penis is fundamental to the psychosexual constitution of the heterosexual male ("Psychological" 187); at other times, the same discovery is given as a leading cause for male homosexuality ("Neurotic" 168; "Infantile" 174). Freud uses the Medusa symbol as an economic illustration of the horror experienced by heterosexual men at the sight of female genitalia yet then attributes the Greek "insight" figured in this mythic emblem to the Greeks' "strongly homosexual" nature, stating that it "was inevitable that we should find among them a representation of woman as a being who frightens and repels because she is castrated" ("Medusa's Head" 213). We might, for the sake of the argument, accept the plausibility of classifying homoerotic practices in ancient Greece with the term *homosexual*—a category that would have been unintelligible to the Greeks. But why would Freud use a symbol from a sexual "anomaly" to explain the sexual dynamics involved in the construction of "normal" male identity and "normal" male antagonistic insecurities in relation to people (women) who are alleged to be the "mature" objects of sexual desire?

In creating a dialogue between gay and feminist theory, it is important to distinguish feminists' anger at phallic privilege from homophobia—the difference between Luce Irigaray and Julia Kristeva, for example. While I share Craig Owens's outrage at the possible consequences of taking literally Irigaray's indictment of patriarchy as a "homosexual monopoly" (Owens 223–24), I would amend his reading of it by stressing her use of the terms "homosexuality" and "hom(m)osexuality" as critical metaphors to illuminate the repressed and thematized contradictions of heterosexual masculine power structures. Irigaray's larger projects—her deconstructive engagement with philosophy and psycho-analysis, her refashioning of sexual specificities and discourses that could accommodate them—are too important and suggestive for gay theory to discard them because of her albeit dangerous collapse of the metaphoric "hom(m)osexuality" and literal "homosexuality" in her pro-nouncement that "homosexuality" is the necessary organizing principle of patriarchies (*This Sex* 192). I would rather recuperate this strategy by clearly demarcating hom(m)osexuality as a diagnosis of heterosexual-ity, as Teresa de Lauretis does when she writes:

> I want to remark the conceptual distance between . . . homosexual-ity, by which I mean lesbian (or gay) sexuality, and the diacritically marked hommosexuality, which is the term of sexual indifference, the term (in fact) of heterosexuality.
>
> ("Sexual Indifference" 159)

Writers (feminists and nonfeminists) who have challenged the phal-locentric exclusion of women in traditional masculine discourses (poli-tics, psychology, religion, etc.) at times continue to hold definitions of male homosexuality uncomfortably close or logically analogous to those in the theories they otherwise deconstruct (for example, Marilyn Frye, Mary Daly, Janine Chasseguet-Smirgel, and Julia Kristeva). The work of Chasseguet-Smirgel and Kristeva is characterized by a literali-zation (and reification) of difference as sexual difference that allows the fear of sexual difference (which, again, was originally established as a characteristic of male heterosexuality) to be reinscribed in the male homosexual as psychological and political pathologies. Kristeva claims that the "pervert [who] invincibly believes in the maternal phal-lus obstinately refusing the existence of the other sex" has played a role—"in antisemitism and the totalitarian movements that embrace it," namely, "the fascist or socialist homosexual community (and all homosexual communities for whom there is no 'other race')" (*Chinese Women* 23). The same pernicious metaphorical slippage underwrites the hostile interpretations of male homosexuality in Roger Scruton, who views male homosexuality as a kind of Hegelian metaphysical failure (299–307).[4]

These examples—not to mention the incessant demonization of gay male sexuality in AIDS discourses—should make it clear with what urgency gay men claim the right to articulate the meanings of their sexuality and its expressions, particularly in its differences from the heterosexual masculinity in which it has been contained. To examine gay sexual practices in their specificity and plurivocality, I borrow the definition of *discourse* developed by Ernesto Laclau and Chantal Mouffe. For them, discourse embraces both linguistic and extralinguistic acts: it is not "a combination of speech and writing, but . . . speech and writing are themselves but internal components of discursive totalities." They explain: "[E]very social configuration is *meaningful*. If I kick a spherical object in the street or if I kick a ball in a football match, the *physical* fact is the same, but *its meaning* is different" (82). If we view sexual acts, their meanings, and their representations as three registers of a discursive field, we can also see how the recontextualization of the erect penis in gay contexts can radically alter its signification. For example, gay male depictions of the heterosexual male act, as in Almodóvar's *Matador*, foreground and parody the aggressive, contradictory, and non-playful use of the penis as a weapon whose penetrative power expresses hostility against the very site of its excitation and orgasmic release. The Trojan War dream in Reinaldo Arenas's novel *Farewell to the Sea* is an idealized paradigm shift that entails transformations in both the significations of the phallus and the social relations among men. In the first half of the dream, in which the warriors attempt to rape Helen, the phalluses are depicted as murderous weapons: "Agenor with a single thrust spits five Lycian captains on his proud rod." After the warriors succumb to the beauty of Paris, they become enamored of one another as well; their penises become sources of mutual pleasure, and the strength of their erections supports the infirm: "Old Priam . . . lean[s] at times on the rigid phallus of his son Hector" (29–32).

Even erogenous zones have valences that differ according to the discursive formation in which they are articulated. Irigaray blames the nonexistence of women in the phallocentric imaginary on an "anal economy" in which sexual difference has not yet emerged (*Speculum* 73–75; *Ethics* 100–01; see also Whitford 164–67). Thus the anus—site of sexual indifference—is the stage of the patriarchal erasure of women, and this "anal eroticism" reinforces Irigaray's conflation of phallocentric hom(m)osexuality with real male homosexuality (*This Sex* 171–72, 192–93.).

Guy Hocquenghem, however, in the discursive practices of post-1968 French political theory, reads male anal eroticism as a radical and liberatory reconfiguration of the male imaginary and its "plugging into" social relations. While he acknowledges that the anus is not sex-specific ("women have one as well as men" [89]), Hocquenghem sees the anus not as the erotic center of the erasure of sexual difference but as another detour around the mystification of the penis as phallus: "The anus does not enjoy the same ambivalence as the phallus, i.e., its duality as penis and Phallus. . . . [T]he desiring use of the anus is inversely proportional to social anality" (83). Therefore, he contends: "To reinvest the anus collectively and libidinally would involve a proportional weakening of the great phallic signifier, which dominates us constantly both in the small scale hierarchies of the family and in the great social hierarchies" (89).

Lee Edelman has argued convincingly that the trauma of the "sodomi-cal scene" often serves to undermine the fixed positionality of sexual difference that the castration complex supposedly guarantees (100–01, 104–07). Here also, male anal eroticism does not elide sexual difference; rather, it liberates social subjects from the hegemonically enforced con-sequences of sexual difference. The force of Hocquenghem's and Edel-man's reading of male anal eroticism comes from a commitment to feminist theory and an awareness of how the politics of sexual difference impinge on gay male self-understanding and political agency.[5]

Many gay male writers focus on particular transgressive sexual prac-tices as somatic strategies to rearticulate a specifically homosexual exis-tential relation to the world: for John Rechy it is public sex; for Takahashi Mutsuo it is fellatio (*Bunch* 66–73; see also Jackson, "Giv-ing"); for Robert Glück it is receptive anal sex (*Elements* 32–34; *Jack* 54–56). In sexual practices, the literal and the metaphoric are not easily distinguishable. An action has metaphoric implications, and the mean-ings of a given act result from negotiations among the agents involved and the interpretative communities in question. Takahashi's meanings of fellatio are in striking contrast to the interpretation of fellatio Sartre imposed on Genet's life and texts (127–28) or the meaning Freud assigns to it in his study of Leonardo da Vinci. Compare the meaning of anal sex in Glück with that in John Boorman's film *Deliverance* or in the social practices of Nazi officers (Theweleit 2: 306–27).

The meanings of sexual acts also differ among gay writers. For Glück, recipient anal sex is a revelatory connection between body and world; for Rechy, it is abhorrent (62). Hocquenghem and Edelman view it as a sexual practice with the power to displace the heterosexist imperative. Takahashi, however, sees anal sex as too easily absorbed into a hetero-sexual parody, preferring to write about oral sex, which maintains its homosexual specificity ("Koko" 54). Finally, Fung notes the other social contradictions that anal sex and sexual roles highlight in cross-racial male pornography (150–54). These contested discourses emerge through our readings of explicit sexual materials—including pornographic ones. Our differences from heterosexual male conventions cannot be ex-pressed within the tranquilized confines of euphemism and elision. We need literary, visual, and performative media that document and explore the ways our sexual practices distinguish us from heterosexuals while affirming us as individuals and as communities. To convey and extend our sexuality into the realm of culture, we often rely on pornography for structural and representational traditions.

Differences in Gay and Lesbian Strategies of Sexual Representation

The problematic interiority of gay male sexuality to conventional male heterosexuality and phallocentrism also grounds its differences from lesbian sexuality and its modes of expression. Although marginalized, gay male sexuality is still recognized under patriarchy. Lesbianism is inconceivable (Frye 155–66; de Lauretis, "Sexual Indifference" 156). Freud's case histories that fail internally are the two that deal with lesbianism ("Fragment of an Analysis" and "Psychogenesis"), although male homosexuality—overt or latent—never confounds his narratives. Our relations to the phallocracy partially determine our contestatory strategies of self-representation as sexual subjects.

We can begin to disengage gay male sexuality from the phallo-centrism of dominant culture by clearly differentiating the political and social overestimation of the penis as phallus in heterosexual phallocra-cies from the erotic investment in the penis among gay men. For one thing, the phallus is monolithic and absolute; gay male attraction to the penis, contextualized in a holistically eroticized body, is not always the focus of sexual desire. An examination of the institution of porno-graphic film itself also helps us distinguish the "worship" in phallo-centrism from the loving irreverence for the penis in gay male porn. Porn films are not "rated X"—they are not rated at all, because of the refusal of the Motion Picture Association of America to rate any film that depicts an erect penis. This refusal is in itself a religious decision: depictions of the erect penis (the stand-in for the phallus) place the film beyond classification ("the phallus can only play its role [as privileged signifier] as veiled" [Lacan 82]). Although a part of this sacrosanct cate-gory, gay male porn demystifies the penis by situating it within the supersaturation of its communal visibility and the ludic praxis of its constant availability. As Tom Waugh observes, "phallocentrism [is] not an explicit text in this fantasy universe where people are not divided according to the presence or absence of cock—everyone has one" ("Men's Pornography" 34). The real scandal that gay male sexuality represents lies in the fact that the playful use of the penis among men resolves the contradictions within phallocentric logic that must remain unresolved for the myth of phallic primacy to remain operative. In other words, if penises become "toys for boys," they are thus at once affirmed (and delimited) within lived experience and jettisoned from the tran-scendence of the ever nonpresent phallus. A toy cannot be an idol, and the god starves.

The erotic centrality of vision in gay porn, however, also establishes our relatedness to phallocentrism. Elizabeth Grosz surmises that the primacy of vision in Freudian and Lacanian thought "privileges the male body as a phallic, virile body and regards the female body as castrated." She notes that "the female can be construed as castrated, lacking a sexual organ, only on the information provided by vision. The other sensori-perceptual organs would have confirmed the presence of a female organ instead of the absence of a male organ" (39).

The scopophilia we share with heterosexual males implicates us in phallocentric epistemology and translates culturally into a specific social privilege:

> [W]hether . . . straight or gay . . . men in our society are conditioned to get off on/by looking. The institutions of heterosexual sexual looking, from advertising to the cinema . . . have always dominated the public space . . . to the exclusion of women's sexuality and . . . of gay people's sexuality. . . . [O]nly in the last generation or two have our rites of looking made a claim on part of that public space to which we are entitled as males in patriarchal society. . . . However, we must not forget that women's sexuality is still by and large excluded from patriarchal public space and that somehow our claim to societal space is complicit in that exclusion. . . .
>
> (Waugh, "Photography" 29–30)

That our claim to public space constitutes part of our "complicity" in the exclusion of women's sexuality from that space foregrounds the paradoxical status of the gay male (particularly the white gay male) in patriarchal society and illuminates a moment of our contradictory relation to that power conceived of as phallocentric heterosexual masculine norms of representation. While "women's sexuality is still by and large excluded from patriarchal public space," the context of Waugh's argument implies that inclusion of women's sexuality in public space would assume a visual form equivalent to that of the male sexuality under discussion. Certainly some women would agree: this philosophy is implicit in both *Playgirl* and *On Our Backs*, and it has been advanced as a specific strategy by Jill Dolan ("Dynamics" 169–71). De Lauretis, however, raises some interesting reservations about this strategy, which we should study carefully in order to understand how issues of lesbian representation differ from those of gay male representation. She writes:

> The simple casting of two women in a standard pornographic scenario or in the standard frame of the hetero romance, repackaged as a commodity purportedly produced for lesbians, does not seem

to me sufficient to disrupt, subvert, or resist the straight representational and social norms by which "homosexuality is nothing
but heterosexuality" nor a fortiori sufficient to shed light on the
specific difference that constitutes a lesbian subjectivity.

("Film" 256)

Merely re-placing women in the fields of sexualized vision (or envisioned sexuality) would not so much appropriate the male prerogative
of the visible as confirm as inevitable the masculinist "occulocentric"
(and thus phallic) conceptions of the sexually intelligible. Monique Wittig also evades a similar trap brilliantly in *Les Guérillères*, in which the
women refer to "the Feminary"—a text that gives cosmological primacy
to the female sexual organs and their imagistic metaphors—as something no longer necessary (30–32, 44–46). By replacing the phallus with
the vulva and the clitoris but then abandoning that project, Wittig first
subverts the hierarchized binarism of sexual difference and relativizes
the primacy of the phallus as transcendental signifier but then eschews
the reversal itself, since a simple inversion of the hierarchy would remain within the phallocentric logic it deconstructs. Wittig thus refuses
intelligibility in the terms of the order she critiques.

Such a refusal is not exceptional in lesbian representational strategies, which often seek to articulate their cultural empowerment and
independence from heteropatriarchy in terms derived from lesbian illeg-
ibility to phallocentric culture. One debate that would be highly unlikely in gay male theater evolved when the University of Michigan
produced Holly Hughes's *Dress Suits for Hire*. Sue-Ellen Case objected
to the contexts of reception (a largely heterosexual audience) and the
Sam Shepard–like style of the script, which made the performance
"available to the young male within his own frame of reference" ("Case"
12; see also Davy)—in other words accessible to the "general public."
Dolan, in her reading of several realist plays, concludes that "structural
codes of realism operate to mark and finally purge the lesbian enigma
from its bourgeois, moral midst" (" 'Lesbian' Subjectivity" 44–45).
Among avant-garde writers, lesbians more frequently dismantle the normally accepted criteria for intelligibility—genres, forms of continuity,
or the language itself—than gay men do. Compare Gide, Proust, and
Baldwin with Stein, Barnes, and Wittig, for example.

The refusal to "be accessible," as voiced in Case's objections to
Hughes's play, is a form of lesbian resistance. For lesbian cultures,
accessibility is often tantamount to erasure or co-optation. This an-
tagonism derives historically from, among other things, the definition
of all sexuality as male (Irigaray, *This Sex* 23–25, 86–87; see also
de Lauretis, "Sexual Indifference"). Because of the masculinist bias

within conceptions of sexuality and discursive practices, women have created forms to interrupt, or to withdraw participation in, phallocentrically determined norms of textual coherence. Sylvia Molloy's third person narrator in *Certificate of Absence* systematically refuses to follow the male traditions of the history, the autobiography, or the novel (8–9, 48–49, 68). Audre Lorde's *Zami* founds a new genre, the "biomythography," fashioned to accommodate the poetics of her own self-creation. Other writers create unclassifiable texts, such as Nicole Brossard's *These Our Mothers*, which destroys the patriarchal mother to create lesbian mother-daughter poetics and paradigm (Parker 313–15). One of the other foundations of the phallopatriarchal norm of cognitive stability is the "I," a monolithic male epistemological privilege from which women, according to both Irigaray and Brossard, have been excluded (Irigaray, *Speculum* 133–46; Brossard, *Aerial Letter* 139–40). Many lesbian writers problematize the "I," most notably Wittig in her creation of the split "J/e" of *The Lesbian Body* (9–11).[6]

In a nearly symmetrical contrast, experimental gay male writing, while usually still within the parameters of ordinary narrative and genre, often embraces and intensifies the "I." In *Funeral Rites*, Jean Genet's first person narrator, Jean, frequently takes over the "I" of other characters, slipping into them narratologically as one might sexually. A similar, pervasive metamorphic "I" appears in Burroughs's *The Wild Boys*. In both *Shy* and *Bedrooms Have Windows*, Kevin Killian's "I," also named after the author, either walks through and manipulates the narrative levels as eavesdropper and organizer of meaning or trains his narrative on the invention of his own "I." These are reappropriations of male epistemological privilege, but they are reconfigured within a narcissism in process that short-circuits the omniscience and ahistoricity of the classic narrator of the bourgeois novel and decenters its ideology from within (just as gay porn disestablishes the theology of the phallus from within the same visual regime). These "I"'s are excessive, just as gay male sexuality is excessively phallic, excessively visible, but they are articulated as transgressive repetition, a revenge of the proximate.

I am drawing a broad connection here between gay men's relation to phallocentrism and the explicitness of their sexual representations, and I suggest that their legibility within the dominant order may also account for less radical deconstructions within gay literary production. Moreover, I educe an antagonistic relation between phallocentric blindness to lesbian existence and the countervailing strategies by which lesbian sexuality is constructed as irreducible to iconography and lesbian subjectivity "as excessive to representation's conventional codes" (Dolan, " 'Lesbian' Subjectivity" 41). These comparisons can account for our potential commonality in contesting heteropatriarchy, while elucidating the differences in our positions vis-à-vis the hegemony and our respective strategies that develop from those positions.

I hope that these observations serve, however sketchily, to contextualize the teaching of gay male sexuality and to show that the use of sexually explicit materials in the gay male classroom is not merely a guerrilla-tactic titillation or an attempt to reify one form of sexuality and sexual expression. Rather, it is one component of a radical educational project of complicating our definitions of sexuality, its expressions, and the means by which other disenfranchised groups realize their sexualities interpersonally, politically, and culturally.

University of California, Santa Cruz

Notes

This essay is dedicated with gratitude and affection to my students, who constantly make my work possible and worth the risks. I am deeply indebted to Todd Baker, for generously sharing his files and his conversation with me. Thanks also to Dorothy Allison, Teresa de Lauretis, Andy Hasse, Neil Levine, Greg Pflugfelder, Takahashi Mutsuo, Jeanne Vaughn, and Benjamin G. White, and to David Jansen-Mendoza, my most constant and passionate critic.

[1] Stewart defines "pornography's predicament" as the impossibility of describing desire without generating desire; the impossibility of separating form and content within the process of sublimation; and, most important, the impossibility of constructing a metadiscourse of pornography once we recognize the interested nature of all discursive practices (163).

[2] I learned later that one woman student decided not to attend this session and wrote an open letter to the class stating that she could not participate in any discussion of pornography that was not based on a definition of violence against women. I take this position seriously and deeply regret that we did not get a chance to discuss it, particularly in the contexts of gay male autoerotic film and the new urgency among gay and lesbian communities for honest and explicit safer sex materials. The research described here is now part of chapter 4 of my *Strategies of Deviance*.

[3] Pronger argues that "heterosexual practice is an erotic and social confirmation of the division of power in our culture through the myth of gender. It is, therefore, a poor standard for the determination of the ethical acceptability of other sexual practices. The legitimacy of homosexuality lies not in its similarity to heterosexuality and orthodox masculinity but in its difference" (22).

[4] On Kristeva's text, see Merck 5–6; lesbianism fares no better in Kristeva, who describes it as a kind of stalled presexuality (*Tales* 80–81). On hostile interpretations of male homosexuality, see Dollimore 260–62. For other examples of this attack on homosexuality as a hatred of difference, see Warner.

[5] This reading is in contrast to both Barthes's and Foucault's versions of "homosexuality" (see Schor).

[6]On the pronoun issue, see also Wittig, "The Mark of Gender"; other means of radicalizing the language are found in Wittig and Zeig.

Works Cited

Arenas, Reinaldo. *Farewell to the Sea.* Trans. Andrew Hurley. New York: Penguin, 1987.

Bad Object-Choices, eds. *How Do I Look? Queer Film and Video.* Seattle: Bay, 1991.

Barry, Kathleen. *Female Sexual Slavery.* Englewood Cliffs: Prentice, 1979.

Blanchford, Greg. "Looking at Pornography: Erotica and the Socialist Morality." *Pink Triangles.* Ed. Pam Mitchell. Boston: Alyson, 1980. 54–67.

Bronski, Michael. *Culture Clash.* Boston: South End, 1984.

Brossard, Nicole. *The Aerial Letter.* Trans. Marlene Wildman. Toronto: Women's, 1988.

———. *These Our Mothers; or, The Disintegrating Chapter.* Trans. Barbara Godard. Quebec: Coach House, 1983.

Burroughs, William. *The Wild Boys.* New York: Grove, 1969.

Case, Sue-Ellen. "A Case concerning Hughes." *Drama Review* 33.4 (1989): 10–14.

———, ed. *Performing Feminisms.* Baltimore: Johns Hopkins UP, 1990.

Cohen, Ed. "Foucauldian Necrologies: 'Gay' 'Politics'? Politically Gay." *Textual Practices* 2.1 (1988): 87–101.

Cooper, Dennis. "Square One." *Wrong.* New York: Grove, 1992. 81–86.

Davy, Kate. "Reading Past the Heterosexual Imperative: *Dress Suits for Hire.*" *Drama Review* 33.1 (1989): 153–70.

de Lauretis, Teresa. "Film and the Visible." Bad Object-Choices 223–76.

———. "Sexual Indifference and Lesbian Representation." *Theatre Journal* 40 (1988): 155–77.

D'Erasmo, Stacey. "The Gay Nineties." *Rolling Stone* 3 Oct. 1991: 83+.

Dolan, Jill. "The Dynamics of Desire: Sexuality and Gender in Pornography and Performance." *Theatre Journal* 39 (1987): 156–71.

———. " 'Lesbian' Subjectivity in Realism: Dragging at the Margins of Structure and Ideology." Case, *Performing Feminisms* 40–53.

Dollimore, Jonathan. *Sexual Dissidence.* Oxford: Oxford UP, 1991.

Edelman, Lee. "Seeing Things: Representation, the Scene of Surveillance, and the Spectacle of Gay Male Sex." *Inside/Out: Lesbian Theories, Gay Theories.* Ed. Diana Fuss. New York: Routledge, 1991. 93–116.

Fletcher, John. "Freud and His Uses: Psychoanalysis and Gay Theory." *Coming on Strong: Gay Politics and Culture.* Ed. Simon Shepherd and Mick Wallis. London: Unwin, 1989. 90–118.

Foucault, Michel. *An Introduction.* Trans. Robert Hurley. New York: Pantheon, 1978. Vol. 1 of *The History of Sexuality.*

Freud, Sigmund. "Certain Neurotic Mechanisms in Jealousy, Paranoia, and Homosexuality." Rieff 160–70.

———. "Fragment of an Analysis of a Case of Hysteria." Freud, *Standard Edition* 7: 3–122.

———. "The Infantile Genital Organization of the Libido." Rieff 171–76.

———. *Leonardo da Vinci and a Memory of His Childhood.* 1910. Trans. Alan Tuson. Freud, *Standard Edition* 11: 59–175.

———. "Medusa's Head." Rieff 212–13.

———. "The Psychogenesis of a Case of Homosexuality in a Woman." Rieff 133–59.

———. "Some Psychological Consequences of the Anatomical Distinction between the Sexes." Rieff 183–93.

———. *The Standard Edition of the Complete Psychological Works of Sigmund Freud.* Trans and ed. James Strachey. 24 vols. London: Hogarth, 1953–74.

Frye, Marilyn. *The Politics of Reality: Essays in Feminist Theory.* Trumansburg: Crossing, 1983.

Fung, Richard. "Looking for My Penis: The Eroticized Asian in Gay Video Porn." Bad Object-Choices 145–68.

Genet, Jean. *Funeral Rites.* Trans. Bernard Frechtman. New York: Grove, 1969.

Glück, Robert. *Elements of a Coffee Service.* San Francisco: Four Seasons, 1982.

———. *Jack the Modernist.* New York: Sea Horse, 1985.

———. "Who Speaks for Us?: Being an Expert." *Writing/Talks.* Ed. Bob Perleman. Carbondale: Southern Illinois UP, 1984. 1–6.

———. "Workload." *High Risk.* Ed. Amy Scholder and Ira Silverberg. New York: Plume, 1991. 253–57.

Grosz, Elizabeth. *Jacques Lacan: A Feminist Introduction.* London: Routledge, 1990.

Hocquenghem, Guy. *Homosexual Desire.* Trans. Daniella Dangoor. London: Allison, 1978.

Irigaray, Luce. *The Ethics of Sexual Difference.* Trans. Carolyn Burke. Ithaca: Cornell UP, 1992.

———. *Speculum of the Other Woman.* Trans. Gillian C. Gill. Ithaca: Cornell UP, 1985.

———. *This Sex Which Is Not One.* Trans. Catherine Porter, with Carolyn Burke. Ithaca: Cornell UP, 1985.

Jackson, Earl, Jr. "Giving Godhead: Fellatio as Countermetaphysical Communion in Takahashi Mutsuo." Fourth Annual Lesbian and Gay Studies Conference, Harvard University. Cambridge, 4 Nov. 1990.

———. "Kabuki Narratives of Male Homoerotic Desire in Saikaku and Mishima." *Theatre Journal* 41 (1989): 459–77.

———. *Strategies of Deviance: Studies in Gay Male Representational Agency.* Bloomington: Indiana UP, 1994.

Jardine, Alice, and Paul Smith, eds. *Men in Feminism.* London: Methuen, 1987.

Killian, Kevin. *Bedrooms Have Windows.* New York: Amethyst, 1989.

———. *Shy.* Freedom: Crossing, 1989.

Kristeva, Julia. *On Chinese Women.* Trans. Anita Barrows. London: Boyars, 1986.

———. *Tales of Love.* Trans. Leon S. Roudiez. New York: Columbia UP, 1987.

Lacan, Jacques. "The Meaning of the Phallus." *Feminine Sexuality.* Ed. Juliet

Mitchell and Jacqueline Rose. Trans. Jacqueline Rose. New York: Norton, 1982. 74–85.

Laclau, Ernesto, and Chantal Mouffe. "Postmarxism without Apologies." *New Left Review* 166 (1987): 79–106.

Lehman, John A. "If Only Mom and Dad Knew . . ." *Redwood Review* 16 May 1991: 6.

Lorde, Audre. *Zami: A New Spelling of My Name.* Freedom: Crossing, 1982.

Lotringer, Sylvere, ed. *Foucault Live.* Trans. John Johnston. New York: Semiotexte, 1989.

Mercer, Kobena. "Imaging the Black Man's Sex." *Photography/Politics: Two.* Ed. Pat Holland, Jo Spence, and Simon Watney. London: Methuen, 1987. 61–69.

———. "Skin Head Sex Thing: Racial Difference and the Homoerotic Imaginary." Bad Object-Choices 169–210.

Merck, Mandy. "Difference and Its Discontents." *Screen* 28.1 (1987): 2–9.

Molloy, Sylvia. *Certificate of Absence.* Trans. Daniel Balderston, with Molloy. Austin: U of Texas P, 1989.

"News around the World." *Out/Week* 12 Aug. 1990: 67.

Owens, Craig. "Outlaws: Gay Men in Feminism." Jardine and Smith 219–32.

Parker, Alice. "Nicole Brossard: A Differential Equation of Lesbian Love." *Lesbian Texts and Contexts: Radical Revisions.* Ed. Karla Jay and Joanne Glasgow. New York: New York UP, 1990. 304–29.

Patton, Cindy. "Visualizing Safe Sex: When Pedagogy and Pornography Collide." *Inside/Out: Lesbian Theories, Gay Theories.* Ed. Diana Fuss. New York: Routledge, 1991. 373–86.

Preston, John. "How Dare You Even Think These Things?" *High Risk.* Ed. Amy Scholder and Ira Silverberg. New York: Plume, 1991. 1–16.

Pronger, Brian. *The Arena of Masculinity: Sports, Homosexuality, and the Meaning of Sex.* New York: St. Martin's, 1990.

Rechy, John. *The Sexual Outlaw.* New York: Grove, 1977.

Rieff, Philip, ed. *Freud: Sexuality and the Psychology of Love.* New York: Collier, 1963.

Rose, Jacqueline. *Sexuality in the Realm of Vision.* London: Verso, 1986.

Sartre, Jean-Paul. *Saint Genet.* Trans. Bernard Frechtman. New York: Pantheon, 1963.

Schor, Naomi. "Dreaming Dissymmetry: Barthes, Foucault, and Sexual Difference." Jardine and Smith 98–110.

Scruton, Roger. *Sexual Desire: A Philosophical Investigation.* London: Weidenfeld, 1986.

Steinem, Gloria. *Outrageous Acts and Everyday Rebellions.* New York: Holt, Rinehart, 1983.

Stewart, Susan. "The Marquis de Meese." *Critical Inquiry* 15 (1988): 162–92.

Takahashi Mutsuo. *A Bunch of Keys.* Trans. Hiroaki Sato. Trumansburg: Crossing, 1984.

———. "Koko, Kotoba, Unmei" [The Oral Cavity, Language, Fate]. *Symposion* 2 (1978): 53–66.

Theweleit, Klaus. *Male Fantasies.* Trans. Erica Carter and Chris Turner. 2 vols. Minneapolis: U of Minnesota P, 1987–89.

Warner, Michael. "Homo-Narcissism, or Heterosexuality." *Engendering Men: The Question of Male Feminist Criticism.* Ed. Joseph A. Boone and Michael Cadden. New York: Routledge, 1990. 190–206.

Waugh, Tom. "Men's Pornography: Gay vs. Straight." *Jump Cut* 30 (1985): 30–35.

———. "Photography, Passion, and Power." *Body Politic* March 1984: 29–33.

Whitford, Margaret. *Luce Irigaray: Philosophy in the Feminine.* London: Routledge, 1991.

Wittig, Monique. *Les Guérillères.* Trans. David Le Vay. New York: Vintage, 1971.

———. *The Lesbian Body.* Trans. David Le Vay. Boston: Beacon, 1975.

———. "The Mark of Gender." *Poetics of Gender.* Ed. Nancy K. Miller. New York: Columbia UP, 1986. 63–73.

Wittig, Monique, and Sande Zeig. *Lesbian Peoples: Materials for a Dictionary.* New York: Avon, 1977.

Wojnarowicz, David. *Close to the Knives.* New York: Vintage, 1991.

Yingling, Thomas. "How the Eye Is Caste: Robert Mapplethorpe and the Limits of Controversy." *Discourse* 12.2 (1990): 3–28.

The Lesbian Narrative:
"The Pursuit of the Inedible by the Unspeakable"

Marilyn R. Farwell

In a book on lesbian ethics, Sarah Lucia Hoagland confronts the problem of defining the word *lesbian* with a refusal: "I choose not to define the term" because any definition will be absorbed by the "context of heterosexualism" (8). Anyone who risks defining the lesbian narrative may be tempted to choose the same alternative because current critical opinion exhibits anything but agreement. Definitions of the lesbian narrative range from a novel by and about lesbians to a metaphoric disruption of the gendered, heterosexual structure of discourse. At one end of the spectrum Catharine Stimpson and Bonnie Zimmerman focus on what Stimpson calls the "severely literal" (244). For Stimpson, not political sympathy but the body, what "partakes of the flesh" (244), determines a lesbian text; in Zimmerman's specialized study of lesbian fiction of the last twenty years, the self-conscious writer and character signal the lesbian novel (15). At the other end of the spectrum is the extravagant claim that Bertha Harris reportedly made at the 1976 MLA convention: "if in a woman writer's work a sentence refuses to do what it is supposed to do," then we have "innately lesbian literature" (Smith 175). In a postmodernist move, Judith Roof declares that the lesbian narrative is determined by absence rather than presence. The direct representation of lesbian images in the movie *Desert Hearts*, for instance, is self-defeating because these images are immediately appropriated by the heterosexual narrative and made into fetishes "that phallicize and control the sexual activity of the scenes" (67). Literature like

Virginia Woolf's *Mrs. Dalloway,* which hints at rather than directly represents lesbian images, is potentially more disruptive because it is not caught in the narrative scheme that Roof believes is inevitably heterosexual (74–75). At the far end of any spectrum, Frann Michel half-jokingly argues the dangerous proposition that William Faulkner is a lesbian author because the relation between "two feminines," the feminized position of the writer and the work of art that is coded as feminine, makes his writing "a lesbian act" (13) and therefore, it would seem, makes his novels lesbian ones.

Amid this wide range of opinion, I suggest a middle ground and risk a definition that is both literal and metaphoric. I argue that the lesbian narrative is not necessarily a story by a lesbian about lesbians but rather a plot that affirms a place for lesbian subjectivity, that narrative space where both lesbian characters and other female characters can be active, desiring agents. This subjectivity is a way to describe the disruption that happens in the Western narrative, which by most current analyses is both male and heterosexual, when female rather than male desire dominates the plot. While I use this definition of lesbian subjectivity metaphorically, I also limit the metaphoric implications to female subjectivity and exclude nongendered agency, which, it has been argued, disrupts the heterosexual linguistic system of binary oppositions. By thus connecting lesbian subjectivity with female desire, I do not argue for an innate truth to a female self or an unconstructed female desire or insist on the equation of lesbian and female but rather claim that lesbian subjectivity is, in Teresa de Lauretis's terms, "a view from 'elsewhere'" (*Technologies* 25), a space in which the existent gender dichotomies are redefined. *Lesbian* is then a place or narrative space that partakes of old definitions of gender and realigns them. Unlike current advocates of queer theory, whose goal is, as Sue-Ellen Case states, to work "not at the site of gender, but at the site of ontology, to shift the ground of being itself" (3), I argue that *lesbian,* including the lesbian narrative, by definition treats the revision of female subjectivity that occurs when the lesbian subject refuses to remain within the old, narrow structures of gender difference.

One way to explore this large subject is to examine the construction of the lesbian body as the core of the lesbian narrative. The body is a particularly fruitful topic because Western ideology equates the female and the lesbian with the bodily and the sexual and because the lesbian body has become the site at which many women writers work to reconstruct and to reclaim female agency. The Western tradition codes the female body as negative and threatening, a body so excessive in its functions and sexuality that it must be controlled. The lesbian body, I argue, is an extension of the excessive female body and therefore the ultimate threat to the dominant order. Cultural discourses make the lesbian body not only an extension of the female body but also at times a silent, potentially frightening figure behind that body. To place the lesbian body in the traditional narrative is to invite conflict, for the old narrative's structure aims, often violently, to contain the woman and the female body. Monique Wittig, Adrienne Rich, Virginia Woolf, and Jeanette Winterson are women writers who work within the cultural construction of the female or lesbian body but also develop this same construction into "a point of resistance and a starting point for an opposing strategy" to use Michel Foucault's terms about the double nature of discourse (101). Before discussing these writers, however, I examine the historical construction of the female body and the lesbian body and the traditional narrative scheme that attempts to control them.

The narrative structure used to house these defiant bodies is built on divisions, differences, and boundaries. Adopting de Lauretis's insightful position on the Western narrative, I argue that the basic plot is intent on mapping out and maintaining not just abstract difference—such as a center/margin dialectic—but also sexual difference: "For if the work of the mythical structuration is to establish distinctions, the primary distinction on which all others depend is not, say, life and death, but rather sexual difference" (*Alice* 119). In a particularly fine distinction, de Lauretis separates these sexually marked spaces from the textual image or character. The function of the hero, she notes, is always gendered male while "the obstacle, whatever its personification (sphinx or dragon, sorceress or villain), is morphologically female—and indeed, simply, the womb, the earth, the space of his movement" (*Technologies* 43). The traditional narrative is the movement of a mobile figure, marked male, through a boundary or passive space, marked female. In this scheme only one gender has agency or subjectivity, and this gender also has the ability to conquer and control its constructed opposite. The bodily differences that are a part of this differential construction leave the female body in the space to be conquered and controlled.

Western thought crafts these gendered bodily distinctions as a way to establish and to confirm a number of oppositional values: pure/ impure, order/disorder, natural/unnatural. What seems most important to this ideology is the maintenance of boundaries between binary opposites. In *Powers of Horror*, Julia Kristeva defines the abject, that which we are repulsed by, not as an innate quality; it is "not lack of cleanliness or health that causes abjection but what disturbs identity, system, order. What does not respect borders, positions, rules" (4). The body that violates rules exceeds itself by exuding some form of culturally defined filth, a figure that "relates to a *boundary* and, more particularly, represents the object jettisoned out of that boundary, its other side, a margin"

(69). In *Rabelais and His World*, Mikhail Bakhtin also defines two bodies as a system dependent on the maintenance of limits or boundaries: the grotesque and the ordered body. According to Bakhtin, medieval and Renaissance thinking defined the grotesque not as unadulterated evil but rather as "a principle of growth" that "liberates the world from all that is dark and terrifying" (26,47); later centuries, he argues, simplified the concept and clothed it in negative connotations. Like the body that exceeds limits in Kristeva's theory, Bakhtin's grotesque body is "not a closed, completed unit; it is unfinished, outgrows itself, transgresses its own limits" (26).

It is not surprising that the body that threatens to destroy boundaries is, in our culture, symbolically female. The two defilements Kristeva identifies—excrement and menstrual blood—"stem from the *maternal* and/or the feminine, of which the maternal is the real support" (71). Although Bakhtin addresses class rather than gender issues, he hints at gender distinctions when he echoes Kristeva's characteristic elements of degradation: "acts of defecation and copulation, conception, pregnancy, and birth" (21). His most potent image of the grotesque body is the pregnant hag (25). In an analysis of *Othello*, Peter Stallybrass overtly genders Bakhtin's distinction when he points to the Renaissance assumption that the woman's body is by definition grotesque: always and "*naturally*" on the verge of "transgress[ing] . . . its own limits" and therefore in need of constant policing (126). Woman's potentially excessive sexuality, not her maternity, is naturally grotesque. Desdemona's perceived promiscuity is a logical result of Renaissance assumptions about women's bodies and sexuality. To find a contemporary image of the grotesqueness associated with the female body, particularly with birth and pregnancy, we need look no further than the popular movie *Aliens*, in which a notoriously destructive bestial insect lives in a dripping womblike chamber and uncontrollably oozes eggs to plant in human bodies, which then die from the horrific second birth. The Western symbolic system justifies this congruence of the grotesquely excessive and the female.

Although the maternal as the elemental female grotesque is the focus of Bakhtin's and especially of Kristeva's analyses, female sexuality, as in *Othello*, is also central to the Western notion of female bodily excess. Since ancient Greece, patriarchal culture has constructed a model of female sexuality that separates female sexual diffuseness from male sexual control. In *One Hundred Years of Homosexuality*, David Halperin attributes to classical Greek male attitudes about woman's desire the belief that it is "an undifferentiated appetite for sexual pleasure" arising "out of a more diffuse and generalized somatic need." What women need, according to this male construction of their sexuality, is "regular phallic irrigation" (36). Other historical periods describe this condition differently, but the same concepts are at work. For the Middle Ages and Renaissance, uncontrolled female desire led women more easily than men to witchcraft and fornication with the devil. The fifteenth-century compendium of witchcraft *Malleus Maleficarum* states this belief simply if not tautologically: "But the natural reason [that a woman is more likely than a man to be a witch] is that she is more carnal than a man, as is clear from her many carnal abominations" (Kramer and Sprenger 44). Another example of the need to control women's sexual lives is the Renaissance concept of the wandering womb, an anatomical phenomenon that is difficult to prove empirically but that can justify the argument that a woman needs regular heterosexual sex and pregnancy to save her from the dreaded consequence of her womb's wandering into her throat and choking her. "The remedy," states Coppélia Kahn, "declares the necessity of male control of this volatile female element" (34). The nineteenth-century concept of the asexual, virginal white woman is a middle-class ideal that depends for its counter on the notion that lower-class women and black women are "naturally" uncontrolled in their sexual appetites. Despite different terms, these ideologies seem to argue that woman is naturally sexually aggressive and uncontrolled and that she must be policed to prevent the destruction of the social order.

The late-nineteenth-century construction of homosexuality as deviance, combined with a time-honored concept of woman's sexuality, led to the condemnation of lesbians as lascivious. Lesbianism, which is not unique in its connection with excess (Roof 237–54), depends on its place in the spectrum of gender construction. Because lesbians are by definition not policed by male sexual desire, they represent to many sexologists the ultimate threat of a rampant and uncontrolled female sexuality. Freud, Havelock Ellis, and Richard von Krafft-Ebing associate this "third sex" with "female lust and with feminist revolt against traditional roles" (Newton 289). Krafft-Ebing summarizes much of the medical opinion when he says that "abnormally increased sexuality is almost a regular accompaniment of anti-pathic sexual feeling" (439). Abnormal sexual activity leads to other excesses such as criminal activity, especially crimes of passion. This threat is palpable in Ellis's description of lesbians: "Inverted women, who may retain their feminine emotionality combined with some degree of infantile impulsiveness and masculine energy, present a favorable soil for the seeds of passional crime, under those conditions of jealousy and allied emotions which must so often enter into the invert's life" (201). The criminal element of which these psychologists speak is not so much in the "invert's" life as it is in the refusal to stay within the accustomed boundaries; these good doctors believe not that the lesbian commits more crimes but that her existence is a crime.

While the fear of women's uncontrolled sexuality places lesbian sexuality on the continuum of female sexuality, lesbian desire ironically seems also to be more ambivalent, less gender-defined, and more likely to imitate (and therefore to usurp) male sexuality. Krafft-Ebing uses one case to claim indirectly that all lesbians show "unmistakable symptoms of *male* libido" (327). Freud attributes libido not to the female, because he views her desire as the goal of male desire, but to the lesbian, because her body and sexuality are outside male control. The lesbian is defined as masculine both in bodily characteristics and in sexuality because her physical independence can only be conceived as destructive of boundaries. It is not that the lesbian body refuses to be contained within the gender system; rather it exceeds that system by being what the system constructs as the ultimate threat: a female body, a woman's sexuality, independent of the male. The early-twentieth-century cross-dressing fad among women, which is familiar through Stephen Gordon in *The Well of Loneliness* (Hall), was, according to Esther Newton, a desire to declare "that women apart from men could have autonomous sexual feeling" (286). The fear, we could say, is that lesbians may become active sexual subjects rather than passive objects and thus usurp not male sexual practices but male subjectivity.

Many lesbian characteristics are constructed as masculine, physically and sexually. Krafft-Ebing devises four stages of what he considers a disease, beginning with masturbation and ending in an androgynous state in which physical and psychological characteristics of the opposite sex dominate the lesbian (399). Although slightly more positive about homosexuality, calling it a congenital rather than a diseased condition, Ellis also defines the lesbian body as contaminated by an excess of masculine characteristics. What Ellis calls the "actively inverted woman" (222) is distinguished by such important masculine characteristics as the angle of the arm (229), bodily movement, intellect (196), and whistling (256). The medical system tries to contain the lesbian by positing her as a threat that can erupt in any woman. The lesbian body and lesbian sexuality, however, are the female body and female sexuality attempting with a vengeance to grasp agency and subjectivity in a linguistic and narrative system that has no place for female subjectivity.

We can understand the traditional narrative as a story that seeks to control female sexuality and the female body. The narrative space coded female is, in bodily terms, that which the male-defined narrative movement intends to control and eventually to transform into nonthreatening—both asexual and nonmaternal—closure: the princess. The dead

Desdemona, a character contained within the narrative's walls, is the epitome of this goal. The Western plot accomplishes this conclusion by explicit or implicit violence, for violence is woven into the fabric of narrative. De Lauretis retells one of Lévi-Strauss's myths to illustrate the narrative's need to take over and to control the female body. In a Cunal tribal incantation to facilitate childbirth, the shaman becomes the heroic figure who seeks to separate the woman from her body, a body "she must come to perceive precisely as a space, the territory in which the battle is waged." He takes over this body for his own meta-phoric journey: "his descent through the landscape of her body symbol-izes the (now) unimpeded descent of the fetus along the birth canal" (*Technologies* 45). Through blatant use of similar imagery, *Aliens* again serves as a narrative example of the threat that the female body poses and the subsequent need for male destruction or control of that body. Played by Sigourney Weaver, the heroic agent is set against another female figure, the immobile obstacle coded as the female otherness of the monster. Ripley, the hero, is a male clone who must contain the excessive body of the female insect and her rampant, threatening repro-duction. Whereas in *Aliens* the capacity for excessive reproduction is the grotesque, in *Othello* it is female sexuality that is seen as grotesque. Because Desdemona chose independently to marry Othello, he is justi-fied within his cultural context in perceiving her as potentially adulter-ous. Since Desdemona's naturally excessive sexuality could erupt at any time, Othello must regain control of it, even if by her death. As Catherine Keller notes from a Jungian perspective, the heroic story is simply a matricide, for the hero "constructs his self-identity by this violent defeat of the values and claims of the female power" (62).

If the female body in narrative is threatening, the lesbian body is doubly so. The female transgresses its own limits because part of its defined nature is to throw off things, to push things outside itself: to menstruate, to give birth, to lactate. The lesbian body, not identified with birthing despite the exploding contemporary phenomenon of les-bian motherhood, seems to be a body not coded female because of its discursive refusal to enter into reproduction. But the sexually indepen-dent lesbian body, even when absent, becomes an archetype of the im-pure female body, and the narrative also violently attempts to contain the lesbian body. In Judith Roof's argument about the two soft-core porn films, *Emmanuelle* and *Melody in Love*, both of which depict lesbian sex scenes on the heroine's way to heterosexual "normality," the narrative movement encloses and excises lesbian authority through violence: "the parallel between narrative and sexuality becomes overtly apparent in a trajectory that links completion to heterosexual inter-course and often to violence" (18). The threat of rampant reproduction is also the threat of rampant sexuality, and the lesbian body represents the threatening, unknown part of female sexuality. One can even argue that the lesbian body is the ultimate transgressor of narrative limits because even when absent it is the silent threat behind the excess attributed to the female body not under male control. The lesbian body, then, transgresses carefully defined sexual boundaries by being "too" female; and at the same time, by refusing to remain the passive, though monstrous, object that the system requires, it also becomes ambiguously gendered. The lesbian body terrifyingly ruptures the distinction on which male, heterosexual power depends.

Injecting this disruptive body into a narrative system that works to contain and to control the female body and female sexuality invites a titanic struggle and demands realignment of the gendered system contained in the narrative. The writers I briefly discuss employ this culturally constructed narrative system as "a starting point of resistance" to the system itself. Each accomplishes this goal in a different way and also presents a different interpretive problem. Wittig's postmodernism in *The Lesbian Body* denies any connection with the system of gender; and in "Twenty-One Love Poems," Rich relies heavily on a romanticized reevaluation of the given gender construction. At the same time, both Rich and Wittig refuse to erase lesbian specificity in coded language. Their lesbian bodies are both literal and metaphoric. Woolf in *Orlando* and Winterson in *Sexing the Cherry* do not, however, have traditionally identifiable lesbian central characters; the texts are not "severely literal." But Woolf's and Winterson's constructions of the female body plays on, indeed depends on, excess, and their fantastic characters, whose bodily excess demands and extends the space of subjectivity in the text, can be called lesbian. Caught within an almost inescapable narrative system, each writer presents her story as a struggle with the system and uses the lesbian body as the center of her disruptive battle.

Wittig's *The Lesbian Body* has become a model of the lesbian postmodernist text that forges a space outside the male/female binary structures and therefore outside heterosexuality. For Wittig, the lesbian body's entry into the text signals a struggle with the narrative. Because the lesbian, Wittig says, is neither man nor woman but occupies a position outside these categories, the traditional narrative structure cannot absorb her vision ("One" 150). Wittig's narrative instead becomes a nonlinear series of poems in which figures like Odyssea replace traditional characters like Odysseus. These lesbianized (not feminized) figures restructure the heterosexual narrative. In a theoretical essay entitled "The Mark of Gender" Wittig describes her intention in *The Lesbian Body* to "lesbianize the symbols, lesbianize the gods and goddesses, lesbianize men and women" (11). Instead of the expected (heterosexual) sexual titillation, we are confronted with a narrative in which, as Elaine Marks claims, the "female body is undomesticated" (372), but undomesticated in violent and unfamiliar terms: "*I* discover that your skin can be lifted layer by layer, *I* / pull, it lifts off, it coils above your knees, *I* pull starting / at the labia, it slides the length of the belly, fine to ex- / treme transparency" (*Lesbian Body* 15). The shock and the antipornographic stance reminds the reader of the norm: the body of the woman and of the lesbian as a sexual object for the male gaze and male narrative control.

But to accomplish this feat of deconstruction Wittig must rely on the code that defines the female body as excessive and threatening and the lesbian body as the extreme version of this gendered body. By highlighting the violence and excessiveness of textuality in confrontation with female sexuality, Wittig exposes the gender system that autonomous female desire threatens. The body and sexuality become unrecognizable because Wittig takes the excess that the system attributes to them and explodes it into an excess that the system will not acknowledge. It is as if she were saying, "If you want excess, I will give you excess; if you want narrative violence, I will give it to you, but beware, you will recognize nothing and everything." Thus skin is torn from the body; hair is torn out by handfuls; the intestines are ripped out—all these acts primarily represent narrative struggle. The excessive body and excessive textuality heighten gender implications but also challenge the system that tries to control them.

In contrast, Adrienne Rich in "Twenty-One Love Poems" seems to romanticize the female body and the lesbian body in order to purge them of the grotesqueness that traditional discourses have insisted on. The one sexual poem, "The Floating Poem, Unnumbered," exists outside the numbered sequence of poems as if to declare idealized isolation from the rest of life. Here the lesbian lovers immerse themselves in each other, not violently as in Wittig's poems, but more gently, like the romanticized natural world to which they are compared: "your lovemaking, like the half-curled frond / of the fiddlehead fern in forests / just washed by the sun" (32). Instead of highlighting the definition of the female body as grotesque, Rich startles us with the opposite, a gentle and female-centered sexuality that the narrative cannot incorporate. The last sentence of the poem, "whatever happens, this is" declares the bodies to be outside history and outside the narrative of the lovers.

Opposed to the sexual body that stands outside the narrative as a constant critique of the narrative's violent gendered structure, is the body represented by the numbered poems, which is, to use Elaine

Scarry's phrase, the body in pain: the female body displayed in pornography, the male body tortured in a political prison, bodies physically separated in a homophobic world. A few moments of gentleness alleviate this pain: hands that through violence make violence obsolete, touch that comforts another in seasickness. Rich's task is to imagine two women together in a world (and in a narrative) that violently excludes them: "Swift / loathing the woman's flesh while praising her mind, / Goethe's dread of the Mothers, Claudel vilifying Gide" (27). Such women can exist in this world only as deformed: "We want to live like trees, / sycamores blazing through the sulfuric air, / dappled with scars" (25). Rich's battle, like Wittig's, is to find a way to incorporate the lesbian lovers in a narrative that the reader can recognize. "The Floating Poem" exists simultaneously as an outsider, as excess, and as a constant presence for each of the numbered poems. Rich redefines the excessive lesbian body not as grotesque but as imagistically lush and narratively excessive.

The female bodies in *Orlando* and in *Sexing the Cherry* are not identified as lesbian, but they succeed in becoming subjects of their own stories only because of their fantastic construction, their excess. In a narrative move I call metaphorically lesbian, these writers take female bodily excess to an extreme and use that excess to burst the narrative boundaries that usually deny female subjectivity. That transgressive body is not only female but also, because of its stubborn insistence on remaining outside as well as inside the system, lesbian. Armed with that definition of a different narrative space, we can examine other texts that, while not depicting self-defined lesbian characters or lesbian themes, do depict a disruptive female body that reorders the traditional narrative structure.

Woolf's *Orlando* playfully confuses the narrative order while trying to contain, or more accurately, not to contain, Orlando's male/female body. Although the book is often considered to be Woolf's lesbian love letter to Vita Sackville-West, its problematic status as a lesbian text has led Sherron E. Knopp to say that if the book "has any claim to be regarded as a lesbian novel, it is one of the best-kept secrets in literary history" (29). The main character is sexually defined primarily as a heterosexual; but sexual and gender confusion reign, for once gender definitions are unclear, sexual definitions also become unclear. In Orlando's relationship with the Archduchess/Archduke, for example, each encounter is determined by male/female symmetry, although the reader discovers later in the book that the Archduke, disguised as a woman, first falls in love with Orlando as a man loving a man. But Orlando's body, which is far from grotesque or lesbian, is excessive because it does not obey boundaries or rules. Orlando begins in the male space of mobile, heroic activity with a charming, although somewhat androgynous body. By switching the character's gender but not the active narrative space in which the character exists, by refusing to change the bodily image in accordance with the space, Woolf creates a transgressive female body that takes over the space of subjectivity. Because boundaries no longer contain the body, the narrative cannot establish clear lines of demarcation between active and passive character functions, between male and female. The space of subjectivity for Orlando's fantastic heroic journey is, I would argue, lesbian because it is carved out by her transgressive body.

Winterson's *Sexing the Cherry* also calls attention to the female body as excessive and transgressive in the main character, Dog-Woman, who also is not identified as lesbian. As the author of *Oranges Are Not the Only Fruit*, Winterson is certainly associated with lesbian writing, but in *Sexing the Cherry*, the specifically lesbian characters are to be found among the twelve dancing princesses. One of the narrators finds these revised fairy-tale figures living together after ridding themselves of the husbands they were forced to marry. Some princesses have found their husbands to be female, some princesses have killed their husbands in favor of women lovers. Dog-Woman, however, is an almost asexual figure, whose few heterosexual episodes are laughingly inept. But they are so because she is what today we would call a woman of size. She outweighs an elephant at a traveling circus; when a child, she broke her father's legs while swinging on his knees; the crowd at the circus compares her to a mountain range (19–21); and she herself says, "I am too huge for love. No one, male or female, has ever dared to approach me. They are afraid to scale mountains" (32). Hers is truly a body in excess. Her physical size, as well as her rejected sexuality, affords her a unique narrative space because her size is the one characteristic by which she demands a speaking voice, a subjectivity. She is the primary narrator and mover of the fantastic plot set in the political chaos of seventeenth-century England. Winterson's concentration on Dog-Woman's physical size makes the character one of the transgressive female bodies that becomes lesbian through excess and through usurpation and rearrangement of the narrative space of subjectivity.

In a 1977 article in *Heresies*, Bertha Harris complains about insipid lesbian literature that merely records "individual turnabouts of homosexual reality" (6); she argues that the "lesbian equivalent of . . . a [traditional] hero in literature is the monster" (7). Lesbian literature should be extravagant, she says, like Oscar Wilde's statement about foxhunting, "*the pursuit of the inedible by the unspeakable*" (5). I further Harris's contention by asserting not only that the lesbian hero must be the monster but also that the monstrous female must be read as lesbian.

The lesbian narrative, then, can be defined as a disruptive story in which the female is given subjectivity, not as a substitute man, but as an oversized, monstrous woman—as a lesbian. This definition, of course, leaves out some traditionally defined lesbian narratives, because the narrative system, not simply the character images, must be the site of transgression. Thus, when writers confront instead of ignore the cultural construction of the female and the lesbian body, when they seize and use these symbols for their own purposes, the narrative in which they place transgressive bodies is changed. The gender boundaries are rearranged; the narrative positioning of gendered subjects and objects is altered. As different as Wittig, Rich, Woolf, and Winterson are, they are all engaged in this radical project.

University of Oregon

Works Cited

Bakhtin, Mikhail. *Rabelais and His World.* Trans. Helene Iswolsky. Cambridge: MIT P, 1968.

Case, Sue-Ellen. "Tracking the Vampire." *Differences* 3 (1991): 1–20.

de Lauretis, Teresa. *Alice Doesn't: Feminism, Semiotics, Cinema.* Bloomington: Indiana UP, 1984.

———. *Technologies of Gender: Essays on Theory, Film, and Fiction.* Bloomington: Indiana UP, 1987.

Ellis, Havelock. *Studies in the Psychology of Sex.* Vol. 1. New York: Random, 1940.

Ferguson, Margaret W., Maureen Quilligan, and Nancy J. Vickers, eds. *Rewriting the Renaissance: The Discourses of Sexual Difference in Early Modern Europe.* Chicago: U of Chicago P, 1986.

Foucault, Michel. *An Introduction.* Trans. Robert Hurley. New York: Pantheon, 1978. Vol. 1 of *The History of Sexuality.*

Hall, Radclyffe. *The Well of Loneliness.* New York: Covici, 1928.

Halperin, David M. *One Hundred Years of Homosexuality and Other Essays on Greek Love.* New York: Routledge, 1990.

Harris, Bertha. "What We Mean to Say: Notes toward Defining the Nature of Lesbian Literature." *Heresies* 3 (1977): 5–8.

Hoagland, Sarah Lucia. *Lesbian Ethics: Towards a New Value.* Palo Alto: Inst. of Lesbian Studies, 1988.

Kahn, Coppélia. "The Absent Mother in *King Lear.*" Ferguson, Quilligan, and Vickers 33–49.

Keller, Catherine. *From a Broken Web: Separation, Sexism, and Self.* Boston: Beacon, 1986.

Knopp, Sherron E. " 'If I Saw You Would You Kiss Me?': Sapphism and the Subversiveness of Virginia Woolf's *Orlando.*" *PMLA* 103 (1988): 24–34.

Krafft-Ebing, Richard von. *Psychopathia Sexualis.* Trans. F. J. Rebman. Rev. ed. Chicago: Login, 1929.

Kramer, Heinrich, and James Sprenger. *The* Malleus Maleficarum. Trans. Montague Summers. 1928. New York: Dover, 1971.

Kristeva, Julia. *Powers of Horror: An Essay on Abjection.* Trans. Leon S. Roudiez. New York: Columbia UP, 1982.

Marks, Elaine. "Lesbian Intertextuality." *Homosexualities and French Literature: Cultural Contexts/Critical Texts.* Ed. Elaine Marks and George Stambolian. Ithaca: Cornell UP, 1979. 353–77.

Michel, Frann. "William Faulkner as a Lesbian Author." *Faulkner Journal* 4 (1988–89): 5–20.

Newton, Esther. "The Mythic Mannish Lesbian: Radclyffe Hall and the New Woman." *Hidden from History: Reclaiming the Gay and Lesbian Past.* Ed. Martin Duberman, Martha Vicinus, and George Chauncy, Jr. New York: Meridian-NAL, 1990. 281–93.

Rich, Adrienne. "Twenty-One Love Poems." *The Dream of a Common Language: Poems 1974–77.* New York: Norton, 1978. 23–36.

Roof, Judith. *A Lure of Knowledge: Lesbian Sexuality and Theory.* New York: Columbia UP, 1991.

Scarry, Elaine. *The Body in Pain: The Making and Unmaking of the World.* New York: Oxford UP, 1985.

Smith, Barbara. "Toward a Black Feminist Criticism." *The New Feminist Criticism: Essays on Women, Literature, and Theory.* Ed. Elaine Showalter. New York: Pantheon, 1985. 168–85.

Stallybrass, Peter. "Patriarchal Territories: The Body Enclosed." Ferguson, Quilligan, and Vickers 123–42.

Stimpson, Catharine R. "Zero Degree Deviancy: The Lesbian Novel in English." *Writing and Sexual Difference.* Ed. Elizabeth Abel. Chicago: U of Chicago P, 1982. 243–59.

Winterson, Jeanette. *Oranges Are Not the Only Fruit.* New York: Atlantic Monthly, 1985.

———. *Sexing the Cherry.* New York: Vintage, 1991.

Wittig, Monique. *The Lesbian Body.* Trans. David Le Vay. New York: Morrow, 1975.

———. "The Mark of Gender." *Feminist Issues* 5 (1985): 3–12.

———. "One Is Not Born a Woman." *Feminist Frameworks: Alternative Theoretical Accounts of Relations between Women and Men.* Ed. Alison M. Jaggar and Paula S. Rothenberg. New York: McGraw, 1984. 148–52.

Woolf, Virginia. *Orlando: A Biography.* 1928. New York: Harcourt, 1956.

Zimmerman, Bonnie. *The Safe Sea of Women: Lesbian Fiction 1969–1989.* Boston: Beacon, 1990.

Anal/yzing the Classroom: On the Impossibility of a Queer Pedagogy

Gregory W. Bredbeck

> Bottoms up.
>
> —Traditional toast

Jane Gallop's discussion of "the student body" in *Thinking through the Body* provides a starting point for what is a relatively bleak project: describing the impossibilities of a queer pedagogy. Analyzing the pedagogical techniques of Sade's bedroom philosophers, Gallop notes:

> One of Sade's contributions to pedagogical technique may be the institution, alongside the traditional oral examination, of an anal examination. The Sadian libertines have a technical term for such an examination; they use the verb *socratiser* (to socratize), meaning to stick a finger up the anus. (43)

This dynamic, Gallop suggests, may well be the basis of all pedagogy: "A greater man penetrates a lesser man with his knowledge. The student is empty, a receptacle for the phallus; the teacher is the phallic fullness of knowledge" (43). What disappears in this second formulation, however, is precisely what leads (or backs) Gallop into the topic in the first place: the anus. It becomes subsumed under the mark of the phallus, erased by a presence that will ultimately fill its absence. Indeed, if we were to follow the logic of this argument closely, we would find that the student becomes the anus, an "empty . . . receptacle for the phallus," but this transformation in turn places the anus *behind* the relatively opaque figure of the student. We might also note here how this argument tends to beg that the anus be compared with something like an anterior vagina (or at least the heterosexual male fantasy of such a thing), even though Dolmancé, the pedagogue in Sade's *Philosophy in the Bedroom*, "refuses on principle 'normal' penile-vaginal intercourse" (Gallop 43). If pederasty is, crudely put, an old prick and a young asshole, it here becomes just another dick and his chick.

The twist of logic derives from Sade's penchant for "heterosexual pederasty," which Gallop calls "a contradiction in terms" (44). I would suggest that this "contradiction" is really the condition of meaning in pedagogy, a condition explicit in the theorization of learning (whether in the classroom or in the bedroom) since at least the time of Plato, a condition that always changes (as Gallop does) the sexual *difference* of the pederastic Ur-scene into what Teresa de Lauretis would call sexual *in*difference.

To begin, I consider the text that subtends both Sade's neologism *socratiser* and all of Western pedagogy, Plato's *Symposium*. The supposed difference of this text has been marked and remarked in gay and queer culture. Clive Durham, for example, attempting to initiate romance with the central character of E. M. Forster's *Maurice*, opens with the quaint pick-up line, "You've read the *Symposium*?" (51). Yet in an already classic essay entitled "Why Is Diotima a Woman?" David Halperin suggests that what motivates Plato's text is a supreme indifference to sexual difference. The essay focuses on Diotima's "education" of Socrates: her lesson that the object of all love, especially pederastic love, is procreation, "the nearest thing to perpetuity and immortality that a mortal being can attain" (Plato 87). Moreover, the strange intrusion of this woman into the masculine world of drinking parties, Greek back rooms, and philosophy can be explained through this allegiance to indifference:

> Diotima's feminine presence at the originary scene of philosophy, at one of its founding moments, contributes an essential ingredient to the legitimation of the philosophical enterprise; her presence endows the paedagogic processes by which men reproduce themselves culturally—by which they communicate the secrets of their wisdom and social identity, the "mysteries" of male authority, to one another across the generations—with the prestige of female procreativity. Diotima's erotic expertise, on this view, constitutes an acknowledgement by men of the peculiar powers and capacities of women; thus, Diotima is a woman because Socratic philosophy must borrow her femininity in order to seem to leave nothing out and thereby to ensure the success of its own procreative

enterprises, the continual reproduction of its universalizing discourse
in the male culture of classical Athens.   (Halperin 144)

I quote at length because this type of argument changes irrevocably the
terrain of knowledge; Halperin suggests that at the basis of this origin
is a profound indifference to difference, a strategy of solidification that,
first, erases the difference between pederasty and the "contradiction"
of heterosexual pederasty by defining both as expressions of the reproduction of sameness and, second, nullifies gender difference by defining
all gender meanings and functions as various types, shadows, and shapes
of the male—a male marked as unified within reproduction, plenitude,
and continuance: *like father, like son*. We might remember that in
reality, there is no woman in the text, only a man's recollection of a
man's retelling of a tale a woman has told to a man.

I underscore the profound effects of Platonic ped(erast)agogy by com-
paring its strategies of indifference with Freud's most pedagogical text,
An Outline of Psycho-analysis. Describing the development of the sexual function—that is, explaining *differences* between "boys" and
"girls"—Freud states that with the dissolution of childhood sexuality
in the phallic phase, "[t]hereafter boys and girls have different histories"
(11). While both sexes "start off from the premiss (sic) of the universal
presence of the penis," development differentiates in the phallic stage
with the boy fixating on the "threat of castration" and the girl on "her
lack of a penis or rather the inferiority of her clitoris" (12). Boys and
girls are different, claims Freud, *but only in relation to the same thing*,
the perception of "the universal presence of the penis." Both gender
difference and sexual difference are secondary constructs recognizable
only in relation to a sustained sameness of one gender, one sex, one
penis. Indeed, Luce Irigaray's unearthing of this buried sameness—her
recognition that "the little girl is (only) a little boy" (25–33)—forced
her exile from the Freudian school and from the University of Vincen-
nes. The woman who questions indifference cannot be tolerated,
whether that woman be Diotima or Irigaray, unless the question is
somehow "used up" by the (re)productive male project, subsumed or
expelled, eaten or defecated. And, it should be noted, the Freudian school
is as much a boys' club as the orgiastic "boy-dello" that houses Plato's
philosophers or the pathologically masculine bedroom that is the center
of Sade's *Philosophy in the Bedroom* is; all are worlds of the same, by
the same, and for the reproduction of the same (but only insofar as that
same is masculine and reproductive).

Teresa de Lauretis best explicates the brutal indifference of these
pedagogical vignettes in "Sexual Indifference and Lesbian Representation," which combines the ideas of Diotima and Irigaray in a critical

formulation that explains the current impossibility of lesbian representation and provides a telling commentary on the ped(erast)agogy of Gallop, Plato, and Freud. As de Lauretis phrases her task,

> with the term *hommo-sexuality* . . . Irigaray puns on the French
> word for man, *homme*, from the Latin *homo* (meaning 'man'), and
> the Greek *homo* (meaning 'same'). In taking up her distinction
> between homosexuality . . . and 'hommo-sexuality,' . . . I want to
> remark the conceptual distance between the former term, homo-
> sexuality, by which I mean lesbian (or gay) sexuality, and the
> diacritically marked hommo-sexuality, which is the term of sexual
> indifference, the term (in fact) of heterosexuality. I want to remark
> both the incommensurable distance between them and the concep-
> tual ambiguity that is conveyed by the two almost identical acous-
> tic images.   (18)

I use de Lauretis's remarking of Irigaray to remark the dynamics of
sameness in all these scenes of pedagogy. In each "classroom," homosexuality is erased by hommo-sexuality; the presence of one self-reproduc-
tive gender (male) subsumes both gender difference and sexual
difference; the seemingly deviant ped(erast)agogy becomes a missionary
spreading the word of gender, which is always already the word of *one*
gender: man without end, (a)men. In this classroom, the hommo-social
woman can be nothing but a reproductive less-than-man, the gay man
can be nothing but a differently reproductive man, and the lesbian, I am
afraid, can be nothing at all. The frame of the classroom has a function
similar to that of the frame de Lauretis traces in the cinema, in which
(re)presentation remains "anchored or contained by a frame of visibility
that is still heterosexual, or hommo-sexual" (35) and in which any
difference only perpetuates sameness. That we should reach this point
of orthodoxy through a path leading from the Sadean anus is no surprise,
for such an outcome indicates the simple truth that heterosexual pederasty is *not* a contradiction in terms. The hommo-sexuality of the heterosexual that marks this supposedly different practice subsumes anything
that is not the same and reproduces any difference as indifference.

> Did you hear about the butcher who backed into the meat
> grinder? He got a little behind in his work.
>
> —Old joke

If the scene of pedagogy is always already a scene of the reproduction
of sameness in both a sexual and a social sense, we might be surprised

to see any discussion of it beginning with the anus. The phallus (Lacan)/ penis (Freud), which governs access to the symbolic and the social, should seem destined to govern such a space; the anus, which is (they say) a passing stage, a dirty and covert orifice, or simply icky, should be an outsider to this space of replication and indoctrination. And yet this outsider has, since the writing of *The Symposium* if not longer, always been the hole at the center of the ped(erast)agogical scene. To understand fully the indifference of the classroom, we must also understand both the privilege and silence that marks the anus in the arena of reproduction.

The place to begin is the essay "On Transformation of Instinct as Exemplified in Anal Eroticism," in which Freud claims that "the concepts *faeces* (money, gift), *baby* and *penis* are ill-distinguished from one another and are easily interchangeable" (*Standard Edition* 17:128). This formulation problematizes the division between the second phase of development, the sadistic-anal, and the third and final stage, the phallic, by suggesting that the "baby" and "penis" of the phallic stage are somehow mere supplements to the aggression and pleasure in the excretory function of the anal stage (cf. Freud, *Outline* 11) and conversely, that the sadistic-anal stage simply prefigures the phallic stage. Like the scene of ped(erast)agogy, this formulation guarantees sameness, for it implies, perhaps inadvertently, that the anal phase is always already part of the social-phallic phase. Lee Edelman has determined a similar continuum within the representation of the anus in the Wolf Man's analysis (Freud, *Standard Edition* 17:7–122); in Edelman's view, the anal trauma that organizes the Wolf Man's history establishes one "coherent narrative that offers itself as the basis for the binary organization of all logic and all thought":

> His anus . . . will be phobically charged as the site at which he traumatically confronts the possibility of becoming "like his mother," while the female genitalia will always be informed by their signifying relation to the anal eroticism he has had to disavow—a relation underscored by the Wolf Man's reference to the vagina as the female's "front bottom." (106)

The Wolf Man's anus becomes the supplement to the female genitalia, which is always already for Freud simply *not* the penis. Such a narrative of supplementarity suggests that the supposed difference of the anal and phallic stages is yet another indifference, another temporary deviation that leads us inevitably to *one* and *the same.*

The basis and implications of this sameness are curiously evident in the terse parenthetical equation of feces with money, which indicates the extent to which the (hommo-sexual) anus is associated with a system of economic (re)production that subtends both phallic and capitalist social relations.[1] The radical French theorist Guy Hocquenghem has explicated roles of the anus and the phallus in the (re)production of capitalism:

> If phallic transcendence and the organization of society around the great signifier are to be possible, the anus must be privatised. . . . The functions of this organ are truly private; they are the site of the formation of the person. . . . Every man possesses a phallus which guarantees him a social role; every man has an anus which is truly his own, in the most secret depths of his person. The anus does not exist in a social relation, since it forms precisely the individual and therefore enables the division between society and the individual to be made.   (82–83)

Hocquenghem's point, pace Gilles Deleuze and Félix Guattari, is that the body's codification into sites of sexual reproduction sustains economic production.[2] In this larger framework, the anus becomes the most crucially (re)productive orifice: "The great act of capitalist decoding is accompanied by the constitution of the individual; money, which must be privately owned in order to circulate, is indeed connected with the anus, in so far as the anus is the most private part of the individual" (Hocquenghem 82–83).[3] The anus is the hole supporting the whole of (re)production, for it is the absence that removes subjectivity into the private space of the individual and in turn assures that there will be private, individualized subjects to (be) (re)produce(d)—whether in the form of progeny (like father, like son) or in the imprinted social relations of the commodity (I shop, therefore I am). For Hocquenghem, the privatized anus functions similarly to the anus in Gallop's analysis, for the privatized anus by definition must "disappear" or "be subsumed" within and behind the social scene, even as it is the very precondition of that social scene.[4]

The function and trauma of privatization within ped(erast)agogy is painfully obvious in one final vignette, this time from Robert Musil's classic 1906 account of young Törless's coming of age at boarding school. The setup for Törless's indoctrination into ped(erast)agogy is a bit complex. During a school holiday, he finds himself in the dormitory with a student named Basini. Three other students—Beineberg, Reiting, and Hofmeier—have previously caught Basini stealing money. These three have blackmailed Basini into a series of sado-sexual sadistic inquisitions, which have become something of an open secret at the boarding school. Törless finds himself compulsively drawn to Basini and to the secret Basini represents in a moment whose imagery blends learning and pederasty:

> [I]n the front there sat Basini, at the back [Törless], holding Basini with his gaze, boring holes into him with his eyes. And it was like this that he wanted to read: penetrating deeper into Basini at the end of every page. That was how it must be; in his way he must find the truth without losing grip on life, living, complicated ambiguous life. . . .   (60–61)

The pederastic dynamic of male-male penetration here is diverted from the anus to the student body across the page of the philosophy book—a diversion that inevitably links sexual and educational penetration and also links this ped(erast)agogical blending with the hommo-sexual dynamic of scopophilia through the substitution of the eye (gaze) for the penis.[5] The "contradiction" of heterosexual (hommo-sexual) pederasty again emerges when Basini disrobes for Törless, for the sexual difference of this scene is drawn in heterosexual terms: "Basini was beautifully built; his body, lacking almost any sign of male development, was of a chaste, slender willowyness, like that of a young girl" (64); "it seemed to [Törless] as though a girl could not be different" (65).[6]

The attraction Basini holds for Törless becomes associated not with a specific practice or physical allure but with an eroticized and almost mystic interiority. Explaining the cross-examination that accompanies each sado-sexual inquisition, Basini recounts Reiting's litany: "First of all he gives me long talks about my soul. He says I've sullied it, but so to speak only the outermost forecourt of it. In relation to the innermost, he says, this is something that doesn't matter at all, it's only external" (68). This idea of the subject being split between inner and outer, between public and private, between anal and phallic becomes Törless's focus of attention when he questions Basini about the physical act of pederasty: "[D]oesn't it make a split go through your whole being? A horror—something you can't describe—as though something unutterable had happened inside you?" (70). Moreover, by the time Basini leaves, Törless himself has become fully inscribed by this division:

> [Törless's] attention was wholly concentrated on this straining to rediscover the point in himself where the change of inner perspective had suddenly occurred.
>
> But every time he came anywhere near it the same thing happened to him as happens to someone trying to compare the close-at-hand with the remote: he could never seize the memory images of the two feelings together. For each time something came in

between. It was like a faint click in the mind, corresponding more or less to something that occurs in the physical realm—that scarcely perceptible muscular sensation which is associated with the focusing of the gaze. And each time, precisely in the decisive moment, this would claim all his attention: the activity of making the comparison thrust itself before the objects to be compared, there was an almost unnoticeable jerk—and everything stopped.

(73)

At the end of the ped(erast)agogical scene, Törless has learned one primary lesson: "In solitude you can do what you will." Yet he has also learned that this private subjectivity is a mark of alienation: "This is not myself! It's not me!" (76). Like the Marxist worker, who labors in private isolation to create that which has meaning only in the public exchange (and hence that which marks the worker's own meaning as, simply, nonmeaning), young Törless exists as that which the social system demands but also excludes.[7] And he is also himself the commodity within this fragmentary system, the object that means only because it bears the imprint of the conditions of production. That this imprint of identity happens through a scene of pederasty only highlights Hocquenghem's point: the anus is at the *seat* of (re)production.

Shoot my head off, darling, and leave me just a highly sensitized anus.

—Andrew Holleran, *Dancer from the Dance*

The point of this rather circuitous meander around the anus is not all that heartening: the form of ped(erast)agogy is such that any difference included in the classroom simply sustains the reproduction of sameness. In each vignette I have discussed, the "classroom" involves two specific components: first, the construction of the base of sameness that will be (re)produced; second, the construction of the pedagogical subject as (re)productive of that sameness. Because the sameness that is the basis of this system is the desire for (re)production, any act of pedagogical production is also always an act of hommo-sexual (re)production. And yet precisely because the classroom is so intimately involved in the (re)production of social sameness, that site demands intervention from any program seeking social change. A passage by Edward Carpenter, one of the greatest and earliest socialist visionaries of the queer cause, demonstrates the double bind we face:

Not long ago the headmaster of a large public school coming suddenly out of his study chanced upon two boys embracing each
other in the corridor. Possibly, and even probably, it was the simple
and natural expression of an unsophisticated attachment. Certainly, it was nothing that in itself could be said to be either right
or wrong. What did he do? He haled the two boys into his study,
gave them a long lecture on the nefariousness of their conduct,
with copious hints that he knew *what such things meant*, and
what they could lead to, and ended by punishing both condignly.
Could anything be more foolish? If their friendship was clean and
natural, the master was only trying to make them feel that it was
unclean and unnatural, and that a lovely and honourable thing
was disgraceful; if the act was—which at least is improbable—a
mere signal of lust—even then the best thing would have been to
assume that it was honourable, and by talking to the boys, either
together or separately, to try and inspire them with a better
ideal. . . .   (229)

The Intermediate Sex, from which this passage is drawn, was published
in 1908 and was probably written sometime earlier—and in the light
of the work's historical placement in the wake of Victorian repression
and of Oscar Wilde's martyrdom, I do not want to minimize Carpenter's
revolutionary vision. I do, however, note the problem of (re)production
of sameness that it highlights. Like the chaste example of neocourtly
Victorian love, homosexuality must be viewed within the pedagogical
institution as "a lovely and honourable thing"; like (re)productive heterosexuality, it must be allowed to be "clean and natural." In arguing
for the acceptance of difference into the classroom, Carpenter also argues
for and validates the same principles that construct all sexualities as
(re)productive hommo-sexualities. The specific content may differ, but
the form remains, intransigent and impermeable, unaltered and unalterable—always, essentially, the same.

Returning to the principles of privatization and sameness that un-
derpin both Freud's anus and Musil's *Young Törless,* I can see no way
at the present that we can avoid this replication of sameness. I cannot
imagine a pedagogy that does not involve the (re)production of anal-
private and phallic-social sameness or one that avoids the binaries of
anal-phallic and private-social that overlie this single coherent narrative. For in the simplest sense do we not all want our students to
leave class with something that is entirely their own, some viewpoint,
perspective, or mode of thinking that they have *internalized* from our
courses? This places us in the position of Dolmancé, diddling with the

capitalist anus and engaging in the "contradiction" of heterosexual, hommo-sexual pederasty, even if what we ask our students to internalize is entirely queer and different. We labor under the illusion that our subjects, having internalized the queer lesson, will continue to reproduce themselves—or else we labor in a Sisyphean void that makes us nonmeaningful by rendering moot the (re)productive codes that have always already produced us as ped(erast)agogues. And hence we labor under the truth that the outcome of queer pedagogy will be the reproduction of reproduction, the reproduction of sameness.

The one possible hope that I see is, again, a risky one: to foreground the classroom *as* hommo-sexual, thereby demystifing it and, in a utopian moment, to render it subject to change. Such an admittedly Pollyannaish project would entail subordinating product to production, decentering our gaze, which is always fixed on the outcome, the *end* result. For we are products of a system of sameness that teaches us that what "matters" is the *bottom* line. Such a fixation of attention replicates and is replicated in the idea of "proper" heterosexual intercourse, which, as Hocquenghem so aptly states, demands that "all sexual acts have an 'aim' which gives them their meaning; they are organised into preliminary caresses which will eventually crystallise in the necessary ejaculation" (81)—an ejaculation whose material meaning will be imprinted only in the boy or not boy sired by the process. Such a notion denies the materiality of the process itself and denies its material significance. If we redirect our attention to the process of production as a material embodiment, even aside from its product, we may be able, if only briefly, to imagine a moment when a large enough quantity of queerness is employed in the production of sameness that sameness itself will appear queer.[8] This concept is, as Wendy Steiner has noted, the oldest crutch of Marxism, "the possibility that a change in quantity eventually creates a change in quality" (351). Yet even as I recognize the fallacy of equating quality and quantity, that fallacy enables me to imagine a classroom in which the deferred authority of *one* hommo-sexual product can be dialogized by other authorities embodied in the material coitus interruptus of process—a form of safer sex that might, perhaps, lead to a safer pedagogy.

University of California, Riverside

Notes

[1] For a summary of the basic premises of the interrelatedness of the evolution of capitalism and the differentiation of individuated sexual roles, see Weeks; for a more extensive and central examination of the topic, see Foucault 75–132.

[2] The androcentrism in Hocquenghem's formulation is, I acknowledge, troubling. The basic formula of one man, one anus is, however, true to Freud, who, according to Irigaray defines woman as not-man and in the process reduces gender to *one* gender much as Hocquenghem does. I do not posit this reduction as an intentionality in Hocquenghem's theory, but I do suggest that the androcentrism present, which in many ways springs from his disenfranchised position as a gay man, does not erase the utility of his theory.

[3] Elsewhere I develop Hocquenghem's (de)construction of the anus and examine the possibility of a gay male semiotics based on the anus (Bredbeck).

[4] Compare Marx's definition of the commodity: "a mysterious thing, simply because in it the social character of men's labour appears to them as an objective character stamped upon the product of that labour; because the relation of the producers to the sum total of their own labour is presented to them as a special relation, existing not between themselves, but between the products of their labour" (436). The private (anal) is the precondition of production, but the meaning of the production is only in the social (phallic) sphere. Hence the private-anal is always a part of the social-phallic.

[5] The substitution of the eye for the penis also recalls the similar mutability of the penetration of the gaze and the penetration of the penis that surfaces again and again in Freud. For an examination of the implications of Freud's "eye-penis," see Irigaray 47–48.

[6] Hocquenghem discusses this scene and finds Törless to be representative of "a polymorphous desire baffled by the signs of the guilt-inducing imaginary" (116). I think that this analysis tends to ignore the extent to which the institutional milieu originates the desire and posits instead the liberational but also largely utopian "body without organs" of Deleuze and Guattari as the Ur-force of desire. See also Deleuze and Guattari 9–35.

[7] The relation between the anus and the private subject is undoubtedly informed in postmodern theory by the significant Marxist scholarship on privatization, domesticity, and production. Engels's *The Origin of the Family, Private Property, and the State,* for example, is an obvious though tacit subtext to Hocquenghem's argument. For a provocative discussion of the problems and benefits of Marxism and homosexual identity politics, see Marshall.

[8] Although I formulated the premises of this argument some time before the argument appeared, it is helpful here to note the complementary relation between this formulation and Judith Butler's: "The task is not whether to repeat, but how to repeat or, indeed, to repeat and, through a radical proliferation of gender, *to displace* the very gender norms that enable the repetition itself" (148).

Works Cited

Bredbeck, Gregory W. "B/O: Barthes's Text/O'Hara's Trick." *PMLA* 108 (1993): 268–82.

Butler, Judith. *Gender Trouble: Feminism and the Subversion of Identity.* New York: Routledge, 1990.

Carpenter, Edward. *Sex*. London: Gay Men's, 1984. Vol. 1 of *Selected Writings*.

de Lauretis, Teresa. "Sexual Indifference and Lesbian Representation." *Performing Feminisms: Feminist Critical Theory and Theatre*. Ed. Sue-Ellen Case. Baltimore: Johns Hopkins UP, 1990. 17–39.

Deleuze, Gilles, and Félix Guattari. *Anti-Oedipus: Capitalism and Schizophrenia*. Trans. Robert Hurley, Mark Seem, and Helen R. Lane. Minneapolis: U of Minnesota P, 1983.

Edelman, Lee. "Seeing Things: Representation, the Scene of Surveillance, and the Spectacle of Gay Male Sex." *Inside/Out: Lesbian Theories, Gay Theories*. Ed. Diana Fuss. New York: Routledge, 1991. 93–116.

Engels, Friedrich. *The Origin of the Family, Private Property, and the State*. London: Lawrence, 1940.

Forster, E. M. *Maurice*. New York: Norton, 1971.

Foucault, Michel. *An Introduction*. Trans. Robert Hurley. New York: Vintage, 1980. Vol. 1 of *A History of Sexuality*.

Freud, Sigmund. *An Outline of Psycho-analysis*. Trans. James Strachey. New York: Norton, 1949.

———. *The Standard Edition of the Complete Psychological Works of Sigmund Freud*. Ed. James Strachey. 24 vols. London: Hogarth, 1953–74.

Gallop, Jane. *Thinking through the Body*. New York: Columbia UP, 1988.

Halperin, David M. "Why Is Diotima a Woman?" *One Hundred Years of Homosexuality and Other Essays on Greek Love*. New York: Routledge, 1990. 113–52.

Hocquenghem, Guy. *Homosexual Desire*. Trans. Daniella Dangoor. London: Allison, 1978.

Irigaray, Luce. *Speculum of the Other Woman*. Trans. Gillian C. Gill. Ithaca: Cornell UP, 1985.

Marshall, Bill. "Gays and Marxism." *Coming On Strong: Gay Politics and Culture*. Ed. Simon Shepherd and Mick Wallis. London: Unwin, 1989. 258–74.

Marx, Karl. *Selected Writings*. Ed. David McLellan. Oxford: Oxford UP, 1977.

Musil, Robert. *Young Törless*. New York: Pantheon, 1955. 116–33. Rpt. in *Calamus: Male Homosexuality in Twentieth-Century Literature*. Ed. David Galloway and Christian Sabisch. New York: Quill, 1982. 59–76.

Plato. *The Symposium*. Trans. Walter Hamilton. Harmondsworth, Eng.: Penguin, 1951.

Steiner, Wendy. "Collage or Miracle: Historicism in a Deconstructed World." *Reconstructing American Literary History*. Ed. Sacvan Bercovitch. Cambridge: Harvard UP, 1986. 323–51.

Weeks, Jeffrey. "Capitalism and the Organisation of Sex." *Homosexuality: Power and Politics*. Ed. Gay Left Collective. London: Allison, 1980. 11–20.

PART 4

Transgressing Subjects

The Disappearance of the Homosexual in *The Picture of Dorian Gray*

Jeffrey Nunokawa

The love that dare not speak its name has never been less at a loss for words than it is in *The Picture of Dorian Gray*, whose sybaritic expanses form a virtual theme park for passions "such . . . as Michael Angelo had known . . . and Winklemann, and Shakespeare himself" (149). Iconography as infamous as the text where it is ensconced gilds Wilde's novel from wall to wall. Processions of homoerotic idols parade through the text, "crowned with heavy lotus-blossoms on the prow of Adrian's barge" (144) or costumed as uppercrust clones of Wilde's own age, "the type often dreamed of in Eton . . . days" (160). All the usual suspects make an appearance: Paterian sentiments, ecclesiastical vestments, anthems to Hellenism, the extremities of aestheticism, a passion for interior decoration, glimpses of cross-dressing, dubious meetings on the waterfront, "the terrible pleasure of a double life" (154), and the threat of blackmail that never ceases to darken it.

More than that, though: homosexual desire is brazen enough in *The Picture of Dorian Gray* to venture past the avenues of intimation where its conduct is generally confined under the rule of canonical standards or family values, out of what one of its recent cartographers calls "the shadow kingdom of connotation" (Miller 125). Not content with congesting the byways of metonymic aside that compose the traditional ghetto, homosexual desire spills out into the wider boulevards of the novel's plot and takes the prouder place of explicit topic.

Basil Hallward, who falls head over heels for Dorian Gray at first sight, is subsequently so "absorbed" (28) by "idolatr[ous]" (145) passion that he offers up his "whole soul" (28) to the beautiful boy. This same "extraordinary beauty" inspires Lord Henry to enlist his considerable powers of eloquence to "make that wonderful spirit his own" (61). For his own part, Dorian Gray experiences an infatuation with Lord Henry intense enough to defy normal restraint: when the older man declares, " 'The only difference between a caprice and a lifelong passion is that a caprice lasts a little longer,' . . . Dorian Gray put[s] his hand upon [Lord Henry's] arm. 'In that case, let our friendship be a caprice,' he murmur[s], flushing at his own boldness . . ." (47).

Such revelations must have a familiar sound for a modern audience; when Basil Hallward confesses his love for Dorian Gray, those who dwell currently under the sign of Hellenism cannot help hearing the opening notes of their own song:

> [A while ago] I went to a party. . . . After I had been in the room about ten minutes . . . I suddenly became conscious that someone was looking at me. . . . When our eyes met, I felt that I was growing pale. A curious sensation of terror came over me. I knew that I had come face to face with someone [who] . . . would absorb my whole nature, my whole soul. . . . I have always been my own master; had at least always been so, till I met [him]. . . . Something seemed to tell me that I was on the verge of a terrible crisis in my life.   (28)

We have no trouble diagnosing Basil Hallward's perturbations as the birth pangs of homosexual identity; we may have trouble diagnosing them as anything else. His attraction to Dorian Gray appears as nothing other than the first act of the now well-developed drama of self-realization we call coming out.

And that in spite of testimony to the contrary: the "curious sensation of terror" that arrests the artist when he encounters the showstopping face of a beautiful boy prophesies a destiny quite opposed to the conclusion that defines the coming-out story. Basil Hallward's homosexual attraction threatens to engulf his identity rather than render it distinct; threatens to force him not from the closet but rather to the vanishing point: "I knew that I had come face to face with someone [who] . . . would absorb my whole nature, my whole soul." Our impulse, nonetheless, to read Basil Hallward's anxiety for his identity as a confirmation of it indicates the ubiquitous contemporary influence of the coming-out story. This narrative, according to what has become its standard history, is the most recent and most liberal administration of a denominational regime first instated by the taxonomic zeal of nineteenth-century sexology, as Foucault describes, and later crystallized in twentieth-century psychoanalysis and psychotherapy; a regime that lodges desire and identity in a tautological relation, a regime that defines who I am as what I want.

The role that Wilde and his work have played in inaugurating this regime has been well documented in recent years (see, for example, Cohen; Sedgwick). Basil Hallward calling his adoration of Dorian Gray "the secret of [his] soul," Lord Henry declaring the "passions" that have "filled [the boy himself] with terror" what the boy "really" is (42)—in the voices thrown off by an outlandish Celt, we may catch the early strains of an identity politics whose anthem will eventually become loud enough to make itself heard even on Saint Patrick's Day.

But as I have noted, Wilde's text declines to cooperate wholeheartedly with its *après coup* canonization as an Old Testament version of the exodus from the closet, a shadowy precursor whose difference from the contemporary coming-out narrative is only a matter of time. Lord Henry's claim that to recognize and to realize Hellenistic passions is to embark on the stairway of "self-development" (42) may be substantiated by the testimony of contemporary gay experience, but it is quite undone by the effect that such passion exerts on the characters who entertain it in *The Picture of Dorian Gray*. For here the expression of homosexual desire cancels rather than clarifies the definition of the character through whom it is conducted. By giving voice to desire, the hero of the coming-out story brings down the walls of the closet and delivers himself to the light of day, his identity confirmed or convicted; in *The Picture of Dorian Gray*, such voicing is less the password by which the self is revealed than the avenue where it is lost from sight.

This vanishing or vaporization is accomplished by a host of arrangements in *The Picture of Dorian Gray*, variously subtle, variously successful, extending from projects of self-sublimation undertaken by characters within the novel to rhetorical features of the text that contains them. It takes form as a simple act of repression when Basil Hallward, appealing to a distinction between art and autobiography whose defensive uses were later publicized in the moment of their defeat at the trial of his author, denies his own impassioned presence in the picture and wishfully declares that the work of art contains no traces of the secret of his own soul: "the artist should create beautiful things, but should put nothing of his own life in them" (34).[1]

The partition separating Basil Hallward from the picture of his love collapses with the certainty of the return of the repressed; his confession—always near the surface—that he has "put too much of [him]self in" (24) this portrait is as destined as the revelation of anything disavowed. But while the artist seeks to conceal himself under the cover of his art, a cover that the slightest hint of scrutiny succeeds in blowing, Lord Henry's self-effacement is more enduring. The painter is only tenuously denied in the painting through which his devotion to Dorian Gray represents itself, but the mentor is altogether sublimated in the course of instruction where his erotic attraction to the young man finds its field of play:

> [H]ow charming the lad had been . . . the night before as, with startled eyes and lips parted in frightened pleasure, he had sat opposite to him . . . the red candleshades staining to a richer rose the wakening wonder of his face. Talking to him was like playing upon an exquisite violin. He answered to every touch and thrill of the bow. . . . There was something enthralling in the exercise of influence. No other activity was like it. To project one's soul into some gracious form, and let it tarry there for a moment, to hear one's own intellectual views echoed back to one with all the added music of passion and youth; to convey one's own temperament into another as though it were a subtle fluid or a strange perfume; there was real joy in that—perhaps the most satisfying joy left to us in an age so limited and vulgar as our own, an age grossly carnal in its pleasures, and grossly common in its aims.   (60)

In the excitements of influence described here, sexual passion is not so much repressed as disembodied: Lord Henry's paean sounds like praise commonly reserved for sex—there is nothing like it—because the spell-binding lecture, whose every touch and thrill the boy answers, rather than furnishing a pale substitute for "grossly carnal pleasures" supplies an erotic charge that surpasses the limits of such ordinary intercourse. This passage sounds less like the frustration of a schoolteacher who finds a substitute for his desires in "just talking" than like the savoir faire of a phone-sex aficionado, for whom the subtle magic of words furnishes the most sublime circuit of erotic expression: "Words! Mere words! How terrible they were! How clear and vivid and cruel. One could not escape them. . . . Mere words! Was there anything so real as words?" (42).[2]

But if the homoerotic enthusiasm that takes form in the exercise of influence remains readily discernible as such, the shape of its subject is sublimated almost beyond recognition. The self-dispersal associated here with the expression of homosexual desire escalates decisively in the shift from the second to the third figure lodged in this passage, from the self's projection into a "gracious form" where it remains intact, ready to return, "echoed back . . . with all the added music of passion and youth," to its alchemical transmutation into "a subtle fluid or a strange perfume." This scent is familiar to us as the atmosphere of pedagogy, the afterlife of the well-known economy of personal sacrifice in which the individuality of the teacher is diffused rather than merely repressed in the manifestation of devotion and translated into the lessons taught: a "new mode of seeing," "the suggestion of a new manner," a habit of aphorism, a valorized text. The self-dispersal through which the erotics of pedagogy expresses itself achieves a climax when Lord Henry's "low musical voice" (41) gives way to "the music[al] cadences" (156) of the yellow book that he assigns his pupil, a shift that John Guillory has marked in a recent investigation of the acts of transference that define pedagogy, from charisma to curriculum. If the teacher's voice grows faint in the course of Dorian Gray's career (we hear Lord Henry lecture less and less as the novel progresses), it is entrusted to the text that Dorian Gray prefers, a text no less capable than its absent sponsor is of entertaining the boy in the erotic embrace of its influence: "For years, Dorian Gray could not free himself from the influence of this book. Or perhaps it would be more accurate to say that he never sought to free himself from it" (158).

The course of depersonalization by which the seductions of the teacher give way to the seductions of teachings that cease to belong to the teacher is the core curriculum of all educational institutions, from the most elementary to the most advanced. What is relevant here is the implication of homosexuality perennially attached to this general dynamic of pedagogy. When Lord Henry imagines the scene for seducing a young man as a classroom rather than a bedroom, he joins a faculty imagined by a well-known tradition of anxiety hard at work in the climate of scandal and controversy that beclouded Oxford and Cambridge during the second half of the nineteenth century, a tradition of anxiety that predates the Victorian period by about two thousand years and shows no signs, even now, of waning. Such anxiety has typically assumed the form of concern for "those young men" taken in by charismatic teachers like Socrates, Winkelmann, Newman, Pater, and Wilde himself.[3] The enduring suspicion that homosexual desire is conducted through schools may reflect the close fit between the homoerotic ambitions exemplified by Lord Henry and the current of depersonalization, that is the *dispersal* of charisma, which forms the currency of pedagogic influence generally.

The homosexual bias of the depersonalizing drift that I am seeking to chart here displays itself by contrast when we consider the effect of heterosexual desire in Wilde's novel. Such passion appears twice in the text, and both times it works to render its subject distinct. Love for Dorian Gray leads Sybil Vane to separate herself from the characters she plays onstage; the prospect of an idyll with a milkmaid is the light by which Dorian Gray attempts to annul the confusion of his soul with Hallward's and Lord Henry's by withdrawing it from the painting where all three are indifferently reposited.

But on the way to Athens, the desiring self is dissolved in the current that carries it: "if one man were to live out his life fully and completely, were to give form to every feeling, expression to every thought, reality to every dream—I believe that the world would gain such a fresh impulse of joy that we would . . . return to the Hellenic ideal" (41). As the "one man" nears the "Hellenic ideal," he dissolves into the elements of a subjectivity that cannot be specified; the possessive pronouns that would mark the particular subject of "every feeling, thought and dream" disappear as they approach Hellenic fulfillment, as if melted into air by the glittering climate of Greece.

The familiar contrivances of art and pedagogy, which appear on the surface of *The Picture of Dorian Gray* to render homosexual desire less a love that dare not speak its name than a lover who never shows his face, are secured at the subterranean level of rhetorical pattern, ratified by a confusion of narrative perspective that habitually arises when such desire gains visibility in Wilde's novel:

> Lord Henry looked at [Dorian Gray]. Yes he was certainly wonder-
> fully handsome, with his finely-curved scarlet lips, his frank blue
> eyes, his crisp golden hair. There was something in his face that
> made one trust him at once.   (39)

The work of self-denial engaged with obvious anxiety or cool facility by the painter and the teacher is sustained in the second and third of these sentences by the ambiguity of indirect discourse, the merging of Lord Henry's vision with the automatic supervision of third person narrative. This confusion is crystallized in the sentence that follows these by an impersonal pronoun ("one"), which enfolds and effaces the particularity of anyone within its vacuous generic contours. When the vision of a man turns to admire the "wonderfully handsome" features of another, the boundary that marks this vision as his own is dismantled, the eye made passionate by homosexual admiration dissolved into the faceless perspective of objective narrative.

Dorian Gray is himself dissolved when he returns Lord Henry's favor:

> [Dorian Gray] could not help liking the tall, graceful young man
> who was standing by him. His romantic olive-coloured face and
> worn expression interested him. There was something in his low,
> languid voice that was absolutely fascinating. His cool, white,
> flower-like hands, even, had a curious charm.   (44)

As this enthusiasm for Lord Henry passes from interest to fascination, Dorian Gray follows the lead of his teacher into a misty region of indirect discourse where the distinctions of his own admiring eyes and ears are given up to an impersonal mechanism of observation.

Such passages mark in miniature a de-individuation of perspective more extensively instated by a general trend in the novel: the men who adore Dorian Gray disappear into the impersonal throng of worshipers that grows and grows as the story proceeds. Basil Hallward's violently literal sublimation is matched by Lord Henry's less melodramatic withdrawal from the scene of *Dorian Gray*. Like the lovers or clients of a male model or movie star who first discover him on the beaches of Malibu or on Santa Monica Boulevard, these early devotees vanish in an anonymous mass of admiration: "There was something about Dorian Gray that charmed *everybody*. It was a pleasure even to see him" (150, emphasis added). Just as they are drawn by the processes of grammar from the bounds of their particularity when they desire Dorian Gray, absorbed by the confusions of indirect discourse and impersonal pronouns, the men who adore him are displaced, as the plot advances, by universal adulation. Basil Hallward and Lord Henry compose an avant garde of desire lost in the crowd they call forth.

Familiar compensations attend such sacrifices. The spirit of Hellenism may lose, as a matter of course, its local habitation in distinct subjects, but it gains a more comprehensive provenance instead. If the face of homosexual desire fades in *The Picture of Dorian Gray*, it fades into the light of common day; if the character of homosexual desire is cancelled, it is also universalized. The self that is lost in the current of homosexual desire has its afterlife in a narrative perspective and a common consensus that are larger than anyone in particular.

This Hegelian bargain distinguishes a central current of homoerotic passion in *The Picture of Dorian Gray* not only from a strain of homosexual desire regularly found there, the strain of homosexual desire where the identity of its subject has its source, but also, paradoxically, from a quite different version of such desire more recently associated with Wilde, a version of desire that simply disbands rather than disperses the character who entertains it. If the homoeroticism that inhabits *The Picture of Dorian Gray* has been deemed interchangeable with the coin of contemporary homosexual identity, it is also hailed as a prophecy of a postmodern sensibility that labors tirelessly to discredit the category of individual identity altogether.[4] Between these two resides the current of homosexual desire we have found at home in *The Picture of Dorian Gray*, the homosexual desire whose subject is finally nowhere and thus everywhere at once.

Princeton University

Notes

[1] On the state's uses of Wilde's fiction as evidence of his homosexuality, see Hyde 271; Ellman 435–65.

[2] I do not mean to claim that disembodiment is not itself a form of sexual repression, either within or beyond *The Picture of Dorian Gray*; I do mean to suggest that what is disembodied within and beyond *The Picture of Dorian Gray* sometimes has its own sexual intensities, that what is disembodied may define rather than deny the object of erotic interest. For an account of disembodiment as sexual denial in *The Picture of Dorian Gray*, see Sedgwick 163–67; for an account of disembodiment as the definition of an erotic object, see Deleuze 15–23.

[3] The phrase is Walter Pater's, and it appears in the famous footnote appended to the conclusion of the third edition of *The Renaissance*: "This brief 'Conclusion' was omitted in the second edition of this book, as I conceived it might possibly mislead some of those young men into whose hands it might fall" (223).

[4] "[F]or Wilde transgressive desire leads to a relinquishing of the essential self" (Dollimore 13). For Dollimore, Wilde's version of homosexual desire is consonant with current projects—Lacanian, Derridean—to promote the decentering of the "authentic" and integral self (3–100). For an especially riveting leaguing of homosexuality with an annihilation of the self that takes no prisoners, see Bersani 197–222.

Works Cited

Bersani, Leo. "Is The Rectum a Grave?" *AIDS: Cultural Analysis, Cultural Criticism*. Ed. Douglas Crimp. Cambridge: MIT P, 1988. 197–222.

Cohen, Ed. "Writing Gone Wilde: Homoerotic Desire in the Closet of Representation." *PMLA* 102 (1987): 801–13.

Deleuze, Gilles. "The Language of Sade and Masoch." *Masochism*. Trans. Jean McNeil. New York: Zone, 1988. 15–23.

Dollimore, Jonathan. *Sexual Dissidence: Augustine to Wilde; Freud to Foucault*. Oxford: Clarendon–Oxford UP, 1991.

Ellman, Richard. *Oscar Wilde*. New York: Vintage, 1988.

Foucault, Michel. *An Introduction*. Trans. Robert Hurley. New York: Vintage, 1980. Vol. 1 of *A History of Sexuality*.

Guillory, John. "The Lesson of Paul de Man: Discipleship, Rhetoric, and the Canon of Theory." *Cultural Capital*. Chicago: U of Chicago P, forthcoming.

Hyde, H. M. *Oscar Wilde: A Biography*. London: Methuen, 1982.

Miller, D. A. "Anal *Rope*." *Inside/Out: Lesbian Theories, Gay Theories*. Ed. Diana Fuss. New York: Routledge, 1991. 119–41.

Pater, Walter. *The Renaissance*. 1888. Chicago: Pandora, 1978.

Sedgwick, Eve Kosofsky. *Epistemology of the Closet*. Berkeley: U of California P, 1990.

Wilde, Oscar. *The Picture of Dorian Gray*. 1891. New York: Penguin, 1988.

Tales of the Avunculate: Queer Tutelage in *The Importance of Being Earnest*

Eve Kosofsky Sedgwick

FOR CRAIG OWENS

Let's begin—but only because everyone else does—with the Name of the Father. *The Importance of Being Earnest* is famous for ending with a scene in which its hero, who never knew his father (having been found as a baby in a handbag in the left luggage office of Victoria Station), tries to ascertain his parentage from his newfound aunt, Lady Bracknell, in order to satisfy a girlfriend who has determined that she can marry only a man named Ernest.

> JACK.   ... Aunt Augusta, a moment. At the time when Miss Prism left me in the hand-bag, had I been christened already?
>
> LADY BRACKNELL.   Every luxury that money could buy, including christening, had been lavished on you by your fond and doting parents.
>
> JACK.   Then I was christened! That is settled. Now, what name was I given? Let me know the worst. . . .
>
> LADY BRACKNELL (*meditatively*).   I cannot at the present moment recall what the General's Christian name was. . . .
>
> JACK.   His name would appear in the Army Lists of the period, I suppose, Aunt Augusta?
>
> LADY BRACKNELL.   ... I have no doubt his name would appear in any military directory.

JACK.   The Army Lists of the last forty years are here. These de-
lightful records should have been my constant study. (*Rushes
to bookcase and tears the books out.*) M. Generals . . . Mallham,
Maxbohm, Magley, what ghastly names they have—Markby,
Migsby, Mobbs, Moncrieff! Lieutenant 1840, Captain, Lieuten-
ant-Colonel, Colonel, General 1869, Christian names, Ernest
John. (*Puts book very quietly down and speaks quite calmly.*)
I always told you, Gwendolen, my name was Ernest, didn't I?
Well, it is Ernest after all, I mean it naturally is Ernest.

(187–89)[1]

No reader of recent critical theory will find it hard to imagine the joy
of recognition that such a passage induces—as if in imitation of the
play's own denouement—in sophisticated critics like Christopher Craft,
who recognizes in Lady Bracknell "a deconstructionist before her time,
a proper Derrida in late Victorian drag" (21). In a condensation with
which Derrida or Lacan would feel equally at home, the Name of the
Father seems here, all but explicitly, exposed as the guarantor and en-
forcer of two things simultaneously: the fiction of a "natural" correspondence between names and things, signifiers and signifieds, titles and
selves; and by the same token the forcible imposition of a "natural"
narrative telos in heterosexual marriage and the family. As Craft puts
it, Wilde

expressly targets the most overdetermined of . . . signifiers—the
Name of the Father, here Ernest John Moncrieff—upon whose lips
. . . a whole cultural disposition is hung: the distribution of women
and (as) property, the heterosexist configuration of eros, the geneal-
ogy of the "legitimate" male subject, and so on.   (36)

In Craft's reading, as in Joel Fineman's influential one of 1980, any
outlets from this monolithic cultural imposition lie in the strains that
can be painstakingly traced within the pseudonatural propriety of the
name—to begin with, of course, the proper and paternal name. For Craft,
as also for Jonathan Dollimore, the occluded gay possibilities of the
play, what are literally (in the homophobic speech prohibition dating
back to Paul) *non nominandum* 'not to be named,' surface mainly as
an oscillation in the relation *to* the name and in the relation, specifically,
of self to name. Finally, in the very concept of self. Craft: "For what
Wilde seeks in desire is not the earnest disclosure of a single and singular
identity . . . but rather something less and something more: the vertigo
of substitution and repetition" (22).

The vertiginous oscillation of "same" and "different" is the sensation most stably valued by this reading, and the one most identifiable with homosexual being. On the phonemic level, Craft argues, punning itself "becomes homoerotic because homophonic. Aurally enacting a drive toward the same, the pun's sound cunningly erases, or momentarily suspends, the semantic differences by which the hetero is both made to appear and made to appear natural, lucid, self-evident" (38). Dollimore, correspondingly, sees in Wilde's propensity for grammatical inversion a destabilization of the essentialist category "self" that has an intimate relation, as well, to what he describes as Wilde's experience of sexual inversion (32–33).

Each of these readings traces and affirms the gay possibility in Wilde's writing by identifying it—feature by feature, as if from a Most Wanted poster—with the perfect fulfillment of a modernist or postmodern project of meaning-destabilization and identity-destabilization. There is no question that the play, like Wilde's other writing, answers spectacularly to any such interrogation. It seems as if Wilde and his sexuality are being strongly validated, in these readings, through the almost uncanny verbal mirrorings they offer to certain already prestigious theoretical projects "after realism," "after Freud," "after metaphysics"—projects that have not themselves, however, had gay affirmation or an antihomophobic problematic at their hearts; arguably quite the contrary. Wilde's sexuality seems to underwrite discoveries of which we have already heard much in the register of heterosexism: a utopian aesthetic of the dizzying, an Oedipally centered demonstration of Oedipal impossibility. We are to admire Wilde for being Derrida or Lacan *avant la lettre;* "inversion" and the "homosexual" are hailed as magically exact precursor-supplements to a line of modernist/postmodern phantasmatic. Magically exact but perhaps not coincidentally exact—if, as one might want to argue, not only have the identities of the "invert" and the "homosexual" already been intimately marked historically by the requisitions of the very same modern phantasmatic, but, as well, that phantasmatic has itself already been intimately marked by the expulsion of the homosexual so neatly destined to arrive as its supplement.

Thus, on the one hand, I find these deconstructive readings of Wilde indispensably interesting and, to an almost tautological degree, "true." There is no question that Wilde is up to what these critics see him as being up to; how could he help being so, if both he and the violently repressive energies that silenced him and filled up the vacuum of his absence were so written into the origin of such interrogations? On the other hand, it also seems as urgent as it is difficult to find some alternative approaches: angles from which it might be possible to perceive the less theorizable resistances that Wilde may at the same time have been offering to these homogenizing modern(ist) interpretive projects.

I would suggest, to give only one reason for my wariness about these deconstructive celebrations, that Wilde "as a person" does not make it particularly easy to assimilate his own sexuality, even insofar as it is oriented toward other men, to either of the then newly available models for male-male sexuality, "inversion" or "homosexuality," the models that so enticingly facilitate the deconstructive project. There is no evidence of Wilde's vibrating very strongly to the chord of gender inversion—to the trope of the woman's soul trapped in a man's body, in the famous 1869 phrase of Karl Heinrich Ulrichs. When he did appeal to its energies, it was always with some extra twist that would make nonsense again out of the supposed schematizations of this model—as when it's *Gwendolen* who pronounces,

> The home seems to me to be the proper sphere for the man. And certainly once a man begins to neglect his domestic duties he becomes painfully effeminate, does he not? And I don't like that. It makes men so very attractive. (162)

Although Wilde's ambience was in many exciting ways charged with forms of gender transitivity, he does not seem very much to have seen or described either himself or those he loved in terms of inversion, even though the critics' assimilation of his characteristic grammatical inversions with a play of gender inversion would seem to depend on some such self-conception. What they depend on much more, however, is the constitution of gender inversion as a transparent and unexaminable part of the "common sense" of twentieth-century sexual tropology—however uneagerly the eros of Wilde himself may answer to such interpretation.

But neither, however, do the associations of the late-nineteenth-century coinage "homosexuality" appear to have engaged much of Wilde's formidable propriodescriptive energy. As David Halperin describes some of the concomitants of "homosexuality" (as distinguished from "inversion"):

> The conceptual isolation of sexuality *per se* from questions of masculinity and femininity made possible a new taxonomy of sexual behaviors and psychologies based entirely on the anatomical sex of the persons engaged in a sexual act (same sex vs. different sex); it thereby obliterated a number of distinctions that had traditionally operated within earlier discourses pertaining to same-sex sexual contacts. . . : all such behaviors were now to be classed alike and placed under the same heading. (16)

Initiating, along with the stigma of narcissism, the utopic modern vision of a bond whose egalitarian potential might be guaranteed by the exclusion of any consequential difference, the new calculus of homo/hetero, on which critics draw in assimilating Wilde's "homo" sexuality to his use of the "homophonic" pun as opposed to "heterophonic" reference (as Craft does [38]) or of the "autological" as opposed to the "heterological" signifier (as Fineman does [88–89])—the new calculus, as I have pointed out in *Epistemology of the Closet*, owes its sleekly utilitarian feel to the linguistically unappealable classification of anyone who shares one's gender as being "the same" as oneself and anyone who does not share one's gender as being one's Other.

It is startling to realize that the aspect of "homosexuality" that now seems in many ways most immutably to fix it—its dependence on a defining sameness between partners—is of so recent crystallization. (The process is also, one ought to add, still radically incomplete and geoculturally partial.) Wilde's work was certainly marked by a grappling with the implications of the new homo/hetero terms. It seems patent that in the paradigm clash among these ways of thinking male-male desire, Wilde's own eros was most closely tuned to the note of the pederastic love in process of being superseded—and, we may as well therefore say, radically misrepresented—by the homo/hetero imposition. Though a passionate classicist, Wilde did not desire only boys; but his desires seem to have been structured intensely by the crossing of definitional lines—of age, milieu, initiatedness, and physique, most notably—sufficiently marked to make him an embattled subject for the "homosexual" homo-genization that is by now critically routine. It is routine, to repeat, not because of its adequacy to Wilde's desiring self— though it was certainly part, a resisted part, of his discursive and creative world—but because it so efficiently fills so many modern analytic, diagnostic, and (hence) even deconstructive needs.

As we have seen, the indispensable—but, I am arguing, insufficient— deconstructive reading of *Earnest* always seems, like the play's hero, to have its origin in a terminus. It doesn't pass Go; it doesn't collect $200; it heads straight for the end-of-the-third-act anagnorisis (recognition or de-forgetting) of the Name of the Father. The sexual different-ness of the play and/or of its author gets subsumed in these readings, under the law of the Father, as that one-size-fits-all "difference" that can always be conscripted to play the same old play with the "same." Bottom line: the totemic force of the Oedipal father-son imperative, its systemic equivalence with everything that could at all be called family, individuation, or meaning, is only strengthened by the congruence with it of these new and glamorous, notionally subversive terms and sexualities—

by the rhetorical sublimity and "dizzying" unthinkability of any alternative topos.

Forget the Name of the Father.

Forget the Name of the Father!

Why can't that, which is after all what these characters remarkably do for the first seventy-four seventy-fifths of *The Importance of Being Earnest*, be said to constitute its imperative—that, rather than the final forced march of the play's amnesiac farce into the glare-lighted, barbed-wire Oedipal holding pen of the very last page?

The injunction to forget, of course, to forget something-in-particular after its jolting anamnesis, as you know if you've ever tried to do it— four in the morning, haplessly alert, knowing you'll never get back to sleep if you can't stop thinking about a certain X—opens an interminably self-defeating involution, self-defeating unless some other term (if only some other fetishistically summoned image, another name, another face, another repeated phrase) can be substituted for X. The only way to forget X is to invoke Y in her place. It can only partially work (your obsessional thought will not cease to be marked by the structuring imperative of X; by analogy, I hardly suppose a coherent textual approach to be possible that would lie fully outside the terms of the anagnoritic ones), but it can work "enough," in the sense of making an unforeseen difference in the effect to which X presides over your obsessional process. I suggest, or I suggest the play suggests: Forget the Name of the Father. Think about your uncles and your aunts.

Think about aunts and uncles because, to begin with, the presiding representative of the previous generation in *The Importance of Being Earnest* is neither the heroes' father nor even their mother but an aunt, Lady Bracknell—a part often played, of course, *Charley's Aunt*–style, by a male actor in woman's dress. Although Aunt Augusta is the very opposite of effeminate, *aunt*, *auntie*, or the French *tante* were recognized throughout the nineteenth century, and are still widely recognized, as terms for (what an 1889 slang dictionary calls) a "passive sodomist" (qtd. in Bartlett 90)—or, more likely, for any man who displays a queenly demeanor, whatever he may do with other men in bed. (Proust's original name for his 1909 essay on "the men-women of Sodom," the real catalyst, apparently, of *Remembrance of Things Past*, was "La race des tantes.") *Uncle*, at the same time, was a common term for a male protector in a sexual relation involving economic sponsorship and, typically, class and age transitivity. *Uncle* has been common, as well, in gradations from the literal, as a metonym for the whole range of older men who might form a relation to a younger man (as patron, friend, literal uncle, godfather, adoptive father, sugar daddy), offering a degree of initiation into gay cultures and identities—like the older man whom a friend of mine, my age, always refers to warmly as his fairy godmother.

Uncle and *aunt* in these very gay-marked meanings don't add up to two complementary male roles, as for instance a "masculine" and a "feminine": even if you wanted to, you couldn't pair an uncle up with an auntie and bundle them off for a happy, heterosexually intelligible honeymoon. *Uncle* and *aunt* aren't even both "figures of speech" in the same sense. Furthermore, *aunt*, used about a man, alludes to a gender-transitive persona that, however, it doesn't particularly pretend to stabilize in the dyadic terms of gender inversion: the *aunt* usage long predates and surely influences, but is not adequated by, the rationalized discursive production of the invert. *Aunt* tells who or how you are (at least sometimes) but not whom you desire. *Uncle* is very different, *not* a persona or type but a relation, relying on a pederastic/pedagogical model of male filiation to which also, as we have seen, the modern rationalized inversion and "homo-" models answer only incompletely and very distortingly. But of course it is the very badness of the fit of *uncle* and *aunt*—the badness of their fit with each other in the first place but also with the streamlined modern models of "family" and of same-sex attachment—that makes them such good places to look for some of the gravity of Wilde's resistance to the sleek "same"/"different" scientism of modern gender and sexual preference.

The interest of uncles and aunts isn't confined to particular, more or less figural usages of the words, though. There are plenty of signals that the constitution and recognition of aunts and uncles has as much as that of parents to do with the identity issues of *The Importance of Being Earnest*. Early in the play, for example, there's a scene where Jack tries to wheedle his friend Algernon into returning his missing cigarette case, without acknowledging to Algernon the existence of his marriageable young ward, Cecily, from whom it was a gift.

> JACK. I simply want my cigarette case back.
> ALGERNON. Yes; but this isn't your cigarette case. This cigarette case is a present from someone of the name of Cecily, and you said you didn't know anyone of that name.
> JACK. Well, if you want to know, Cecily happens to be my aunt.
> ALGERNON. Your aunt!
> JACK. Yes. Charming old lady she is, too. Lives at Tunbridge Wells. Just give it back to me, Algy.
> ALGERNON. But why does she call herself little Cecily if she is your aunt and lives at Tunbridge Wells? (*Reading.*) "From little Cecily with her fondest love."

JACK.   My dear fellow, what on earth is there in that? Some aunts
are tall, some aunts are not tall. That is a matter that surely
an aunt may be allowed to decide for herself. You seem to think
that every aunt should be exactly like your aunt! That is absurd!
[There is a great variety in aunts. You can have aunts of any
shape or size you like. My aunt is a small aunt.[2]] For Heaven's
sake give me back my cigarette case.

ALGERNON.   Yes. But why does your aunt call you her uncle?
"From little Cecily, with fondest love to her dear Uncle Jack."
There is no objection, I admit, to an aunt being a small aunt,
but why an aunt, no matter what her size may be, should call
her own nephew her uncle, I can't quite make out.   (120–21)

What may be at stake in the making visible of aunts and uncles in
this play? In some cryptic but very provocative paragraphs in his essay
"Outlaws: Gay Men in Feminism," Craig Owens suggests that the turn-
of-the-century Freudian recasting of the (supposedly universal) incest
taboo—from being, as anthropologists describe it, a prohibition that
chiefly involves avuncular and sibling-in-law relations to being, in the
Oedipal, a prohibition of directly cross-generational relations between
parent and child—may have had gravely obfuscatory consequences for
modern understandings of sexuality. The possibility of an uncle-cen-
tered rather than a parent-centered reading of traditional cultures suggests, Owens says, "that the incest taboo may actually work to integrate
homosexual impulses into the sexual economy, and that the 'repression'
of homosexuality may be less [than] universal" (228).

In saying this, Owens may be drawing on some formulations of Juliet
Mitchell's that are not themselves particularly concerned with homo/
hetero issues. In *Psychoanalysis and Feminism*, Mitchell, too, points
to the distance between, on the one hand, the broadly filiated "anthropo-
logical" incest taboo, involving men's circulation of sisters, to be rewarded by the acquisition of brothers-in-law and nephews (as formulated
by, for example, Lévi-Strauss), and, on the other, the more nuclearized
incest taboo formulated as the Oedipus complex, "its internalized
form," in Freud (375). The difference, essentially, seems to be the drop-
ping out of a fourth term that had complicated and rendered "cultural"
the biological triad: that fourth term being the maternal uncle. In the
avuncular relation, Mitchell summarizes,

[t]he maternal brother offers his sister to his thereby future brother-
in-law, within this generation he therefore acts as mediator between his brother-in-law and the latter's wife (his sister); furthermore, he mediates between these parents and their child (his

nephew]; he thus has a horizontal and vertical role. The uncle ensures that the vicious cycle [of incestuous brother-sister endogamy] cannot come again. . . . The holy (bestial) family will not reign supreme. There always has to be some other term that mediates and transforms the deathly symmetry, the impossibility for culture, of the biological family: within the kinship structure, classically this term is the maternal uncle. (375)

Mitchell gives a Marxist-inflected account of the transition from kinship societies to modern ones:

In economically advanced societies, though the kinship exchange system still operates in a residual way, other forms of economic exchange—i.e. commodity exchange—dominate[,] and class, not kinship structures prevail. It would seem that it is against a background of the *remoteness* of a kinship system that the ideology of the biological family comes into its own. In other words, that the relationship between two parents and their children assumes a dominant role when the complexity of a class society forces the kinship system to recede. (378)

Craig Owens's speculations invite us to ask, as Mitchell doesn't quite do, not only about the excisions involved in this avunculosuppressive move from "kinship" to "family," but also—within the postkinship culture of the now weirdly resurrected "holy (bestial) family"—about the importance of residual, re-created, or even entirely newly imagined forms of the avunculate. To begin with, of course, the fact that we don't so much as have names to distinguish our mother's from our father's brother (or sister), or any of those from an aunt or uncle related to us only by marriage to a parental sibling, shows that a far less specified set of avuncular roles and relations now obtains—to the extent that, first, the term *avunculate* actually does seem usable for both men and women who occupy these relations to us and, second, many geocultural settings allow us to call *aunt* or *uncle* people older than ourselves who aren't related to us by either blood *or* marriage.

Because aunts and uncles (in either narrow or extended meanings) are adults whose intimate access to children needn't depend on their own pairing or procreation, it's very common, of course, for some of them to have the office of representing nonconforming or nonreproductive sexualities to children. We are many, the queer women and men whose first sense of the possibility of alternative life trajectories came to us from our uncles and aunts—even when the stories we were allowed to hear about their lives were almost unrecognizably mangled, often in demeaning ways, by the heterosexist hygiene of child rearing. But the space for nonconformity carved out by the avunculate goes beyond the important provision of role models for proto-gay kids. After all, many of us don't turn out all that much like "artistic" Uncle Harvey; "not the marrying kind" Cousin David, whose engagements always fell through at the last minute; or (the best-loved people in my family) Aunt Estelle and Aunt Frances, sisters who slept in the same room for most of their eight decades. But if having grandparents means perceiving your parents as somebody's children, then having aunts and uncles, even the most conventional of aunts and uncles, means perceiving your parents as somebody's sibs—not, that is, as alternately abject and omnipotent links in a chain of compulsion and replication that leads inevitably to *you* but rather as elements in a varied, contingent, recalcitrant, but re-forming seriality, as people who demonstrably could have turned out very differently, indeed as people who, in the differing, refractive relations among their own generation, can be seen already to have done so.

It follows that a family system understood to include an avuncular function might also have a less hypostatized view of what and therefore how a child can desire. When "the family" is stylized as the supposed biologically based triad,[3] as it now is both in psychoanalysis and in the modern mass ideology that psychoanalysis in this respect both reflects and ratifies, the paths of desire/identification for a given child are essentially reduced to two: identification ("Oedipal"), through the same-sex parent, with a desire for the other-sex parent or identification ("negative Oedipal"), through the other-sex parent, with a desire for the same-sex parent. If the so-far undiminished reliance of psychoanalytic thought on the inversion topos were not enough to ensure its heterosexist bias,[4] its heterosexist circumscription would nonetheless be guaranteed, if it is not already caused, by the fact that the closed system of "the family," within which all formative identification and desire are seen to take place, is limited by tendentious prior definition to parents—to adults already defined as procreative within a heterosexual bond.

Within this ideological system, accounts of the desire of any child must in turn be disfiguringly ritualized. The dispiriting debates on "the seduction theory," for example, have pitted a psychoanalytic-identified view of the totally volitional, unproblematically "active" child against a feminist-identified view of the child as the perfect victim, totally passive and incapable of relevant or effectual desire. But suppose we assume for a moment the near inevitability of any child's being "seduced" in the sense of being inducted into, and more or less implanted with, one or more adult sexualities whose congruence with the child's felt desires will necessarily leave at least many painful gaps.[5] (I mean here to designate a continuum that extends to, but is not fully defined by, the experience of a child who is in fact assaulted or raped.) That a child, objectively very disempowered, might yet be seen as being sometimes in a position to influence—obviously to radically varying degrees—*by whom she or he may be seduced,* as having some possible degree of choice, that is to say, about *whose* desire, what conscious and unconscious needs, what ruptures of self, and what flawed resources of remediation are henceforth to become part of her or his internalized sexual law: such a possibility is thinkable only in proportion as the child is seen as having intimate access to some range of adults, and hence of adult sexualities. At the utopian limit: "There is a great variety in aunts. You can have aunts of any shape or size *you like.*"

Part of the interest of the avunculate is, as we have seen, that its thinkability also renders more thinkable (across and perhaps therefore within generations) the sibling relation. *The Importance of Being Earnest* places the sibling plot in many ways prior to, and hence more tellingly in question than, the marriage plot—especially as a locus for explorations of gender and sexuality. The first effect of the anagnoritic ending is not, after all, to enable the play to bring about its three hetero-sexual marriages but rather to locate Jack/Ernest within a sib network.

> LADY BRACKNELL.   You are the son of my poor sister, Mrs. Moncrieff, and consequently Algernon's elder brother.
> JACK.   Algy's elder brother! Then I have a brother after all. I knew I had a brother! I always said I had a brother! Cecily,—how could you have ever doubted that I had a brother? (*Seizes hold of Algernon.*) Dr. Chasuble, my unfortunate brother. Miss Prism, my unfortunate brother. Gwendolen, my unfortunate brother. Algy, you young scoundrel, you will have to treat me with more respect in the future. You have never behaved to me like a brother in all your life.
> ALGERNON.   Well, not till to-day, old boy, I admit. I did my best, however, though I was out of practice.   (187–88)

Only Gwendolen's prodding reminds Jack that the questions of his name and hence of his marriage are also at stake. ("Good heavens! . . . I had quite forgotten that point" [188].)

An important switch point between the avuncular and the sibling relations in *Earnest* is, rather oddly, the word and notion *German.* But maybe not *absolutely* oddly, if we suppose that an important switch point between any avuncular and sibling relations is likely to be the cousin—the first cousin, more precisely called cousin-german, meaning the child of a parental sibling (someone of the same "germ" as the parent), from the same germ as, for instance, Spanish *hermano* 'brother.'

Of course it would, no doubt, be anachronistic to connect the Germanities of *Earnest* fully to the usage in the next decade, in the wake of the Eulenburg scandal in Germany, of "Do you speak German?" as a pickup line for gay Frenchmen; in 1895 homosexuality is not yet referred to as *le vice allemand*. But German is already, as Miss Prism enthuses in the four-act original of *Earnest*, famous as the tongue "whose grammar displays such interesting varieties of syntax, gender, and expression" (52). Lady Bracknell prefers German vocal music to French, she says because unlike French "German sounds a thoroughly respectable language, and indeed, I believe is so" (128). A truer reason for this avuncular preference may be Aunt Augusta's own none-too-latent Valkyrie tendencies. "On this point, as indeed on all points, I am firm" (176)—"when my heart is touched, I become like granite. Nothing can move me" (*Importance . . . Four Acts* 160). In her capacity of aunt she is instantly recognizable ("Ah!" says Algernon, hearing the doorbell, "that must be Aunt Augusta") for announcing her presence in a "Wagnerian manner" (124–25).

Wagner is an important figure in many cultural systems by 1895, but not least in the systems of sexual signification. Himself certifiable as heterosexually active, if not hyperactive, Wagner nonetheless crystallized a hypersaturated solution of what were and were becoming homosexual signifiers. This was possible partly because the newly crystallizing German state was itself more densely innervated than any other site with the newly insistent, internally incoherent but increasingly foregrounded discourses of homosexual identity, recognition, prohibition, advocacy, demographic specification, and political controversy. Virtually all the competing, conflicting figures for understanding same-sex desire—archaic ones and modern ones, medicalized and politicizing, those emphasizing pederastic relations, gender inversion, or "homo-" homosexuality—were coined and circulated in this period in the first place in German and through German culture, medicine, and politics. (At a time after the Wilde scandal when the author's name and work were elsewhere in total eclipse, his popularity in Germany, appropriately, was undimmed—including the 1903 publication of a play called *Ernst Sein*.) The intensely sexualized and nationalized Wagnerian opera, accordingly, set up under the notorious aegis of Ludwig II, represented a cultural lodestar for what Max Nordau, in *Degeneration*, refers to as "the abnormals"; the tireless taxonomist Krafft-Ebing quotes a homosexual patient who is "an enthusiastic partisan of Richard Wagner, for whom I have remarked a predilection in most of us [sufferers from "contrary-sexual-feeling"]; I find that this music accords so very much with our nature" (123). Dorian Gray, too, an Englishman, hears in Wagner's music "a presentation of the tragedy of his own soul" (150).

And an 1899 questionnaire by the pioneering gay sexologist Magnus Hirschfeld, designed to help readers gauge the degree to which they themselves might be "At All An Uranian" (i.e., an invert), included the indexical question "Are you particularly fond of Wagner?" (Bartlett 72). The "Wagnerian" "ring" of Aunt Augusta, thus, however it may seem to her a guarantee of perfect sexual rectitude, invokes very different relations in the nephews who attend it as spectators and who circulate in an urbane world where the very name Wagner is a node of gay recognition and attribution.

The germaneness of the German in *Ernst Sein* isn't only through aunts, however, but through brothers, the alibi of the *hermano*—indeed German *is* the alibi of Jack's *hermano* in his urban mode. The German text is what's left guarding his aunt/niece/ward Cecily in the Hertfordshire place where brother Ernest isn't—where "Uncle" Jack isn't when he goes to London to be (with) Ernest; it is what Ernest as Algernon interrupts when he escapes Jack and finds his way to Hertfordshire. Miss Prism chides Cecily that Jack "laid particular stress on your German, as he was leaving for town yesterday. Indeed, he always lays stress on your German when he is leaving for town" (Cecily: "Dear Uncle Jack is so very serious!" [141]). And when the brother alibi begins to unwind, the threat of too much éclaircissement, of revelations that won't fit in with the marital telos, is wafted on the now familiar east wind:

> GWENDOLEN.   Mr. Worthing, what explanation can you offer to me for pretending to have a brother? Was it in order that you might have an opportunity of coming up to town to see me as often as possible?
> JACK.   Can you doubt it, Miss Fairfax?
> GWENDOLEN.   I have the gravest doubts upon the subject. But I intend to crush them. This is not the moment for German scepticism.   (174)

German, then, as befits the thick, complex, incoherent sexual valences of the label, both enables and threatens (what Christopher Craft describes deconstructively as) the treatment of fraternal bonds in this play as pure alibi: brotherhood as Bunburying, the empty, disavowed position "beside themselves" into which men may move at will, becoming "Ernest, in the city" and "Jack in the country" (24, 25), the imaginary bond by which Algernon (masquerading as Ernest) may try to relate to Jack as Jack (also masquerading as Ernest) relates to himself (40). Thus, insofar as the name *brother* functions as alibi, as pure structure, it is homologous with a modern/deconstructive understanding of men's bonds with other men as "homo," as relations to an (always absent, lacking, elusive or eloping) same, in the homogenizing heterosexist scientism of homo/hetero.

Abstract brotherhood, then, is seen as Bunburying; but the highly cathected noun and verb *Bunbury* itself, the nonfamilial alibi in the play, as distinct from the term *brother*, alludes (as several critics note) to surreptitious sexuality in terms of a particular genital practice: anal sex as "burying in the bun." The practice wasn't Wilde's own, but the repeated reference to it does add to the specific gravity of the play's resistance to homo/hetero scientism, in this case by appealing to the premodern (though by no means obsolete) understanding of sexual nonconformity in terms of acts (e.g., "sodomy") rather than types (inverts, homosexuals) or even relations (pederastic).

> ALGERNON.   A man who married without knowing Bunbury has a very tedious time of it.
> JACK.   That is nonsense. If I marry a charming girl like Gwendolen, and she is the only girl I ever saw in my life that I would marry, I certainly won't want to know Bunbury.
> ALGERNON.   Then your wife will.   (124)

So little is this transgressive practice seen as tied to the modern homosexual type that Wilde doesn't even confine its attribution to his own gender: the same Gwendolen who's dangerously attracted to effeminate men is also, and apparently not as part of the same rhetoric, ascribed an eager anal sexuality that nothing in turn-of-the-century (and little enough in contemporary) sexological "common sense" could have made any space for.[6]

What Jack means in saying, when they turn out to be brothers, that Algy has "never ['till to-day'] behaved to me like a brother" is, of course, that they have been very close friends. Unlike the glitteringly implausible cross-gender marriages that dramatically, inevitably arrive to cement the glitteringly implausible cross-gender courtships, the much less foregrounded arrival of a literal sibling bond to cap the bond of male attachment makes it seem more unsettling that something may really be changing—something may be lost. That there is something to be lost. The effect of something to be lost in this relation, something at a different ontological level from the other relationships in the play, is clearly traceable to a grammatical effect. The prevailing grammatical mode of the play is, of course, pointed wit—its almost ascetic paring down to the bare surface of the inversions, epigrams, double entendres that Camille Paglia rightly describes as "smooth with Mannerist spareness," "spasms of delimitation," "attempts to defy the temporal character of speech" (94). Wilde's "greatest departure from the Restoration dramatists," Paglia points out, is to "[detach] the witticism from repartee, that is, from social relationship" (93). It isn't so much that nothing is spared as that nothing is to spare—nothing doesn't pay off; almost literally, not a word of the play fails to contribute its full quantum to the clockwork mechanisms of syntactic and semantic parsimony and hypersalience.

The exception to this law of salience is, then, precisely subliminal in its operation, a pattern of dull spots, single-entendre phrases, unnecessary words. They occur in the middle of the utterances Algernon and Jack address to each other. Here are some from one otherwise spectacularly quotable scene: "[M]y dear Ernest," "My dear fellow," "[D]ear Algy," "[M]y dear fellow," "My dear fellow," "My dear fellow," "[O]ld boy," "My dear fellow," "[D]ear boy," "[M]y dear fellow," "My dear Algy," "[M]y dear Algy," "[M]y dear fellow," "[M]y dear young friend," "My dear fellow" (117–24). The most commonplace list of interpellatory endearments; murmurs from where?—clubland, the fifth-form study, the darkened bedroom; the earth tones of *The Importance of Being Earnest*. Neither figures of speech nor puns nor even constative propositions, these phrases, purely phatic, raising no issues of the "proper" or "improper" name, mean nothing but relation—do nothing but situate in an intimacy of two. In a play in which every relationship (including several that don't exist) is named and explicitly accounted for, sometimes several times over in conflicting versions, the unspecified bond of Jack to Algernon is taken as requiring no account. For the play's purposes, it is the natural. At least, it is so until it is naturalized in the name of the family—when it becomes the stressful, invidious thing at which Algy can only strain at doing his best, "though I was out of practice."[7] If, as Algernon says in the four-act version of the play, relations "are a sort of aggravated form of the public" (34), the main aggravation seems to consist in how the public grows less individual, less differentiated, even less lovable as it is brought within the holy bounds of family privacy.

Supposing we wanted to ask whether the play, as a play, narrows or extends, "stabilizes" or "destabilizes," the holy name of the family as our culture hands it to us. We would have to ask conclusively, at this point, a difficult question: what it means that the play's central marriage, the one between Jack and Gwendolen, can't take place until Jack is demonstrated to be not only Algernon's "true" brother but (as Ernest) his own "true" brother; Aunt Augusta's "true" nephew; at once Algernon's big nephew and big uncle (as Algernon is also marrying his "little aunt" cum "little niece" Cecily)—and, finally, his own wife's first cousin, mediator between the sibship and the avunculate, in the chiasmic, diagonal relation that in most cultures even now forms the immediate defining demarcation, from one side or the other, of the boundary legally called "incest": that between inside and outside the family.

To pose the question in this way, however, would be not only to frame the play yet again in terms of its conclusion but to enlist this entire reading in the service of two projects about which I think we now have the ability to make some more critical interrogations. I borrow a term from Leo Bersani (215) in saying that what's limiting about both projects is that they are redemptive—that they presume and hence reinforce the essentially theological assumption that any cultural manifestation under study must respond first and last to the moralistic questions "Can it be saved?" and "Can it save us?" In the political register, it seems that the question toward which this reading might tend is, "Can the family be redeemed?" In the literary register it would be, "Can the play be redeemed?" Both of these questions deserve, I think, to be resisted.

Can the family be redeemed? The easiest path of argument from some of my starting points here would be advocacy of a more elastic, inclusive definition of *family*, beginning with a relegitimation of the avunculate: an advocacy that would appeal backward to precapitalist models of kinship organization, or the supposed early-capitalist extended family, in order to project into the future a vision of *family* elastic enough to do justice to the depth and sometimes durability of nonmarital and/or nonprocreative bonds, same-sex bonds, nondyadic bonds, bonds not defined by genitality, "step" bonds, adult sibling bonds, nonbiological bonds across generations, and so on. At the same time, as we have seen, a different angle—perhaps an avuncular angle—onto the family of the present can show this heterosexist structure always already awash with homosexual energies and potentials, even with lesbian and gay persons, whose making-visible might then require only an adjustment of the interrogatory optic, the bringing to the family structure of the pressure of our different claims, our different needs. Clearly, there is a very great deal that is imaginatively exciting and politically important in such programs, beginning but not ending with their affordances for lesbian and gay filiation and survival. Such programs are right at the center of a lot of present contestations around gay/lesbian issues, in terms of broadened definitions of domestic partnership; moves to pluralize what counts as "family" for legal, welfare, insurance, and real-estate purposes; debates over whether a politics called "pro-family" need somehow necessarily be antichoice, antiwoman, antichild, and antigay; and, maybe most tellingly, the Thatcher government's framing of Clause 28, its charter of censorship against gay-affirmative speech, as a rebuttal of queers who present ourselves as what the legislation terms "pretended families." In America, I suppose the best definition of family is whom you spend Thanksgiving with. The people I like to spend Thanksgiving with, joined to one another by being friends, lovers, companions, sometimes parents and children, and people who like to spend Thanksgiving together, proudly call ourselves after Clause 28: the Extended Pretended Family.

At the same time it seems that too much, too important ground is given up in letting the problematic of *family* define these intimate and political structurations—*family* even in the most denaturalized and denaturalizing, the most utopian possible uses of the term. One gay scholar/activist, Michael Lynch, said in a 1989 interview that he finds *family* a "dangerous word": "I don't like the idea of the gay family, it's a heterosexist notion. I'd like a straight family to see themselves in terms of friends. I'd rather see same-sex friendship be the model to straights" (7). The very difficulty of conceiving this, a difficulty that the whole plot of *Earnest* underlines, points to the worst danger about "family": how much the word, the name, the signifier *family* is already installed unbudgeably at the center of a cultural value system—so much so that a rearrangement or reassignment of its signifieds need have no effect whatever on its rhetorical or ideological effects. You will have noted a certain impatience, in this reading of *Earnest*, with the concept of the Name of the Father. That is partly because I see what may have been the precapitalist or early-capitalist functions of the Name of the Father as having been substantially superseded, in a process accelerating over the last century and a half, very specifically by what might be termed the Name of the Family—that is, the name Family. (Within this family, the position of any father is by no means a given; there are important purposes, including feminist ones, for which the term *familialism* may now usefully be substituted for *patriarchy*.) Now, the potency of any signifier is proved and increased, over and over, by how visibly and spectacularly it fails to be adequated by the various signifieds over which it is nonetheless seen to hold sway. So the gaping fit between, on the one hand, the Name of the Family and, on the other, the quite varied groupings gathered in that name can only add to the numinous prestige of a term whose origins, histories, and uses may have little in common with our own recognizable needs. Redeeming the family isn't, finally, an option but a compulsion; the question would be how to stop redeeming the family. How, as well, to stop being complicit in the process by which the name Family occludes the actual extant relations—for many people, horrifyingly impoverished ones; for everyone, radically changed and unaccounted for, indeed highly phantasmatic ones—that mediate exchanges between the order of the individual and the order of capital, "information," and the state.

Duke University

Notes

This essay—written in the summer of 1990—was sparked by the work of Craig Owens, cited in the essay, and any pleasure in its writing came from the anticipation of showing it to him when a draft of it might be completed. That was the least of the things that suddenly became impossible on his death from AIDS-related illness, on 4 July 1990, at age thirty-nine.

The piece also owes a lot to very enabling conversations with Jonathan Goldberg and Michael Moon. A version of it was published in my *Tendencies*, and it appears here with permission of Duke University Press.

[1] Quotations from *The Importance of Being Earnest* are from the 1985 Signet–NAL edition unless otherwise indicated.

[2] Brackets mark additional text present in the four-act version of the play.

[3] I say "supposed" because there is nothing more biological about a family of three than there is about a kinship group of two hundred.

[4] The inversion topos depends on a view of desire as something that can subsist only between a masculine self and a feminine self, whatever the sex of the bodies in which these notional selves may be housed.

[5] This account depends both on Ferenczi and on Laplanche.

[6] My argument here is not the same as Fineman's when he writes,

> For now, remembering their etymology, we may rechristen the autological as the autosexual, or rather, the homosexual, and we may equally revalue the heterological as the heterosexual. This leaves us with the psychoanalytic conclusion that the fundamental desire of the reader of literature is the desire of the homosexual for the heterosexual, or rather, substituting the appropriate figurative embodiments of these abstractions, the desire of the man to be sodomized by the woman. . . . This would also explain why the only word that ends up being naturally motivated in *The Importance of Being Earnest* is not *Earnest* but *Bunbury* itself. . . .   (88–89)

[7] Interestingly, the introduction of the naturalizing name of the father in this play refers not to his surname, the legitimating aegis supposed to extend vertically to every child of his, but rather to the accident of his given name, which depends on the contingent seriality of the sib relation ("Being the eldest son you were naturally christened after your father" [188]). If the paternal name is something you get from Canon Chasuble, everyone can be Ernest; if you have to get it from your father, only the *erst* can *Ernst sein*. Algernon, in a sense, loses his father by becoming a brother; loses his father as Jack wins him, at the same time winning Jack in the more indisseverable calculus of fraternity.

Works Cited

Bartlett, Neil. *Who Was That Man?: A Present for Mr Oscar Wilde*. London: Serpent's Tail, 1988.

Bersani, Leo. "Is the Rectum a Grave?" *AIDS: Cultural Analysis, Cultural Activism*. Ed. Douglas Crimp. Cambridge: MIT P, 1988. 197–222.

Craft, Christopher. "Alias Bunbury: Desire and Termination in *The Importance of Being Earnest*." *Representations* 31 (1990): 19–46.

Dollimore, Jonathan. "Different Desires: Subjectivity and Transgression in Wilde and Gide." *Genders* 2 (1988): 24–41.

Ferenczi, Sandor. "Confusion of Tongues between Adults and the Child." *Final Contributions to the Problems and Methods of Psycho-analysis*. Ed. Michael Balint. Tr. Eric Mosbacher et al. New York: Brunner, 1955. 156–67.

Fineman, Joel. "The Significance of Literature: *The Importance of Being Earnest*." *October* 15 (1980): 79–90.

Halperin, David M. *One Hundred Years of Homosexuality and Other Essays on Greek Love*. New York: Routledge, 1990.

Krafft-Ebing, Richard von. *Psychopathia Sexualis: A Medico-forensic Study*. 1939. Intro. and supp. Victor Robinson. New York: Pioneer, 1953.

Laplanche, Jean. *New Foundations for Psychoanalysis*. Trans. David Macey. Oxford: Blackwell, 1989. 89–149.

Lynch, Michael. Interview. "Fighting Words." With Nick Sherman. *Xtra!* 138 (1989): 2–8.

Mitchell, Juliet. *Psychoanalysis and Feminism*. 1974. New York: Vintage, 1975.

Nordau, Max. *Degeneration*. 4th ed. New York: Appleton, 1895.

Owens, Craig. "Outlaws: Gay Men in Feminism." *Men in Feminism*. Ed. Alice Jardine and Paul Smith. New York: Methuen, 1987. 217–32.

Paglia, Camille. "Oscar Wilde and the English Epicene." *Raritan* 4.3 (1985): 85–109.

Sedgwick, Eve Kosofsky. *Epistemology of the Closet*. Berkeley: U of California P, 1990.

Wilde, Oscar. The Importance of Being Earnest *and Other Plays*. Intro. Sylvan Barnet. New York: Signet–NAL, 1985.

———. *The Importance of Being Earnest: A Trivial Comedy for Serious People: In Four Acts as Originally Written*. 2 vols. New York: New York Public Library, 1956.

———. *The Picture of Dorian Gray*. Middlesex, Eng.: Penguin, 1981.

Private Affairs: Race, Sex, Property, and Persons

Phillip Brian Harper

THE KISS

I begin this inquiry into the social significance of privacy at
what may seem an unlikely point: recent criticism of modern
painting and sculpture. While Auguste Rodin, Constantin
Brancusi, and Gustav Klimt worked in different styles and
in different mediums, these artists share a title that desig-
nates one or more of each one's best-known works. I refer,
of course, to *The Kiss*. Each artist's rendition of that subject
is stylistically distinctive, but as the commonality of the
title suggests, all the works depict the same theme: a male
and a female figure engaged in a full embrace and in the
aforementioned kiss. The stylistic variation has led critics
to assert that each work has a unique effect. And yet the
language in which these assertions are couched suggests
more congruence among the different conceptions of the kiss
than is generally acknowledged. Indeed, it would seem that
one particular formulation of the kiss's cultural significance
has achieved hegemony worth interrogating.

Let us consider, for example, Bernard Champigneulle's
description of Rodin's sculpture *The Kiss* (1886; fig. 1) as
"that luminous symbol of love and of the twofold tenderness
of man the protector and woman stirred to the depths of her
being" (157). What is perhaps most familiar in this assessment is the positing of the man as stolidly protecting the
woman yet acting on her in such a way that she, by contrast,
is utterly moved. The degree to which this conception of
heterosexual communion has been stereotyped is best indicated by its pervasiveness in both soft- and hard-core pornography, in which the woman's groans and facial expressions
generally register the pleasure that is supposed to characterize

Fig. 1. Auguste Rodin, *The Kiss*, 1886.

the sexual encounter while the man appears comparatively unaffected, despite his customary energy and athleticism. Champigneulle does not identify the characteristics of the sculpture that indicate to him the subjects' emotional states (and, frankly, I cannot identify any such characteristics); instead, his claim acquires plausibility through recourse to representational conventions of the heterosexual relationship.

While Champigneulle notes the different moods of the two figures, he also comments on their formal continuity with each other: "From lips to feet both figures are pervaded by the same fluidity" (157). The interplay between this continuity on the one hand and the distinction of masculine and feminine sensibilities on the other provides the basis for the characteristic conception of the heterosexual coupling as the necessary overcoming of a fundamental difference between the genders—a conception that is reflected in much of the critical commentary on Rodin's sculpture. For instance, having noted the "incredulous" critical reaction to the stolid "reticence" of *The Kiss*'s male figure, Albert E. Elsen suggests that the sculptural "fusion" of male and female quells that incredulity (136–37). This argument clearly indicates that such fusion is considered "natural" in the heterosexual encounter and is construed as a convergence of polarities whose teleological imperative of union is represented in the kiss itself.

This postulation of the heterosexual kiss's significance as the overcoming of gendered difference also marks commentary on the work of the Romanian-born French sculptor Constantin Brancusi. Brancusi completed numerous versions of his own *Kiss*, most in stone, and according to Sidney Geist, these frankly abstract works are "the antithesis of *The Kiss* of Rodin" (142). However accurate this assertion may be, Geist's commentary implicates Brancusi's work in the same conception of the kiss's import that is manifested in Champigneulle's comments on Rodin. Geist describes Brancusi's first version of the work (1907–08; fig. 2) as follows: the "two lovers . . . are eye to eye, their lips mingle, the breasts of the woman encroach gently on the form of the man" (28). Geist stresses the merging of the two figures—"[t]he unity of the bodies"—but faults their arms, whose "round, ropelike *separable* character . . . violates the continuity of the stony matter" (28). Brancusi repairs this violation, according to Geist, in a more columnar version of *The Kiss* (1909; fig. 3), which presents the two figures with full bodies, "the legs of the woman embrac[ing] those of the man" (36). Geist claims that this *Kiss* "accomplishes the weaving of forms without destroying the integrity of the stone," whose continuity "marks an advance . . . over the first *Kiss*" (36), and he concludes that Brancusi's "image of two figures locked in an embrace is a permanent expression of the unity of love, which Plato called 'the desire and pursuit of the whole' " (37).

Fig. 2. Constantin Brancusi, *The Kiss*, 1907–08 (Craiova).

In Geist's privileging of the "pursuit of the whole," which is evidently figured in the heterosexual union, and his enthusiasm for Brancusi's abstractionism, lies a dichotomy similar to the one that characterizes the Rodin criticism: formal continuity set against emotional distance. Moreover, Geist, in his anxiety to render this schema in clearly heterosexual terms, seems to betray his own modernism (evident in his clear appreciation of Brancusi's abstractionism) by insisting that *The Kiss*'s representation of heterosexual union is based not only on realism but also in biography. In assessing the first *Kiss*, Geist notes the peculiarities of the figures in the sculpture:

Fig. 3. Constantin Brancusi, *The Kiss*, 1909 (Montparnasse Cemetery).

The man's hair falls over his brow, much as Brancusi wore [his] in 1904. The line of the hair starts at a higher point on the woman, giving her a somewhat longer face than the man, and making her appear slightly taller (and Brancusi was short). It is reasonable to speculate that this carving . . . celebrates a consummated kiss. If it does, we must conclude that what seems to be a set of formal variations has a biographical origin.   (29)

And Geist implicitly faults what is arguably Brancusi's best-known version of the work (1912; fig. 4) for "los[ing] the immediacy of the earlier versions as it moves toward pure design" (40). Thus, Geist's celebration of Brancusi's modernist aesthetic for its "timelessness, simplicity and autonomy" (28) is attended by a certain uneasy desire to recuperate the sculpture in a narrative of recognizably heterosexual love of which the kiss is the necessary and inevitable "consummation."

So pervasive and versatile is the mythology of heterosexual love that the dichotomous impulse that characterizes Geist's response to Brancusi's work might be incorporated into a completely different interpretational scheme without in the least forfeiting the scheme's ultimate significance. In a study of the work of the Austrian artist Gustav Klimt, Frank Whitford notes the contemporaneity of Brancusi's sculpture and Klimt's famous painting *The Kiss* (1908; fig. 5) and claims that

> to compare them is to see instantly the differences between Klimt's work and that of another, more completely modern artist. . . . [W]hereas Brancusi simplifies, reduces and rarefies, Klimt complicates, allows his ornament to proliferate and adds layer after layer of effect and allusion.   (118)

In short, as a less "modern" artist, Klimt is less abstract in his work than Brancusi, and thus Klimt's painting needs less to be reclaimed by a realistic narrative of heterosexual love than to be rescued from an overly specific interpretation derived from autobiographical realism. Consequently, while Geist underscores the extent to which Brancusi's *Kiss* can be traced to the artist's own experiences and thus presumably reinvested with the heterosexual significance that it threatens to lose through high abstraction,[1] Whitford denies the biographical significance of Klimt's painting (whose heterosexual meaning is clear) in order to cast the work as emblematic of the "universality" of the love it depicts:

> In some of the preliminary drawings the man is depicted with a beard and it has therefore inevitably been suggested that the male figure is Klimt himself and the woman an idealized portrait of Adele Bloch-Bauer, whose affair with Klimt was supposedly continuing when *The Kiss* was painted. The only evidence for this, however, is the awkward position of the woman's right hand

Fig. 4. Constantin Brancusi, *The Kiss*, 1912 (Philadelphia Museum of Art Collection).

[Adele Bloch-Bauer had a disfiguration of the right middle finger] (but this masks the fourth, and not the disfigured middle finger). The painting is not autobiographical but a symbolic, universalized statement about sexual love.   (118)

Whitford takes as universal the notion, which Klimt's work apparently espouses, that the kiss represents the logical end of the heterosexual relationship—a notion also evident in the title of a forerunner to *The Kiss*, Klimt's *Fulfillment* (1905–09; fig. 6), which depicts a scene similar to the one presented in the later work. (One notable difference, according to Whitford, is that in *The Kiss* "the woman's ecstasy . . . [is] revealed in her face" (117), just as I have suggested is usual in depictions of heterosexual encounters.) It is necessary, I think, to examine this notion critically, for if we view the kiss merely as an emblem of the consummation of

Fig. 5. Gustav Klimt, *The Kiss*, 1908.

Fig. 6. Gustav Klimt, *Fulfillment*, 1905–09.

heterosexual love, we miss its import in other social contexts; at the same time, it is necessary to understand the extent to which that consummation is the primary significance of the kiss before we can fully appreciate its meanings in the other economies of signification that I consider here.

If, as the art criticism discussed above suggests, the kiss generally signifies the logical consummation of the heterosexual encounter, then conversely any relationship between a man and a woman, in order to register as heterosexual, must be considered to be founded on an erotic charge that is "hidden" beneath the relationship's quotidian aspect and that achieves public expression in the kiss. The kiss, in teleologically "fulfilling" that relationship, retroactively invests all the interactions that have heretofore constituted the relationship with an inevitably erotic significance. Furthermore, the notion of the sexualized encounter as fulfillment is so strong a force in Western culture that we "know" that any heterosexual relationship "really" represents an erotic engagement, however "innocent" of eroticism the constituent interactions of that relationship may appear. The status of the properly heterosexual relationship, then, is always that of the "open secret" whose revelation (through the kiss, for example) startles us only because, as D. A. Miller points out, "we too inevitably surrender our privileged position as readers to whom all secrets are open by 'forgetting' our knowledge for the pleasures of suspense and surprise" (206). Miller refers to "readers" in this passage because he is discussing the experience of novelistic narrative. Yet reading seems an apt description of the decoding of social texts as well as fictional ones. After all, as Miller notes, "the social function of secrecy [is] isomorphic with its novelistic function," and that function is "not to conceal knowledge, so much as to conceal the knowledge of the knowledge" (206). The necessity for this concealment, in Miller's assessment, derives from a subject's desire to disavow the degree to which the social totality has accounted for and absorbed that subject. That is, secrecy serves as a sort of "defense mechanism" by which

> the subject is allowed to conceive of himself as a resistance: a friction in the smooth functioning of the social order. . . . [It is] the subjective practice in which the oppositions of private/public, inside/outside, subject/object are established, and the sanctity of their first term kept inviolate.   (207)

Secrecy, then, creates the notion of privacy (to focus on the first of the oppositions Miller lists), which obviously is operative in the epistemology of the heterosexual relationship but which is also a crucial category (just as the kiss is a signal phenomenon) in the more socially and politically troublesome realms to which I now turn.

WHO'S AFRAID OF MISCEGENATION?

Insofar as interpersonal relationships are conventionally taken to be an expression of personal emotions, which are in turn considered essentially internal to our psychic mechanisms, the modern conception of the social entity routinely consigns interpersonal relationships to the private realm. Nonetheless, we need not look far to find the state or some other entity external to the private sphere regulating the supposedly free and unconstrained private realm where people choose with whom to interact socially. Indeed, it is precisely when such regulation encroaches on personal choice that we are most likely to find the irreducibly private nature of interpersonal relationships—and thus their sanctity—strongly asserted. The African-American writer Frances Ellen Watkins Harper offers an example of this phenomenon in the novel *Iola Leroy* (1892).

The title character of Harper's novel, which is set during the Civil War and Reconstruction, is a young woman of "mixed blood," the daughter of a wealthy white planter from the Mississippi Delta and a white-skinned octoroon woman who was the planter's slave before their marriage. Iola and her brother, Harry, are raised to believe that they are of purely European heritage, and they are disabused of this notion only after their father, Eugene, dies, and his evil cousin remands them and their mother, Marie, to slavery. Following a fortuitous confluence of events, Iola escapes from bondage to work as a nurse in the camps of the Union army during the war. While there, she meets Dr. Gresham, a white physician from New England who falls in love with her and requests her hand in marriage repeatedly, even after he learns the secret of her racial heritage. At the final proposal, Iola informs Dr. Gresham that despite his affection there is an "insurmountable barrier" between them. When he asks what it is, she replies, "It is the public opinion which assigns me a place with the colored people." Unconvinced, Dr. Gresham marshals the argument of privacy to which I have alluded: "[W]hat right," he demands, "has public opinion to interfere with our marriage relations?" (230–31). Iola notes that she and Dr. Gresham are constrained to conform to public opinion because "it is stronger than we are" (231). That strength derives largely from legal authority, since public disapproval of miscegenation was encoded in laws prohibiting interracial marriage or interracial sexual relations in some states well into the twentieth century.[2]

So it is evident that the bar separating the public and the private realm is not so impermeable as it has often seemed. This conclusion is not a revelation: a tradition of feminist critique, along with other schools of social theory, has already called into question the public/ private dichotomy (see, for instance, Pateman). I focus here, however, on how the problematic public/private distinction is inscribed not only in the relationships between social subjects but also in the individual subjects themselves in a way that complicates profoundly the constitution of minority identity.

A prime character through which to interrogate these issues is Iola Leroy, since her status as a white-skinned mulatto situates her on the line that distinguishes public from private in conventional assessments. By this assertion I mean that the very existence not only of Iola but of light-skinned blacks in general destabilizes the conventional link between socially constituted racial identity and the apparent biological fact of skin color. Indeed, since Iola's skin color does not correspond to her racial identification (once she learns of her ancestry Iola fully identifies with black people) that racial identification remarkably takes on the status of a secret—one whose revelation always shocks because it disrupts the standard association between skin color and racial identity. A key passage from Harper's novel makes clear the fundamentally private nature of Iola's racial identification. After a series of amazing coincidences that reunite Iola with her mother, brother, and uncle after the war, Iola decides to seek employment in the northern city where she has settled. She is twice thwarted in her efforts when her fellow employees at the stores where she finds work as a saleswoman learn that she is a Negro. Nonetheless, as she tells her Uncle Robert,

> "I am determined to win for myself a place in the fields of labor. I have heard of a place in New England, and I mean to try for it, even if I only stay a few months."
>
> "Well, if you *will* go, say nothing about your color."
>
> "Uncle Robert, I see no necessity for proclaiming that fact on the house-top. Yet I am resolved that nothing shall tempt me to deny it. The best blood in my veins is African blood, and I am not ashamed of it." (208)

Note that Robert specifically enjoins Iola not to say anything about her color. This word choice is not a slip, since the term *color* is a conventional euphemism for racial identification. But the remark demonstrates the problems of this usage, since Iola's skin color, which is visible to anyone who looks at her, needs no explanation unless the secret of her racial identification is revealed; it is this disclosure that Robert is warning against. Thus, racial identification, which is normally a matter of public knowledge, is for Iola a private matter whose disclosure affects her private life, including her personal relationships, such as the one with Dr. Gresham.

The elements of this narrative are the same as those featured in the narrative I have discerned in the commentaries of the art critics, which I call the narrative of the standard heterosexual relationship. These elements include a social existence bifurcated into public and private realms and an erotic attachment situated somewhere on the border between those realms. In the narrative of the standard heterosexual relationship, that attachment is figured in the kiss; in *Iola Leroy*, in Dr. Gresham's romantic overtures. The context in which those elements figure in the novel, however—Iola's status as a light-skinned, black-identified mulatto woman—transforms their function and significance. In the narrative of the standard heterosexual relationship the culminatory kiss exposes the fundamentally erotic nature of the relationship between the key figures and confirms our knowledge of that relationship's primary "secret"; but the revelation of Iola's secret—her racial identification—works a transformation in her erotic attachment (and in the rest of her "private" life) that prevents the "fulfillment" prescribed in the narrative of the standard heterosexual relationship.

Such a transformation need not interrupt an erotic relationship (though when Iola first confronts Dr. Gresham with the possibility that their union might produce children who show "unmistakable signs of color," he is stymied in his marriage proposal [117]); on the contrary, in the light of the configuration of sociosexual relations in the United States, such racial "unclosing" can actually effect an erotic relationship. This scenario occurs in *Iola Leroy*, though ironically when Iola does not know her racial status.

Once Iola's father dies, his cousin Alfred Lorraine sends two envoys, Camille and Bastine, to the North, where Iola is enrolled in a private boarding school. Their mission is to trick her into returning to the South with them so that she can be sold into slavery before she learns either that her father is dead or that she is legally considered black. While the party is waiting between trains in a large southern hotel, Iola drifts off to sleep:

> In her dreams she was at home, encircled in the warm clasp of her father's arms, feeling her mother's kisses lingering on her lips, and hearing the joyous greetings of the servants and Mammy Liza's glad welcome as she folded her to her heart. From this dream of bliss she was awakened by a burning kiss pressed on her lips, and a strong arm encircling her. Gazing around and taking in the whole

situation, she sprang from her seat, her eyes flashing with rage and scorn, her face flushed to the roots of her hair, her voice shaken with excitement, and every nerve trembling with angry emotion.

"How dare you do such a thing! Don't you know if my father were here he would crush you to the earth?"

"Not so fast, my lovely tigress," said Bastine, "your father knew what he was doing when he placed you in my charge."   (104)

This last sentence, while not literally true, certainly is true metaphorically if the "father" in question is the white patriarchy that governs the disposal of slave women in the United States. For Iola is a slave woman, and Bastine's behavior toward her indicates that the disclosure of that fact reconfigures her relation to the private and public realms. Previously Iola's racial identity has been almost completely secret—unknown even to her—a perversely private affair. With the revelation—the making public—of that identity comes Iola's inscription into a literal economy in which her person becomes someone else's private concern; that is, she effectively becomes the private property of any white man who conceives an interest in her, and the erotic relationship that might develop between her and such a man (symbolized by the kiss that Bastine forces on her) becomes the expression of that new privatized status.[3]

This private-property status need not be literalized as slavery to be socially significant; it is still implicated in many forms of the white male–black female relationship long after the signing of the Emancipation Proclamation. Because a woman's sudden discovery of her African heritage provides for a particularly dramatic transition to a privatized status, the light-skinned black woman consistently illustrates the social dimensions of such privatization in various representational contexts. For instance, in the 1949 movie *Pinky*, directed by Elia Kazan, the light-skinned title character, who has returned to her small segregated southern hometown after passing as a white woman in Boston for some years, is warned by two white men in a car that she should not be out walking in the "nigger section" of town. When she informs them that she is walking there because she lives there, they realize that she must be black and immediately sexually accost her. One nearly succeeds in kissing her before she is able to break away and escape to her grandmother's house.[4]

Both instances illustrate the degree to which sexual exploitation of black women by white men in the United States is characterized as the man's exercising his rights with respect to his private concern, represented in the person of the woman, whose availability for sexual use (which is identical to her racial affiliation) is a matter of public knowledge. This arrangement, while it may cause many individual citizens discomfort, does not, I daresay, produce among social conservatives the great degree of anxiety that we usually consider to be engendered by miscegenation. But I would not characterize this type of relationship as miscegenational for the purposes of my discussion here.

In the scenarios I have considered, the disclosure of the women's secret (their true racial identity) immediately alters their relation to the private realm such that they become objects in someone else's private domain—specifically, the white man's—and not active subjects governing their own private domains. Thus the relationship between the white man and the black woman in the narratives I have cited is no threat to the subjective power of the white patriarch—indeed that relationship solidifies the white patriarch's subjectivity by emphasizing that he is master of his private realm, king in his castle, while simultaneously voiding the black woman's subjectivity by depriving her of a private realm over which she can hold sovereign sway.[5] Miscegenation, as I narrowly define it, is a sexual relationship between two people who, while of different racial identifications, are equal subjects in that they agree to behave as though each has command of a private realm and consents to "wed" it with the other's realm in a common interest—the "marriage relations" of which Dr. Gresham speaks to Iola (231). I contend that social subjectivity depends on a person's having control over a body of interests that all concerned parties agree are private to that person. The problem, from the perspective of white patriarchal interests, is that such a recognition with respect to certain historically oppressed populations necessarily compromises the white patriarchy's subjective power.[6] Thus, miscegenation, insofar as it implies the reconceptualization of a nonwhite individual not as privatized object but as private subject (by definition entitled to hold private property) represents a profound threat to the political status quo and thus becomes a source of anxiety throughout "official" culture. According to Eva Saks's analysis of miscegenation case law in the United States,

> Miscegenation, which threatened the existing distribution of property and of blood (law's title to race), was therefore a crime by people against property. . . . Interracial sex and marriage had the potential to threaten the distribution of property, and their legal prohibition was an important step in consolidating social and economic boundaries.[7] (48–50)

This statement recalls Iola Leroy's assertion about her racial identity: "I see no necessity for proclaiming [it] on the house-top. Yet I am resolved that nothing shall tempt me to deny it." Iola makes this assertion in the context of her search for gainful employment—for her own private income, which is what is at stake in the struggle to manage interracial sexual relationships. What impresses me most strongly every time I read this passage, however, is how much it sounds like a post-Stonewall assertion about the private nature of gay or lesbian identity. Indeed, it seems to me that if we interrogate the apparent parallel between the political significance of mixed-race relationships and that of homosexual identity in the light of the economic dimension of the concerns I have examined, we may discover that antimiscegenation sentiment and homophobia—or at any rate, the versions of them prevalent in the United States—derive their impetus largely from a common organizing principle: the sanctity of the private realm as a means of controlling the flow of economic capital.

HOMOSEXUAL IDENTITY AS FOREIGN THREAT

To get at the fundamental economic concerns that constitute the core of these phenomena—antimiscegenation sentiment and homophobia—I first consider some cultural manifestations. I have discussed the significance of the kiss in the narrative of the standard heterosexual relationship—the teleological function whereby the kiss retroactively invests the heterosexual relation with a fundamentally erotic character, confers on that character the status of open secret, and founds a realm of personal privacy from which the heterosexual relationship derives its social meaning. I have also discussed the distinctive significance of privacy in representations of a certain type of mixed-race relationship, which dictates that the kiss, too, must signify differently in that context than in the heterosexual narrative: instead of implicating a realm of personal privacy, the kiss expresses a private-property relation in which the white man's sovereignty over his private dominion is solidified at the expense of the black woman's control over her private realm. Now the question before us is, What does the same-sex kiss signify?

The same-sex kiss can serve a function similar to that of the kiss in the narrative of the standard heterosexual relationship: that is, the same-sex kiss makes manifest the erotic character of a relationship previously presented as nonerotic. If we see two men or two women kiss—on the lips, in particular—we instantly recast previous knowledge about that relationship in erotic terms. But the same-sex kiss reveals a secret not only about the relationship between the persons who kiss but also about those persons themselves. Because of Western culture's presumption that everyone is heterosexual unless proven otherwise, the same-sex kiss speaks to identity in a much more highly charged way than does a kiss between a woman and a man, and in this respect the same-sex kiss resembles the signal kiss in the narrative of racial secrecy and revelation discussed above.

Given this potential of the same-sex kiss to bespeak a homosexual identity—and the threat to social status that such an identity generally constitutes—it is not surprising that extensive cultural safeguards have been constructed to short-circuit that threat in the contexts where such a kiss is likely to occur. The extreme scarcity of such contexts attests the degree of social danger in the same-sex kiss.

One such context is the masculine realm of professional sports, of which Brian Pronger claims, "[A] homoerotic text can be gleaned from [its] common discourse" (191). In partial support of this statement, Pronger presents a photograph of the now famous scene in which the professional basketball players Isiah Thomas and Earvin "Magic" Johnson kiss before a tip-off during the 1988 NBA finals (fig. 7). After Magic Johnson's public announcement of his HIV positivity in 1991, it is impossible not to consider this scene a constitutive factor in the popular problematization of his sexual identity—the widespread, albeit fairly tacit, recognition that that identity may implicate homosexual activity, despite Johnson's continued insistence that his sexual encounters have been only with women. I would argue that before Johnson's announcement, however, the kiss between the two players was never considered to have a homosexual import or to indicate that Thomas and Johnson

Fig. 7. Earvin "Magic" Johnson and Isiah Thomas, during the 1988 NBA finals.

were gay. On the contrary, the extensive cultural sanctioning of professional sport's profoundly homosocial character sublimates to a conventional hypermasculine significance whatever homoerotically inflected behavior takes place in that context. Consequently, individual players are immunized against being identified as homosexuals, and the threatening effects of such identification are concomitantly displaced to (and defused in) the abstracted professional sports "discourse" in which Pronger locates the "homoerotic text" to which he refers. (This fact may even make redundant the disclaimer that appears on the copyright page of Pronger's book: "The presence of the image or name of any person in this book does not necessarily imply that they are homosexual.")

A similar strategy of displacement is evident in a 1989 story in the *New York Times* about the former New York Mets outfielder Darryl Strawberry. Printed with a photograph of Strawberry kissing teammate Keith Hernandez on the cheek (fig. 8), the story by George Vecsey asks, "Was Darryl Strawberry warming up for an exodus to Los Angeles by planting a show-biz smooch on Keith Hernandez's cheek?" Vecsey then continues with some cultural explication: "This kind of behavior goes over very well on the Left Coast, where Strawberry hopes to perform in 1991." In this example, the kiss's homoerotic potential is rendered

Fig. 8. Darryl Strawberry and Keith Hernandez, 1989.

manageable by framing the kiss as characteristic of some other place, away from here, wherever here may happen to be.

A June 1990 installment of the sports comic "Tank McNamara," by Jeff Millar and Bill Hinds (fig. 9), recapitulates the identification of the homoerotic as a foreign characteristic. In the strip, which consists of one long panel, two patrons at a bar are watching a sports match on television and exclaiming incredulously about the behavior of the men on the field, "They're *kissing* each other." The bartender responds, "Millions of people are watching the World Cup. Don't you guys want to be cosmopolitan?" The invocation of cosmopolitanism, along with the reference to soccer—that most alien of sports in the United States—neatly implicates foreignness so as to manage the potential homoeroticism of the players' kiss in two divergent and yet complementary ways. On the one hand, these aspects of the bartender's remarks—like Vecsey's discussion of the Darryl Strawberry incident—suggest that that homoeroticism need not be threatening, because it is characteristic of a foreign people who are not at all "like us." On the other hand, to the degree that the bartender seeks to nudge his customers out of their resistance to foreign sports custom, he may be seen as trying to make the soccer players' kiss intelligible to the bar patrons—implicitly suggesting the kiss's comparability to conventional instances of masculine homosocial affection in American professional sports and thereby rendering the kiss similarly void of recognized homoerotic import.

The engineered comparability of characteristic practices in different public interactions usefully underscores the properly private quality of the interpersonal relationships within which the same practices routinely occur. Indeed, it is in the private realm that the principle of comparability operates most powerfully, since the beauty of the private domain in capitalist society is that anything in that domain can be rendered equivalent to, and thus exchangeable for, any other private

TANK M^cNAMARA®   **by Jeff Millar & Bill Hinds**

Fig. 9

interest. I do not suggest that the social meanings of, say, a kiss between two persons of different sexes and a kiss between two persons of the same sex are identical; I do suggest, however, that in the cultural economy as in the market economy comparable social values can be extracted from otherwise disparately signifying phenomena. According to this logic, not only do homosexual relationships begin to look a lot like heterosexual ones, with the same claims to protection as private interests,[8] but homosexual relationships also metaphorically represent the possible encroachment of "foreign" interests on the conventional domestic economy. Thus homosexual panic—the fear of a sort of domino effect by which homosexuals inexorably recruit to their cause ever-increasing numbers of heretofore "innocent" parties—resembles anxiety over the encroachment of alien claims on the domestic sphere. A notorious legal case indicates the extent to which such anxiety founds officially sanctioned homophobic activity in American culture.

Until 1983 Sharon Kowalski and Karen Thompson lived a closeted lesbian existence in Saint Cloud, Minnesota. They made no legal provisions to protect their relationship. In 1983 Kowalski was so seriously injured in a car accident that afterward she could neither speak nor walk. When Kowalski's father obtained sole guardianship of his daughter, he moved her to a nursing home in rural Minnesota and prohibited Thompson from visiting her. Thompson fought in the courts from 1985 until 1989 for the right to see her lover and eventually won a court order granting her visitation rights. Kowalski's father, citing poor health, resigned as his daughter's guardian in May 1990; however, State District Court Judge Robert Campbell, who chastised Thompson for violating Kowalski's privacy by informing Kowalski's parents and a concerned gay and lesbian constituency of Kowalski's lesbian involvement, denied Thompson's request to be made guardian (for a concise overview of the case, see Hunter). In December 1991, the Minnesota Court of Appeals reversed Campbell's decision and granted guardianship to Thompson (see Schmitz), but the decision had already powerfully demonstrated the infinite manipulability of the private realm to lesbian and gay activists, who had long considered privacy a practically unassailable defense against moral challenges to homosexual behavior. For the state was interested in maintaining as inviolate not the privacy of the homosexual relationship (the fundamental terms of that privacy would have to have been violated already in order for the relationship to be rendered recognizable) but the private interest of the heterosexually constituted nuclear family against which the claims of the lesbian couple represented a serious foreign threat. That threat may appear to us to consist merely in the alienation of affective ties among the blood relatives who constitute the nuclear family because we have been carefully trained to recognize as mere affective interest what is really at stake in the constitution of the family unit—distribution of property and other material benefits through, among other mechanisms, legal inheritance.

The common sociopolitical significance of homosexual relationships and the mixed-race relationships discussed above is clear. For the fracturing of the heterosexually oriented boundaries that have traditionally defined the family structure portends as profound a disruption in the orderly distribution of material wealth in the twentieth century as did the subversion of clearly traceable blood lines by miscegenation in the nineteenth. What this fact means, for those of us who are interested in the construction of cultural mechanisms by which to understand and combat the social and political forces that keep lesbians and gay men in check, is that the history of racial politics in this country, beyond providing us with a model for activism—as has long been acknowledged—may prove to be the context in which the terms of our predicament are founded and therefore a domain to which we must recur if we hope to struggle effectively in the contemporary moment.

Harvard University

Notes

This essay has benefited from critical attention accorded it in a number of contexts between the fall of 1990 and the winter of 1992. For helpful comments and suggestions, I would like to thank audiences at the University of Pennsylvania, the University of Rochester, and the 1991 Modern Language Association convention and participants in the "homotextualities" conference at the State University of New York, Buffalo, in April 1991. Particular thanks are due to Brian Johnson for photographic services and to David Halperin for his invaluable editorial assistance.

[1] Indeed, in commenting on one of Brancusi's later renditions of the theme (*Medallion*, c. 1919), in which the figures are barely differentiated, let alone gendered, Geist negotiates the unease caused by the unisexual aspect of the piece by rendering the figures not human but rather immortal. This version of the work, he says, "echoes Donne: 'Difference of sex no more we knew than our guardian angels do' " (81); Geist thus casts the lack of sexual differentiation in the sculpture as angelic purity rather than human decadence.

[2] Saks provides a comprehensive analysis of miscegenation case law from the early nineteenth through the late twentieth century.

[3] Obviously, my argument exploits the dual meaning of the word *private*, which denotes both proprietorship and secrecy or social discretion. This apparently fortuitous coincidence actually indicates the degree to which these two

concepts are linked. What is perhaps most interesting about this linkage, however, is the counterintuitive order of legal-historical precedence: the sense of inviolability that is implied in secrecy derives from the subjective sovereignty that characterizes proprietorship, rather than the other way around.

In tracing the development of the legal right to personal privacy—which most legal commentators claim is distinct from the right to own private property—the authors of a 1981 article derive that right in part from nineteenth-century case law against eavesdropping, which determines that "no man has a right . . . to pry into your secrecy in your own home" ("Right to Privacy" 1896). The authors thus conceive of personal privacy predominantly as a function of the private-property context in which it is recognized (the implicitly operative legal maxim "a man's house is his castle" connoting possession by occupation if not by title), despite the putative independence of the two concepts. For more on various legal conceptions of privacy—and further evidence of the degree to which the relation between personal privacy and private property is purposefully and suspiciously obscured in conventional legal thought—see also Samar 13–49; Warren and Brandeis.

However strenuously legal commentators may deny the personal privacy–private property link, it nonetheless seems to enjoy a high degree of popular recognition. For instance, a recently aired radio advertisement for a Boston-area reproductive health clinic claims that "Repro Associates is a private practice devoted to reproductive health—because in some matters, it's privacy that counts" and thus powerfully identifies the corporation's private status with its clientele's private concerns (*Matty in the Morning*).

[4] I am grateful to Cindy Patton for directing my attention to this scene.

[5] Clearly, then, property relations are a key factor in the constitution not only of personal privacy but also of private (i.e., domestic) life. Engels inaugurates the theorization of this function.

Williams addresses the ramifications of this particular type of interracial, intergender relationship.

[6] The centrality of the white subject's interest in the phenomenon of miscegenation is indicated in a dictionary definition of the term: "marriage between white and nonwhite persons" ("Miscegenation").

[7] Another novel from roughly the same period as *Iola Leroy* makes this point particularly explicit. In Chesnutt's *The Marrow of Tradition* (1901), a white character's profound hatred of her mixed-race half sister is based on her fear that this sister will lay claim to a portion of their dead father's estate. When the white sister confesses her anxiety to her husband, he reassures her in terms that resonate with the point I make above—that the black woman's relative powerlessness as a private subject is a function of her effective status as private property: "Who was she," he demands, "to have inherited the estate of your ancestors, of which, a few years before, she would herself have formed a part?" (256). I am indebted to Lee Edelman for suggesting to me the pertinence of Chesnutt's work to my argument.

[8] These claims are characteristically invoked by conservative gay activists whose objective is to achieve the extension of "civil rights" to gay men and

lesbians without calling into question the basis on which those rights are founded. See, for instance, LaFontaine and Ward.

Works Cited

Champigneulle, Bernard. *Rodin*. Adapted and trans. J. Maxwell Brownjohn. New York: Abrams, 1967.

Chesnutt, Charles W. *The Marrow of Tradition*. 1901. New York: Arno, 1969.

Elsen, Albert E. "When the Sculptures Were White." *Rodin Rediscovered*. Exhibition Catalog. Ed. Elsen. Washington: National Gallery of Art; Boston: New York Graphic Society, 1981. 127–50.

Engels, Friedrich. *The Origin of the Family, Private Property, and the State*. 1884. New York: International, 1942.

Geist, Sidney. *Brancusi: A Study of the Sculpture*. New York: Grossman, 1968.

Harper, Frances Ellen Watkins. *Iola Leroy*. 1892. Intro. Hazel V. Carby. Black Women Writers Series. Deborah E. McDowell, series ed. Boston: Beacon, 1987.

Hunter, Nan D. "Sexual Dissent and the Family." *Nation* 7 Oct. 1991: 406–11.

LaFontaine, David, and Patrick Ward. "Why Our Future Is in the GOP." *Gay Community News* 4 Feb. 1991: 5.

Matty in the Morning. WXKS, Medford, MA. 13 Jan. 1993.

Millar, Jeff, and Bill Hinds. "Tank McNamara." Cartoon. 27 June 1990.

Miller, D. A. "Secret Subjects, Open Secrets." *The Novel and the Police*. Berkeley: U of California P, 1988. 192–220.

"Miscegenation." *American Heritage Dictionary*. 1973 ed.

Pateman, Carole. "Feminist Critiques of the Public/Private Dichotomy." *The Disorder of Women: Democracy, Feminism and Political Theory*. Stanford: Stanford UP, 1989. 118–40.

Pinky. Dir. Elia Kazan. Twentieth Century–Fox, 1949.

Pronger, Brian. *The Arena of Masculinity: Sports, Homosexuality, and the Meaning of Sex*. New York: St. Martin's, 1990.

"The Right to Privacy in Nineteenth-Century America." *Harvard Law Review* 94.8 (1981): 1892–1910.

Saks, Eva. "Representing Miscegenation Law." *Raritan* 8.2 (1988): 39–69.

Samar, Vincent J. *The Right to Privacy: Gays, Lesbians, and the Constitution*. Philadelphia: Temple UP, 1991.

Schmitz, Dawn. "Kowalski and Thompson Win!" *Gay Community News* 22 Dec. 1991: 1+.

Vecsey, George. "Strawberry: One Kiss, One Homer." *New York Times* 5 Mar. 1989: sec. 8: 2.

Warren, Samuel D., and Louis D. Brandeis. "The Right to Privacy." *Harvard Law Review* 4:5 (1890): 193–220.

Whitford, Frank. *Klimt*. World of Art Series. London: Thames, 1990.

Williams, Patricia J. "On Being the Object of Property." *The Alchemy of Race and Rights*. Cambridge: Harvard UP, 1991. 216–36.

Memorial Rags

Michael Moon

"Where do we find ourselves? In a series of which we do not know the extremes, and believe that it has none. We wake and find ourselves on a stair; there are stairs below us, which we seem to have ascended; there are stairs above us, many a one, which go upward and out of sight." Thus opens Ralph Waldo Emerson's essay "Experience," with its striking and memorable evocation of waking to find that one has lost one's way. When I recently taught the essay once again, its opening lines struck me as a powerful emblem of the collective mourning and grieving that have unexpectedly become central activities in the lives of gay men and our friends in the wake of AIDS. And Emerson's essay does not cease to speak to our experience after its famous opening but goes on to become a powerful, if largely implicit, meditation on ultimate loss, on the pain of the deaths of others—in the essay, on the death of Emerson's five-year-old son Waldo two years earlier.

The "scandal" of the essay is that Emerson unequivocally disowns the traditional association of grief and mourning with deep feeling, with coming into profound self-knowledge, or with undergoing a transforming ascesis:

> The only thing grief has taught me is to know how shallow it is. . . . In the death of my son, . . . I seem to have lost a beautiful estate—no more. I cannot get it nearer to me. . . . [T]his calamity . . . does not touch me: something which I fancied was part of me, which could not be torn away without tearing me . . . falls off from me, and leaves no scar. It was caducous. I grieve that grief can teach me nothing. . . .   (287–88)

This passage has generated a remarkable series of comments from Emerson's critics, some of whom have posthumously chided him for his apparent lack of feeling or for his perverse pretense of indifference toward the death of his son. Sharon Cameron has eloquently rebutted this interpretation of Emerson's expressed relation to death and grief. She demonstrates with exemplary rigor how the figure of the dead son, unmentioned after the essay's opening pages, pervades "Experience," making it a threnody—albeit one that refuses all the traditional means of mourning, including those still enshrined in all kinds of consolation literature, highbrow and pop alike, for bereaved persons: what Cameron calls "ideas of depth, integration, internalization," and "acknowledgment." Rather, Cameron relates Emerson's ideas about grief and mourning to those of the psychoanalytic theorists Nicolas Abraham and Maria Torok, who "resist the idea that mourning is a process that can be completed . . ." (37).

More recently, Mark Edmundson has related the fierce resistance to conventional notions of mourning that Emerson articulates in "Experience" and other texts to Freud's theories of mourning and melancholia and to the centrality of melancholia in the high tradition of Romantic lyric poetry. Edmundson observes that Emerson's cultivated oscillation between melancholia and mania, his refusal to uphold mania (or any other state) over melancholia, is a practice profoundly "at odds with our humanistic ethical principles," principles of the kind Freud's theory of the work of mourning in the influential essay "Mourning and Melancholia" (1917) represents: moderation, resolution, and closure in the form of a return to "health" and "normalcy."

According to Cameron's and Edmundson's studies, Emerson's position must be set against the tradition that Freud's essay embodies, in which grieving and mourning are completable tasks, private psychological projects with teleological internal structures. In Freud's essay—and there, as at some other moments in his work, his theory is as one with conventional wisdom—mourning is, in an often quoted phrase, an elaborate process of "working through," a gradual and effortful journey back from the initial sheer, unassimilable pain of grief to acknowledgment and eventually to acceptance of loss, psychological reintegration, and the discovery of new objects.

Mourning is work for Freud, but there is a payoff at the end of the job: acceptance, reintegration, the "fresh woods, and pastures new" that Milton holds out at the end of "Lycidas." There are of course other ways of understanding work besides the capitalist ones that have long predominated in American culture, but one of the things that seem most wrong with the notion of grief and mourning that informs Freud's idea of "working through" is the considerable degree to which that idea is constructed under the signs of compulsory labor and the cash nexus.

One must dig one's way out of grief, advisers in Freud's tradition say, to be rewarded by a return to "normalcy."

As lesbians and gay men, most of us have been categorically excluded from "normalcy" at critical junctures in our lives. In the light of our personal and collective struggles for recognition, acknowledgement, acceptance, and fulfillment of our needs the Freudian model of mourning may look fundamentally normalizing and consequently privative and may seem to diminish the process and to foreclose its possible meanings instead of enriching it or making it more accessible to understanding. Those of us who are students, teachers, and critics of literature may assume that we are especially well qualified to recognize and to interpret for ourselves and others the utterances of the dead and the discourses of death and grieving. What classroom exhibit have professors of literature had over the past century that is more central than the elegy is? Perhaps more of us have cut our critical baby teeth by participating in classroom close readings of the aforementioned "Lycidas," for example, than by studying any other single text. And beyond the classical elegy, reading many other kinds of texts we study and teach—realist fictions, tales of the macabre and the uncanny, lyric poems, dramatic texts of many kinds—in ways that privilege elegiac modes of perception and interpretation accounts for much of our critical and pedagogic practice.

If we are to make, to read, and to teach memorials to the dead in the light of models of mourning that do not contain and repress urgent needs and feelings, as the traditional elegiac model does by presenting the process as a set of conventional tasks with a preordained beginning, middle, and end, where are these models to come from? I suspect that we have much to learn from those who have written against the "task-oriented" school of grief and mourning. The "scandal" of Emerson's ostensible refusal to mourn is one locus for such thinking, but there are others. Among contemporary gay male writers, Michael Bronski has written evocatively on mourning and sexuality. Bearing in mind Bronski's seasonable exhortations to his fellow mourners not to suppress but rather to cultivate actively the erotic component of grief and sorrow, I consider another, later essay of Freud's and a number of passages from Walt Whitman's poetry. Taken together, these texts raise questions that may be useful for us to consider in relation to the project of restoring the "scandal" of sexuality, specifically of gay male sexuality, to the mourning process.

In discussing matters of sexual rights and rights to representation, supposedly well-intentioned persons often attempt to limit discussion by making such supposedly jocular remarks as, Where is this sexual rights stuff going to end? Are we going to end up defending necrophiliacs? Rather than companionably laugh off the suggestion, I interrogate the notion that sexual desire for the dead constitutes some kind of universal limit case for acceptable sexualities. I also consider how we may extend our relationships, including our sexual relationships, with and to the dead instead of submitting to the kinds of coercions and prohibitions, jocular and otherwise, that label all such practices necrophilia. Critics and theorists of elegy and the elegiac now routinely acknowledge the erotic dimension of mourning, but since they tend to derive their terms from a post-Freudian ego-psychology model of the self, their primary terms for the mourner's sexuality tend to be negative ones. These accounts of the sexuality of the mourner tend to focus on the experience of symbolic states of "impotence" and "castration": bereavement is coextensive with the rupture, the sudden "cutting off," of the possibility of erotic connection with the dead. Again because of our particular histories as gay men and lesbians, we bring to the practice of mourning complex relations to body images—our own and other people's—that may well make us want to challenge ideas of significant relationships—including our own significant relationships with and to our beloved dead—that are based on notions of bodily deficiency and abnormality. Such pathologizing ideas—for example, that being gay is a consequence of physiological deficiency or abnormality—have been central to homophobic constructions of homosexuality over the past century. What if, instead of focusing on bodily deficiency in thinking about our own mourning practices, we focus on bodily abundance and supplementarity? Resisting thinking of the deaths of others as the making deficient of our own bodies or body parts and resisting thinking of death as absolutely rupturing the possible erotic relation of a living person to a dead one may make an important difference in our mourning practices.

The form of bodily supplementarity I am particularly interested in considering in relation to mourning and memorializing is the fetish. Parts of the body (such as feet); items of apparel associated with body parts, such as socks and shoes; other "intimate" garments, such as underwear; certain styles of occupational dress, such as athletic gear and cops' or nurses' uniforms; certain substances associated with various human and nonhuman "skins," such as leather, rubber, and silk—all have had significant careers as fetishes in the modern period. Freud's 1927 essay "Fetishism" effectively disperses the tendency to hypostatize the fetish. In the face of a conventional understanding of fetishism in which the fetishist is a relentless specialist—supposedly not just any color of sock or style of shoe will do—the young male fetishist Freud takes as a specimen case vibrates not to socks or underpants, bustles or baseball caps, but to what he calls the "shine on the nose." According to the young man's testimony, his getting off depends entirely on his being initially turned on by noticing a "shine" on a woman's nose. Proceeding by the classic Freudian analytic principle *Cherchez la bonne d'enfant* 'Look for the nursery maid,' Freud establishes that his patient has been reared in an anglophone nursery. He is then able to interpret the young man's curious-seeming fetishization of the *Glanz auf der Nase* not as the "shine on the nose" that it literally is in German but as an unconscious translinguistic pun between the German word *Glanz* and the English word *glance*: the *Glanz auf der Nase*, Freud argues, means not a shine on the nose but a *glance* at the nose, which is by the psychoanalytic logic of upward displacement and, here, displacement across genders a peek at the penis.

The crucial part of the Freudian argument—its own fetish, one might say—is that the penis at which the fetish allows the young man to peek is not his own or another male's but, phantasmatically, the penis that the young man as a small boy once imagined that his mother had lost. In a series of feminist revisions of psychoanalytic theories of sexual difference, Juliet Mitchell, Jacqueline Rose, and Mary Jacobus, among others, have over the past twenty years critiqued these scenes in which Freud's small boys (re)discover sexual difference in mistaking women's (here their mothers') genitalia for signs of castration. In a not unrelated series of critiques, several other feminist theorists—most notably, Naomi Schor—have in recent years presented thoughtful accounts of representations of female fetishism. I appropriate the dispersive and linguistic emphases of Freud's account of male fetishism while dislodging fetishism from castration, Oedipalization, and the maternal phallus in his writing. Most of all, I disengage male fetishism from its primary function in Freud, which is to allay not only castration anxiety but also "homosexual panic," or, as Freud puts it, to "save . . . the fetishist from being a homosexual by endowing women with the attribute which makes them acceptable as sexual objects" ("Fetishism" 217).

Rather than accept Freud's unwavering identification of the fetish with the maternal phallus, we may find in fetishes a broadly conceived means of extending our own bodies, as well as the bodies of our beloved dead, and in fetishistic practices further means of exploring and extending our relationships, including our sexual relationships, with the dead. For models we cannot look to someone as timorous about fetishism and homosexuality as Freud is. Rather, let us look to one of the great collections of male-homoerotic memorial writing, Walt Whitman's *Drum-Taps* poems.

In writing about *Drum-Taps* a while back, I became aware of a transformative process in Whitman's Civil War poetry that to my knowledge had not previously been noted in print—the kind of subtly but unmistakably eroticized process that many of Whitman's critics have been blind to. The early war poetry, written just before or just after the outbreak of the war, shows a remarkable fixation on the American flag that I think justifies the term *fetish*. The banner of the Union is represented as beautiful, enticing, lovable, and irresistible, the sign of everything desirable, something worth defending with one's own life and with the lives of others. (Freud's comment that "grown men" grasp at fetishes not in direct response to castration anxiety but "when the cry goes up that throne and altar are in danger" may be relevant here ["Fetishism" 215].) But the cloth of the banner that is compulsively admired and saluted in Whitman's early war poetry returns in quite different form in the later, much more highly regarded and well-known elegiac poetry, which represents the poet serving the sick and wounded and also grieving over the war dead. These poems are full of cloth, not flags or banners, which correspond with Freud's notion of the fetish as a sign of masculinist triumph, but rags, bandages, torn garments, and blankets that cover the dead and enfold them for burial. In poem after poem, with the aggression characteristic of a person acting out feelings of intense grief, the voluminous folds of the war pennant under which *Drum-Taps* is elaborately inaugurated are ripped apart into wound dressings and shrouds. There is finally almost nothing left of this material, textual or textile, but ragged strips of bloody cloth: "No poem proud, I chanting bring to thee / But a cluster containing night's darkness and blood-dripping wounds, / And psalms of the dead," Whitman writes in "Lo, Victress on the Peaks" (lines 7–9).

The superabundance of wounds and ragged bandages in this poetry, I would argue, functions superficially to de-eroticize Whitman's representations of the extraordinarily rich variety of homoerotic exchange between the poet and his patients: undressing, bathing, drying, and dressing the patients and their wounds, lifting and holding the patients, burying the patients' bodies, and elegizing the dead. These famous elegies seem to abjure the erotic in favor of representing what has conventionally been considered to be the stern and grievous business of war and war deaths, and many of Whitman's critics have rushed to concur with such a reading, apparently with the homophobic assumption that here in Whitman's poetry at least, they would find relief from the insistent, indeed ubiquitous, vein of male homoeroticism in his writing. On the contrary, what becomes vivid in reading these poems in the context of the rest of *Leaves of Grass*, into which the *Drum-Taps* poems were incorporated several years after the end of the Civil War, is how the poems represent care-giving as erotically charged. "I am faithful, I do not give out, / The fractured thigh, the knee, the wound in the abdomen, / These and more I dress with impassive hand, (yet deep in my breast a fire, a burning flame)," reads a representative passage from the poem "The Wound-Dresser" (lines 27–29). One need not ignore the shattered state of the flesh that is lovingly specularized, tended, dressed, undressed, and memorialized in this writing to perceive that "The Wound-Dresser" is a poem not only about literally shattered flesh but also about the shatterings—not least of all erotic shatterings—one can experience in response to flashes of flesh, the unexpected uncoverings and re-coverings of desired or beloved flesh that are as much a part of the everyday of the sick as they are of numerous other quotidian practices. The equation of the glance at the nose, or peek at the penis, with the specific imaginary object of the maternal phallus is proleptically deconstructed in a text like Whitman's "The Wound-Dresser," which, unlike Freud's fetishism essay, is a text emphatically not "saved from homosexuality," a text in which visions of the flash of flesh and the rag or fetish that veils and unveils the flesh take different paths from the sexist, heterosexist, and homophobic trajectory of Freud's account.

Recognizing and accepting the possible restorative effects of such processes can perhaps be helpful in reconstituting our relationship to the dead. Such recognition and acceptance can be part of a process that is not a displacement or a dismemberment—not a castration—but a re-memberment that has repositioned itself among the remnants, the remainders, and reminders that do not go away; loss is not denied, but neither is it "worked through." Loss is not lost.

Duke University

Works Cited

Bronski, Michael. "Death, AIDS and the Transfiguration of Grief." *Gay Community News* 24 July 1988: 14.

———. "Death and the Erotic Imagination." *Taking Liberties: AIDS and Cultural Politics.* Ed. Erica Carter and Simon Watney. London: Serpent's Tail, 1989. 219–28.

Cameron, Sharon. "Representing Grief: Emerson's 'Experience.' " *Representations* 15 (1986): 15–41.

Edmundson, Mark. "Emerson and the Work of Melancholia." *Raritan* 6 (1987): 120–36.

Emerson, Ralph Waldo. "Experience." *Ralph Waldo Emerson: Selected Essays.* Ed. Larzer Ziff. New York: Penguin, 1982. 285–311.

Freud, Sigmund. "Fetishism." *Freud: Sexuality and the Psychology of Love.* Ed. Philip Rieff. New York: Collier, 1963. 214–19.

———. "Mourning and Melancholia." *Sigmund Freud: Collected Papers.* Trans. James Strachey. Vol. 4. New York: Basic, 1959. 152–70.

Moon, Michael. " 'The Blood of the World': Gender, Bloodshed, and the Uncanny in the Fourth (1867) Edition of *Leaves of Grass." Disseminating Whitman: Revision and Corporeality in* Leaves of Grass. Cambridge: Harvard UP, 1991. 171–222.

Whitman, Walt. Leaves of Grass: *A Textual Variorum of the Printed Poems.* Ed. Sculley Bradley, Harold W. Blodgett, Arthur Golden, and William White. 3 vols. New York: New York UP, 1980.

Index